Alexander the Great's Legacy

*To Janet, Joe, Katie, Rich and my
wonderful new granddaughter Emmy.*

Alexander the Great's Legacy

The Decline of Macedonian Europe in the Wake of the Wars of the Successors

Mike Roberts

Pen & Sword
MILITARY

First published in Great Britain in 2022 by
Pen & Sword Military
An imprint of
Pen & Sword Books Ltd
Yorkshire – Philadelphia

ISBN 978 1 52678 852 8

Typeset by Mac Style
Printed and bound in the UK by CPI Group (UK) Ltd,
Croydon, CR0 4YY

Pen & Sword Books Limited incorporates the imprints of Atlas,
Archaeology, Aviation, Discovery, Family History, Fiction, History,
Maritime, Military, Military Classics, Politics, Select, Transport,
True Crime, Air World, Frontline Publishing, Leo Cooper, Remember
When, Seaforth Publishing, The Praetorian Press, Wharncliffe
Local History, Wharncliffe Transport, Wharncliffe True Crime
and White Owl.

For a complete list of Pen & Sword titles please contact

PEN & SWORD BOOKS LIMITED
47 Church Street, Barnsley, South Yorkshire, S70 2AS, England
E-mail: enquiries@pen-and-sword.co.uk
Website: www.pen-and-sword.co.uk

Or

PEN AND SWORD BOOKS
1950 Lawrence Rd, Havertown, PA 19083, USA
E-mail: Uspen-and-sword@casematepublishers.com
Website: www.penandswordbooks.com

Contents

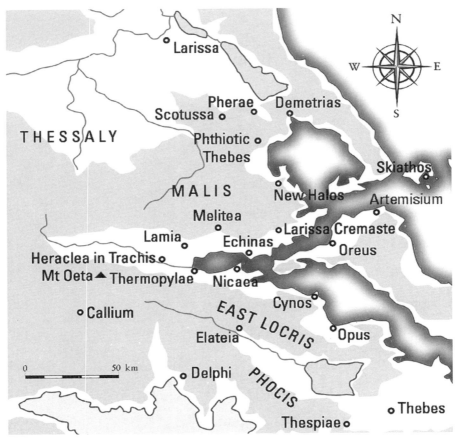

Detailed Map of Thermopylae and Demetrias region.

Map of East Central Greece.

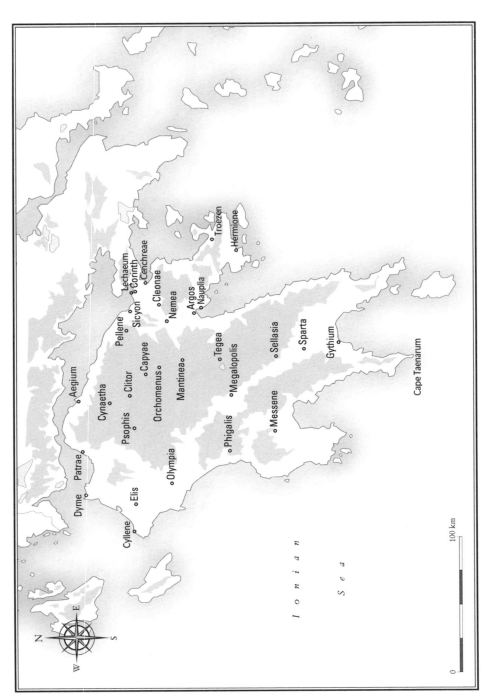

Map of the Peloponnese.

Map of West Central Greece.

Introduction

There are a number of memorable archaeological sites in what was ancient Macedonia: there is Pella itself, a considerable and fascinating location that was probably originally Illyrian, situated between the ancient Haliacmon and Axios rivers, near Mount Paiko and formerly connected to the Thermaic Gulf by a navigable inlet. This hybrid foundation where Thracian and Illyrian influences were strong in the people's original pantheon was later thoroughly Hellenized; cultural influences were displayed in terrific late fourth-century pebble mosaics in the House of Dionysos and the House of the Abduction of Helen. Not far away is the picturesque and shady glen at the Nymphaion of Mieza where Aristotle is supposed to have taught Alexander and his youthful companions, and beyond these central locations there is a plethora of archaic burial grounds and a plentiful scatter of Greek cities: the likes of Amphipolis with its famous lion, probably set up to honour Laomedon of Mytilene, and the Kasta Tomb, a recently-excavated late fourth-century vault of unusual size protected by a pair of sphinxes. However, the jewel in the crown is the set of graves at Aigai exposed by Manolis Andronikos as recently as 1977 and the dramatic feel of descending into the tumuli and discovering the pediment entrances is a museum experience that for the author has only been matched by entering the cavernous gloom of the Vasa Museum in Stockholm to see the shape of the resuscitated seventeenth-century galleon emerging into view.

There has been plenty of debate concerning the two undisturbed tombs containing bones sufficiently disfigured to lead to endless controversy about who they might belong to and wonderful artefacts including body armour and greaves, but what is uncontested is that they are royal burials from the end of the fourth century. Yet this regal necropolis near the ancient capital of Macedonia and containing the remains of many of the dynasty whose most famous representative had just conquered most of the world was, within half a century of Alexander's death, almost laid to ruins. Gallic mercenaries, dispatched to the area by their employer, the flame-haired Pyrrhus, king of Epirus, who had once again taken control in the kingdom, pillaged a number of graves, showing the kind of shocking impiety that most Hellenes considered typical of people who a few years before had run amok in the old dominions of Philip and Alexander, bringing death, destruction and chaos to Macedonia, Illyria, Thrace and Greece. How was it possible for a kingdom that had risen so high to so quickly succumb to find itself in the humiliating predicament of not being able to protect the resting-place of the royal family that had ensured that little Macedonia, hardly bigger than Denmark or Estonia, had risen to become ruler of the world?

Embarrassment over an Imperial past is surely a proper indicator of intellectual and moral progress; to understand that hokum of being a chosen people or bringing the benefits of civilization to the benighted and backward, advancing the barbarian or fetching heathens into the light of the Lord was never anything but a paper-thin fig leaf to obscure the profits of rapine and pillage. Yet during recorded time when the stronger was fated to crush and exploit the weaker has been an absolute theme of the ages, it has generally been the case that those polities that trod an Imperialist road benefited greatly – that was the point – and were for a considerable period of time much stronger and in many cases able to use the Imperial dividend to dominate the world around them. It is almost axiomatic that for all such adventures in history, ancient and modern, the homeland of the successful Imperial people will receive major benefits; not just the immediate profit of riches looted from the victims but the longer-term exploitation of the natural resources of the defeated foe. That Imperial homelands were normally augmented in the long term is obvious and evident from blood tribute that might come directly when vanquished enemies were enslaved or transported as communities to labour for their new rulers or when the fruits of their exertions produced in their own lands were appropriated for the new rulers' benefit. Exemplified by the songs of longing for home sung by Jews by the rivers of Babylon where they toiled for neo-Babylonian masters, the vast hordes of enslaved captives that fuelled Roman economic expansion and the steppe lords Genghis Khan and Tamerlane dragging off the best artists and artisans of half the continent of Asia to beautify their capitals at Karakorum and Samarkand literally draining the wealth and skilled manpower of their new subjects to enrich and empower the homeland. All this was apart from the massive trade revenues accruing to people who can control or at least influence by dint of military might so many of the levers of commerce to their advantage. While direct seizing of items of value, people and economic assets is usually only the most immediate advantage, gaining access to critical trade goods can be equally pivotal, such as competition over control of the spice trade involving European, Iberian, Dutch and English Imperialists over several centuries. Controlling access to markets could also be of crucial concern, with one of the most dishonourable examples in our own Imperial past being that of Victorian drug-dealing on a grand scale with the enforced opening of China to the opium trade by British gunboats in the nineteenth century.

In their time Hittite Hattusa and Assyrian Nineveh had tumbled and been consumed by raging flames, while Persian Persepolis was ordered to be torched by an inebriate Alexander, and even Rome finally fell to a reluctant Visigoth prince after he had been rebuffed repeatedly after entreating the promotion and reward in a Roman Imperial context that he really craved. Yet if the snubbed applicant sacked the city that, if not eternal, got as close as any, like the others this termination came after centuries of supremacy, and to this pattern ancient Macedon seems an exception. Within a couple of generations the state ruled from Pella was not even as significant a player on the world stage as it had been when her armies had started on the road that led across the Hellespont to the conquest of the bountiful lands of Achaemenid Persia. This is hardly usual; that the conquerors seemed to benefit for so short a time from their exploitation of the people and resources of the new domains they had brought under their sway. Not that there were not initially clear bonuses. Pella had become a place of stately halls and temples, showing the impact of Eastern wealth siphoned back to beautify the town. Immediate rewards would have been visible with gorgeous purple and saffron robes becoming a common sight in the corridors of Pella's palaces and indeed the streets of other Macedonian towns brought back by soldiers from the vast amounts distributed to them from the treasure cities of Susa, Babylon and Persepolis. Resources were not used just to beautify; investment was made in weapons manufacture to arm the next generation of soldiers and factories are known at Pella, Cassandreia, Amphipolis and Thessaloniki. Regular folk also benefited: families of veterans back home got tax exemption, while the old soldiers themselves enjoyed front-row seats at athletic and dramatic competitions. Even non-Macedonians would have stood out as beneficiaries like the blowhard Greek mercenaries replete with the riches of the Orient who crop up in the New Comedy of the Hellenistic age.

The experience of the Imperial homeland was never just going to be one of basking in the wealth siphoned off from subject peoples; there was always bound to be a downside with an ongoing brain and brawn drain that even growing generations would find hard to replenish. How many active young Macedonians left either with the army or as logistical support cannot be absolutely known; perhaps 10 per cent of the available manpower would have been serving in the military, but it must have been a considerable proportion that travelled to service the Imperial court and war machine. While some returned with satchels full of Eastern treasure, many did not, either dying or settling as a new ruling elite in some conquered region. Also over the years those not part of Alexander's enterprise, able and adventurous members of the new generations would have left to become administrative, commercial or even artistic participants in the rich new world of Macedonian Asia and Africa with all its myriad opportunities for members of the Imperial nation. Yet this is surely not in itself sufficient to explain why Macedonia seemed to benefit so much less than most other successful imperialists, or why her people were so disappointed in their giddy anticipation of continued pre-eminence.

This was no case of a vigorous warrior people becoming louche and enervated due to the impact of luxury and power or even an economy becoming perverted by their commercial classes being directed in parasitic directions. Nor was it that they were not adept at operations of regional exploitation from even before the extravagant Imperial pulse initiated by Alexander. From the earliest days the Macedonian rulers had not been shy about exploiting mineral-rich Chalcidice and terrific quality wood grown from the Bermion Mountains across to the Argos peninsula. Further from home Philip had planted Heraclea Lyncestis, Philippopolis and Philippi to exert control in Lynkos, the Strymón (modern-day Struma) valley and rich Thracian goldfields. They had done a bit of people-trafficking too, if not on an Assyrian or Persian scale. Philip had transported Illyrians and Thracians in his time, while artisans and weapon-makers were brought from the cities in mainland Greece,

Chalcidice, Thrace and even further afield in the year of expansion, and later Cassander planted 20,000 Illyrian Autariatae refugees near Mount Orbelos. Yet after they hit the Achaemenid jackpot, instead of basking in the light of Imperial splendour, the Macedonians soon found themselves having to fight for survival, needing to find a resilience sufficient not to splinter into the urban leagues and domains of regional dynasts or highland clan chiefs; a situation pretty much like that which had faced Philip II when he usurped the throne from his infant nephew Amyntas IV in 359.

For more than forty years the polity became subject to waves of dangerous misfortunes thundering against its borders that only finally yielded to a more peaceful time when a stoic prince grew ancient on a throne he had inherited almost by accident: a monarch who, appropriately for his diminished state, was far from plotting the kind of expansionist course taken by his more famous antecedents, behaviour that he had neither the inclination nor the wherewithal to attempt. The strain of continual conflict and years of spoliation and repeated invasions by familiar neighbours as well as by unknown and terrible barbarians that brought defeat in battle to soldiers whose predecessors had conquered the world ensured that the economic and financial base of Macedonia could not help but fracture. If two of the greatest of the ancient world's monarchs ensured that their people had from the middle of the fourth century punched massively above their weight after they left the stage, things singularly failed to continue in an upward trajectory. In fact, soon enough the kingdom faced a threat of extinction with an impending dissolution of the political and social attachments that had allowed the flowering of Imperial Macedonia from the start.

Surviving tough struggles from Philip's accession, the kingdom of Macedonia that was almost created by this remarkable king had burst like a whirlwind into the lives of those who inhabited both the Hellenic and barbarian expanse of the Balkans. The hard man, whose one-eyed image probably looks out at us from one of the small busts found in the tombs at modern-day Vergina, had gained a particular military education when held hostage at the Thebes of Epaminondas. Weapons training, an almost Spartan discipline and contest for prizes practised in the local gymnasia were typical of Hellenistic armies from Philip through the later kingdoms and much of it was inspired by this experience when the

Macedonian prince may have been the lover of the general Pelopidas and where he probably met the Athenian Condottieri Iphicrates, famous for exposing his men to mock battles, ambushes, assaults, betrayals and panic. Utilizing what he had learned, he re-formed or completed the reformation[1] of a primitive near-feudal army, transforming it into an almost professional force based around an unstoppable infantry phalanx armed with sarissas (pikes) and backed by the excellent cavalry drawn from Macedon's landed gentry. This military force was completed by formidable auxiliaries from the regions of Thrace and Illyria he dominated, and supported by the latest engineering train using torsion artillery first pioneered by the tyrants of Syracuse in Sicily. Such an army allowed him to achieve not only conquests in Thrace, Illyria and along the Pontic shore but the imposition of an almost universal hegemony over the bickering communities of mainland Greece institutionalized by the League of Corinth which, as *strategos autokrator*, he could mobilize militarily to abet in forwarding his plans for expanding at the expense of a temptingly fragile Achaemenid Empire.

How was it possible that the state Philip had formed had within a couple of generations of his son's death been downgraded as a world power? That by the time Antigonus Gonatas, a prince influenced in his young manhood at Athens by the great Stoic Zeno, finally settled down to bed his dynasty firmly in at Pella, Macedonia was just not in the same league it had been when Philip was assassinated. The answer to this conundrum lies in the unique character of Alexander, so different in his world view and vaunting ambition from his contemporaries that it is not impossible to believe that he may really have considered himself a demi-god, if not a full-blown deity. With Alexander things are always exceptional. The contention that if a particular historical figure had not come along somebody very like them would have and the direction of history not been dramatically altered is usually a reasonable one. That if no specific Scipio Africanus had emerged young and unconventional, another such or group of others learning so much under the lash of Hannibal's awful brilliance would have become available to lead the Roman comeback that finally won the Second Punic War. If Julius Caesar had not been born, another ambitious Roman warlord would have encompassed the overthrow of the republic in a similar time frame. Sulla and Pompey had shown the way and somebody would have followed, who through successful foreign campaigning would have made himself the greatest power in mid-first-century Rome and then not have been prepared to retire to the back benches of the Senate. These things were almost bound to happen, just as it was pretty inevitable that that person or one of his successors would have set up a kind of empire based on a standing army. That Augustus was so long-lived and subtle enough to establish that super-state with such foundations to last so long was important, but if it had not been him, somebody like him would have almost certainly achieved a similar outcome. The vastly expanded Roman Empire required some such organization and the ruling class that had fought and died in its civil wars would always finally have been prepared to accept a potentate offering life, peace, status and riches; however much that person's supremacy eliminated the contest for a limited period of supreme power had been the very raison d'être of so many of their forebears.

However, Alexander was truly exceptional and the world would have been different had he not lived. Part of what made him so significant was not only that he won the greatest empire the world had ever seen in an extraordinary short period of time, but also singularly failed to make provision for a secure and smooth succession that might have promised a brighter, richer and more potent future for his homeland. The point has been made often and well how important was the absence of a viable heir who could have pledged a continuation of legitimacy and made probable a future of stability and security. However, to designate this as failure[2] is perhaps hardly reasonable as a lack of interest in this kind of normal dynastic forethought was just a part of the way in which Alexander was exceptional. That kind of orthodox thinking was just not his style and it is not at all far-fetched to think that he who had lived for personal glory and reputation might have found a smooth succession for his huge realm a real disappointment and that his expectations around a war of succession comprising his funeral games were not just prescient, it was what he would have wanted.

Alexander was different, and from this difference so much flowed. It was not just his military success which, though outstanding, can be imagined under the leadership of others of his compatriots who showed as so impressive in the generations around 300. It was the extent of his ambition that set him apart from those who accompanied him over the Hellespont in 334. The exceptionalism of his aspirations and the fact that he was able to carry so many of them through, even if finally failing to reach the far ocean he sought, made all the difference. It was not just that his conquests ensured a period when a vast Hellenistic *koine* (common language) included so much of the East Mediterranean and West Asia but that the distance he pushed the borders of his empire formed the context in which his homeland failed significantly to reap the Imperial dividends that it might have expected. An outcome that was conditional on Alexander hardly setting any limit on conquests that ended stretching as far as the wide steppes of central Asia, the mountain fastness of the Hindu Kush and the great delta of the River Indus. So at the king's death at the romantically youthful age of 32, not only was there no clear line of succession but the very size of the new empire meant that to have tried to rule it all from almost anywhere would be hugely difficult and from Pella almost impossible. This mint new realm stretched thousands of miles from its borders in the east and south and the inexorable judgement of geography alone would have meant entropy, that centrifugal forces would be bound to split the new Imperial entity into a number of fragments, never mind the coterie of talented, ruthless and militarily powerful officers who controlled the levers of command in the Macedonian army, hovering round Alexander's deathbed.

Almost as important was that the overthrow of the whole Achaemenid Empire had made available a vast amount of specie released from the treasure houses of Babylon, Susa and Ecbatana. The fabulous reports were that by 330 Alexander had access to 200,000 talents, dwarfing the 1,000 talents of income Macedon could boast at the end of Philip's reign and worth several centuries of revenue of the Athenian Empire at its height. All this, together with the tribute available from so many rich provinces, ensured that the ambitious Macedonians and Greeks who would contest for the world Alexander left behind had the wherewithal to mobilize armies that could not only challenge for prizes in Asia but could return to Europe in an attempt to wrest control there from those left behind when Alexander departed. Alexander had shown by calling on his provincial governors to collect arms for his army, a policy that ensured the disarming and dispersal of Achaemenid soldiers who might have been the focus for revolt, that he could replenish the panoplies of his huge number of followers several times, a capacity for logistical organization inherited by his successors. That these puissant warlords were drawn back home with the intention of occupying the throne at Pella was hardly a surprise, but the consequence included years of warfare in Greece, Macedonia and Thrace, guaranteeing that Macedonian Europe was a markedly weakened entity when the dust finally settled in the late 270s and a grandson of one of the most powerful of the original successors was finally able to oversee a period of peace and reconstruction. Magnates based in Asia and Africa, cash-rich from the treasuries of the Persian Empire with manpower and armaments to burn, kept on coming back to try to take over or at least have an important say in what was happening in what was, after all, their familial homeland. Antigonid, Seleucid and Ptolemaic armies and navies all played their part in battering on the door of Macedonian Europe, fostering the kind of insecurity that was never likely to be conducive to any kind of reinvigorated legitimacy. That a mere 50 talents had been enough to ignite the Lamian War in 323 is indicative of the kind of damage this sort of extremely well-funded intervention could potentially inflict.

Yet the likelihood is that without Alexander's peculiar personality, the men who led the Macedonian army into Asia would not have been drawn to the ends of the world. After all, the environment from which came so many of the great Macedonian marshals did not suggest world travellers. Many were from the highland country of upper Macedonia; Perdiccas and Craterus were princes of Orestis; Polyperchon came from Tymphaea on the Epirot march; Antigonus was from Elimiotis; Leonnatus came from Lyncestis; Neoptolemus was an Epirot; and Pithon may have had Illyrian roots. In many ways it had been the incorporation of these fighting clansmen into Greater Macedonia, swapping their sheep and goatskins for the chlamys[3] (an ancient Greek cloak), that allowed Philip to reinvent his people as well constituted warriors and build a new model army of pike-wielding infantry and heavy companion cavalry. Many of these men when children would have had horizons constrained by their native hills and valleys, princely upbringings but probably only occasionally enlivened by a journey to Pella that would not have entailed much more than 100 miles there and back. Certainly their fathers or the more mature of them had their vistas expanded by following the colours of their conquering king Philip east to Thrace and the Hellespont and south in mainland Greece, but still the travel prospects of the elite of even this expanded marcher kingdom were largely constrained by the limits of a Balkan and Greek world. The younger generation of the highland ruling families lived and were educated as royal pages or in the company of Alexander, doubling as hostages for people only recently coming to terms with the authority of a lowland king, mingled with plainsmen like Philotas and Parmenion's other sons, Antipater's son Cassander, his brothers and the likes of Peucestas and Lysimachus who seemed to have Thessalian roots, but none of these could have conceived that in a few years they would be storming fortresses in the clouds in the Hindu Kush or outdoing the demigod Heracles at the great rock fortress of Aornos on the borders of India.

These Macedonians were not steppe nomads or desert Arabs for whom great journeys across trackless wastes was a way of life. Such men would surely not have followed so far down the path taken by Alexander unless they had a leader who thought in a manner unconstrained by the norms of his people or his generation. Nor does this matter have to remain in the realms of conjecture as it was tested at the time. In the summer of 332 while his army was battering the famous city of Tyre, Alexander received a letter from Darius III of Persia offering a huge sum of money, the King of King's own daughter as a wife and all Persian territory west of the Euphrates River in return for peace. This is the setting for a conversation in which Parmenion remarks that if he were Alexander he would accept the offer, before the king quips back 'So would I if I were Parmenion.' The trope of Alexander contradicting his great lieutenant, as before the proposed night attack on the enemy near Gaugamela, should not incline us to disbelieve this exchange, nor that the desire to stop at this point in the avalanche of conquest is anything but real for not just many officers but for most of the village boys who manned the victorious phalanx as well. Sense must have screamed in the heads of many that the amount of real estate they had already acquired and would be confirmed by this agreement was beyond enormous and would need years of further struggle to properly subjugate and assimilate. After all, so far they had hardly done any more than establish control over the key cities and main roads; to spread out and incorporate the rest into an Imperial Macedonian state would be bound to be the work of years, if not decades, never mind the chance to exploit and enjoy it.

Yet Alexander would not stop, refusing the offer to divide the world he conquered Egypt and defeated Darius in a climactic battle at Gaugamela before diving into the astonishing spaces east of Babylonia on the road to the Punjab. There was not just plenty of fighting with Scythians, Bactrians, Sogdians and eventually Indians, but significant troubles with his own followers along the way during Alexander's progress, and among the gripes of those concerned was almost always a desire to stop and enjoy what had already been won and not to career crazily on into the unknown. Developments finally came to a head when a halt was put to their endless wanderings not far from the banks of the Ganges. The army just would not have gone this far without the demands of their overbearing leader; most would not have denied their hankering for home, and to take back the eastern treasures that would make them the greatest men in their local communities. On top of this, many were distressed by the changes that they saw taking place in the headquarters the further east they went as Alexander seemed to leave behind traditional Macedonian ways and succumb to Persian habits. Proskynesis (obeisance) and Median trousers raised eyebrows and few could sympathize with a vision, however necessary, of co-opting the defeated ruling elite into the new Imperial administration, never mind the enrolling of Persian youths into the elite units of the army. Even many of those who did understand, who had no idea of returning to the home they had left so long before, would have wanted to see an end to their leader's interminable peregrinations to put down roots and enjoy what they had won as a planted ruling class in the rich and fertile regions they had already traversed.

The huge and diverse political entity that was the Macedonian Empire remaining after the death of Alexander the Great in 323 in Babylon might have developed in a number of directions and the eventual outcome would not have been in the least clear at the time or indeed for years after, although conflict was surely almost inevitable. The subsequent campaigns in the Asian and African lands turned into an astonishing epic, with a brief doomed attempt to hold the new empire together under Perdiccas, acting as regent for Alexander's half-brother Philip Arrhidaeus and his baby son by Roxana, ending with his death at the hands of treacherous Macedonian soldiery on the banks of the Nile. Then another power reshuffle at Triparadisus on the Orontes River, on the road from Egypt to Anatolia, was soon reformulated into a reality that saw Macedonian Europe, outside of Thrace, settled under the steady hand of Antipater, who had remained as regent in Pella when Alexander crossed the Hellespont, while Antigonus the One-Eyed was deputed to eradicate the remnants of those factions still loyal to Perdiccas remaining in the Asian lands. Years of hard fighting in Anatolia, Mesopotamia and Persia saw an opposition led by the brilliant Greek general Eumenes of Cardia finally reduced when he, like Perdiccas years earlier, was deserted by his Macedonian veterans and handed over to his adversary Antigonus.

These dramatic years of duelling from 318 to 315 between two military exemplars had been accompanied by considerable developments in Europe. From the start the centre never threatened to hold as the peoples of Greece, appreciating the odour when 'the stench of the corpse would have filled the world' that Demades prophesied on the great Macedonian oppressor's death finally entered their nostrils, utilized the money that Alexander's errant treasurer Harpalus had banked at Athens to try to throw off the yoke imposed since the bloodletting at Chaeronea fifteen years earlier. Barely had this Lamian War been concluded with the help of reinforcements from Alexander's eastern army brought back by Leonnatus, Craterus and Polyperchon than the Wars of the Diadochi themselves migrated to Europe. An Antipatrine disposition hardly lasted at all after Triparadisus and in a few years Antigonus, trying to make himself number one in Asia, backed Cassander in a conflict with Polyperchon, Antipater's designated successor at Pella, and his new-found ally Alexander's formidable Epirot mother Olympias. Four years of vicious civil strife followed, with armies of Macedonian levies, Greek mercenaries, Thessalian cavalry, Epirot and Thracian warriors and many more promenading destructively up and down Greece from the Peloponnese in the south to Aetolia, Acarnania, Epirus in the west and the upper Macedonian cantons before a very temporary conclusion was reached in 315 after Olympias was captured at Pydna and assassinated by the relatives of those victims she had dispatched in her days of power.

These traumatic times were only the beginning, and just after Cassander had established himself in power outsiders began to intervene, a process that scarcely halted for forty years. Almost every great name in the gallery of the first generation of Alexander's successors would stir the stew of Macedonian Europe: from the Antigonids, father and son, making their presence felt for decades, through Lysimachus first as the ruler of Thrace and after Ipsus, a power from the Danube to the Taurus, to Seleucus, the final man standing in the game to win west and central Hellenistic Asia and who, as his last act, was also intent on returning to Pella.

Even Ptolemy, whose ambitions are generally considered more limited, kept a finger in the pie, and it would not be just familiar and cultivated antagonists that would tear and shred the economic and societal fabric of Macedonian Europe. Dangerous strangers from the north on the lookout for glory, loot and perhaps land to settle would provide the devastating finale to these agonal decades. There was hardly a few years together when the region from the Peloponnese to the Hellespont was at peace; when farmers could sow their fields with confidence that they would be able to peacefully reap the rewards of their labour, when merchants might with conviction finance trading expeditions in a world made so much wider in Macedonia's Imperial era. Monarchs would come and go in bewildering succession and a bloated elite made immediately rich by the winnings of their belligerent children brought back from wealthy and exotic Mesopotamia, Egypt, Iran and further east would be divided and manipulated by new masters emerging from royal bloodlines ensconced in Epirus or Egypt or from the first generations of warlords coming out of Thrace and Anatolia.

Eventually there was an end game to the sanguine winnowing of the peoples in the huge expanse of country where so much fighting had taken place. Finally it turned out to be fairly simple. East and south of the Hellespont where two dynasties – the Seleucids and the Ptolemies – roughly divided the continents of Asia and Africa between them, though the rivalry for control of Coele-Syria ran down the generations and almost from the start the emergence of embryonic Bithynian and Pontic states on the edges and a Galatian rump in the centre ensured that Anatolia was never fully secure. Similar failure to keep control in the Far Eastern satrapies would probably have been equally noticeable if the evidence was there to substantiate it. There was, however, nothing simple about developments in Europe, and from 318 when Cassander, son of Antipater, had taken over in Macedonia despite his father initially disinheriting him and one of Alexander's intimates Lysimachus establishing himself in Thrace, a fiefdom he had received at the first post-Alexander settlement at Babylon in 323, the story is fascinating and complicated and its outcome significant, despite the fact that after 301 the paucity of sources is challenging.

The number of contemporaries who wrote about this period is considerable, but none survive outside quotations or references in the likes of Pausanias and Plutarch and the most important is the principal source for the relevant sections of Diodorus of Sicily. It is necessary to contend with great gaps in this first-century purveyor of universal history, leaving us largely dependent on evidence that has suffered coruscating criticism in its time, such as Justin's epitome of Pompeius Trogus and a local history of Pontic Heraclea by Memnon. Even the man who gives us the lives of two of the most exciting actors in the years we are contemplating is often traduced as the purveyor of hackneyed moral tales whose interest in political and military matters is cursory at best. Pausanias contains much in what is overtly a tourist guide and a fund of inscriptions particularly from Athens contributes an important take on events. Generally facts are vague and few, and details are often lost or confused, allowing a variety of explanations, and it cannot be denied that those used to several continuous accounts of the kind we have for the life of Alexander or the eruption of Rome into the Hellenistic world might find the period frustrating. Yet these kinds of epochs depending on gossamer-thin evidence have their appeal, fitting shadowy clues together in an effort to paint a picture that makes sense and if sometimes the endeavour can be exasperating with just glimpses of clarity in a shadowy landscape, nothing can completely obscure epic encounters and great clashing characters painted in colours as garish as would have been the decoration on those wonderful temples and sculptures that the modern observer is used to seeing as pristine marble.

Chapter One

An Old, Old Man

Sometime in the 600s impecunious, land-hungry and adventurous people from Miletus and Clazomenae, both Greek cities on the Aegean shore of Asia, sailed north along the coast to reach the head of the Gulf of Melas (today the Gulf of Saros) and there on the margins of Europe they planted the town of Cardia. Mixing with folk from the local Dolonci[1] the place thrived, getting a population boost from Athens late in the next century when Miltiades of Marathon fame was a big man in the region and the town became an important post on the grain route that fed the maw of the Athenian people in the days of that city's pomp, as indicated by the ears of corn shown on the city's money. A hard-won but fragile autonomy for this most important city of the Thracian Chersonese terminated in alliance with Philip II of Macedon by 346, if not earlier, such that the orator Demosthenes in the Peace of Philocrates specifically designated the people of Cardia as enemies of Athens.

In the 350s a man was born there from whom we derive so much of what is known of the period of Alexander's successors. Hieronymus the historian and his kinsman Eumenes grew up in the privileged milieu of a cultivated urban upper class with close Macedonian ties. Eumenes' father, also called Hieronymus,[2] was recorded as a guest friend of King Philip himself. The future historian would have been in his late teens or early 20s when he accompanied Eumenes, possibly an uncle and a senior functionary in the chancellery that accompanied Alexander's army in the conquest of the Persian Empire. Belonging to one of the great families of the city, these two were bitter rivals of Hecataeus who became the local tyrant; indeed, it may well have been for their own safety that they removed themselves so far from home where a malignant nemesis was eager to encompass their demise. Certainly in the year after Alexander's death when for his own purposes a general called Leonnatus was trying to get both Eumenes and Hecataeus to support his bid for power as husband of Alexander's sister Cleopatra, it became clear that Eumenes was afraid if he co-operated in this foray into Europe, Antipater, still in power at that time, might have him killed to gratify the Cardian strongman.

The significance of this man who would wear out so many years – one suggestion is that he lived to 104[3] – is first properly noticed in 320 when he headed a diplomatic mission from Eumenes to Antipater, although before that he would have already been a senior member of that capable man's administrative staff when he was ordered by Perdiccas to take over troublesome Cappadocia, a region where these well-connected Greeks born in a city so close to Anatolia would have been worth their weight in gold. In 318 when Eumenes, notorious and outlawed for having defeated Craterus near the Hellespont in a battle where that Macedonian military exemplar died, a figure of almost kingly stature who wrapped himself in a purple cloak when he received Greek envoys after the victory at Crannon ended the Lamian War,[4] was tracked down by Antigonus the One-Eyed to a fortress in Cappadocia called Nora at the foot of the Taurus Mountains. This contemporary of Philip had been in charge of Phrygia in Alexander's time, but had taken charge of the Asian army Antipater left behind on returning to Macedonia at the end of his one foray east of the Hellespont. There, besieged in his eyrie, Eumenes tried to intrigue his way out by directing Hieronymus to win terms from the man entrenched tenaciously below his walls. The scheming during these exchanges is opaque, but Hieronymus and Eumenes showed cunning in the context of a world just ruptured by the news of Antipater's death, apparently first accepting an alliance with Antigonus to earn their release from Nora, but then reneging and gaining from Antipater's successor Polyperchon access to enough of the treasure kept at Cynda in Cilicia that it was possible to fund an army spearheaded by those formidable old veterans of all Alexander's battles, the Silver Shields. These were men that Eumenes would lead with such subtly and intelligence that Antigonus would only just get the better of him in two years of hard campaigning over a vast Eastern amphitheatre.

The winter of 316/315 saw Hieronymus penned up with other prisoners following his leader and compatriot being sold by the Silver Shields to his death as the price of their women and baggage. However, if the victor of the Iranian war felt that Eumenes was too dangerous to live, this was not at all the case with his talented protégé. Transferring to the victor's party from the defeated one was anyway a norm in these successor wars and the Cardian already knew Antigonus from the Nora transactions. The administrator-historian was soon established at the heart of Antigonid headquarters, on familiar terms with both Antigonus and his son the future Demetrius Poliorcetes (the besieger of cities). At the time this highbrow joined the entourage of the one-eyed dynast he had been campaigning deep in upper Asia for two years and when starting out on the road to Mesopotamia and the upper satrapies Antigonus had been but one of a number of significant power-players in the splintered world that had emerged in the half-decade since Alexander's death. However, when in 315 he returned to the west, his position was exponentially different: now he was the dominant power, the richest by far of the Diadochi with the strongest army in Europe, Africa or Asia. He had even resuscitated those old dazzling Persian arrangements that meant exploiting the resources of an Asian realm of vast distances and hugely varied terrain would be so much easier: 'He himself established at intervals throughout all that part of Asia of which he was master a system of fire-signals and dispatch-carriers, by means of which he expected to have quick service in all his business.'[5]

The product of success was inevitably envy and fear. Antigonus was worrying everybody now after his removal of local potentates like Pithon, Seleucus and Peucestas, the latter two who had been enjoying control of the wealthy old provinces of Babylonia and Persia. The size of his fortune was alarming: he had already taken 10,000 talents from the Cyinda treasury and had an annual income of more than that. Such military might, founded on the combined Macedonian veterans, minus the Silver Shields sent off in small units on what was intended to be fatal duty on the Indian frontier, of both his own and Eumenes' armies and the best mercenaries his ample money could buy, was bound to raise anxiety among his peers. Ptolemy of Egypt became the architect of a joint reaction instigated by the arrival of the exiled Seleucus, so it was his envoys that covered the hundreds of miles on roads well maintained since the Persians had been in charge that it took to reach Antigonus in upper Syria. What they had on offer was extraordinary: the confederates' demands laid before the old warrior and his council if accepted would have chopped great chunks of real estate out of the empire he had won so there was little real chance of accommodation. Yet refusal meant war and, after accepting the gage thrown down at his feet, we hear of Ptolemaeus, a nephew of Antigonus, being sent to raise the siege of Amisus, to clear Cassander's men out of Cappadocia and occupy the Hellespont to prevent him interfering in Anatolia again. Hieronymus would have known this man well: they had met as far back as the siege of Nora when Antigonus had dispatched him as a hostage to Eumenes, but still Ptolemaeus' efforts were largely peripheral; it was Antigonus' maritime offensive against the Lagids of Egypt that was at the centre of the great man's exertions. The generation of naval muscle with which to control the Aegean and its islands was crucial in dominating the routes east and west from Phoenicia to Greece as far as Carthage and Spain and north-south where control from Rhodes to Paros would cut communications between his enemies in Europe and Africa. As part of this strategy, the Peloponnese, Attica and Euboea were also crucial in monitoring the whole East Mediterranean, as were the Cypriot powers who Antigonus was soon assiduously wooing.

This involvement in Europe was a process, not an event, and had emerged as a serious prong of Antigonus' strategy by 314. He might have sponsored Cassander before when he needed a counterweight to Polyperchon, having his own hands full in dealing with Eumenes, but that time was past and it hardly needed the ruler of Macedon to have made demands for compensation in Cappadocia and Lycia as part of the list of requirements forwarded by Ptolemy to make him an enemy, but from that moment onwards he certainly was one, meaning that there would be another dimension to the next successor war. Once returned to the coast of Syria, the Antigonid chancery, where Hieronymus cheerfully sat, would have collated the reports on the situation in the Macedonian homeland and what had been for almost a generation her Greek adjuncts. Not that the hard-hand hegemony impressed by Philip and reinforced by Antipater had been uncontested: there were always factions, often fuelled by savage class hatred, eager to oust the garrisons or apparatchiks that had long been keeping them subservient. The Lamian War had almost looked like it might introduce a new dawn of autonomy, and if these reveries had been stillborn, in more recent years the bloody divisions between their Macedonian masters had offered the opportunity of finding freedom between the cracks. If Cassander's success in establishing himself in Pella suggested a return to the bad old days of his father's time, there were still sparks glowing and perhaps the more prescient of Hellenic observers realized that exploitation of dynastic fault lines might engage the power of those to the east who possessed the fuel to start a mighty fire of freedom.

It was the history written by the minister Hieronymus of Cardia who had long ago left his birthplace on the Thracian Chersonese and freighted via Diodorus of Sicily that highlights the impact of a newly-conquered Asian world rebounding west across the Aegean against the homeland of its conquerors. Down to modern times Diodorus has suffered, being considered an entirely unoriginal copyist despite him having no inclination to try to hide his character as a compiler. Yet at least the quality of Hieronymus as a source, concerned as he was to discover the practical motives of leaders and qualities of subordinates with less emphasis on the impact of sacrilege or piety, makes him invaluable, whether from the geographic itinerary compiled in the last year of Alexander's life with information from his chancery or from the Diadochi period with military details never reproduced in Diodorus' pages when he was not available. Nonetheless, as Pausanias suggests: 'If Philistus was justified in suppressing the most wicked deeds of Dionysius, because he expected his return to Syracuse, surely Hieronymus may be fully forgiven for writing to please Antigonus.'[6] Such an association with power ensured that he could not help but show a certain bias.

The details of the European contest would have been personally familiar to the man who would chronicle it, listening to the intelligence reports in Antigonus' headquarters and relaying what his proxies in Europe had achieved. He must inevitably be partial, making grand and tragic his sponsors' reputation by suggesting that he alone really had the ambition to reunify and rule the whole of Alexander's Empire, the most deserving for trying for the supreme prize, for contemplating world conquest. Such a verdict fails to register that if Ptolemy and Cassander may have had largely more local ambitions, certainly Seleucus shared the aspiration and was but a short step from achieving most of it when he fell foul of a despicable fatality. Yet despite this preference, Hieronymus had the considerable advantage of being contemporary with events and as such was able to verify the narratives heard from eyewitnesses and directly understand the personalities of those involved. Following a historical tradition well over 150 years old, his analysis remained to be not just tapped but sometimes virtually plagiarized by not a few of those whose works are still left to us and, like Polybius, the historian of

Rome's climb to greatness, with first-hand knowledge of the world he was describing and intimate contact with major figures, he also probably had just as elevated an understanding of his own significance in what he understood as an age of giants. We know much more about him than many ancient historians. We may hear of Thucydides in command of a naval squadron near Amphipolis and his subsequent exile or Polybius as a world traveller and sycophant and tutor in the houses of the Scipio Aemiliani, but Hieronymus remained significant through to his demise, dying sound in mind and body at over 100 years of age.

Since Antipater had straddled the Balkan world, the family programme continued by his son had been to keep a grip on the Greek cities in their purview, either by the presence of a military garrison or the rule of congenial oligarchies generally guaranteed by the restriction of the citizen franchise to men of very considerable means. This enfeebling of democratic factions was for years the norm in mainland Greece, only entrenched after the debacle of the Lamian revolt had dampened recalcitrant spirits in blood. Yet these Macedonian rulers were not the only kids on the block: of those already on the spot when the successor conflict flared again there was Alexander, the able son of Polyperchon who had been reported as active on his father's behalf in Attica in 318 in his high days when he was, as the guardian of Alexander's heirs designated by Antipater, besieging Megalopolis. The family pairing may have fallen in the world since Cassander had taken Macedonia from their ally Olympias, but the industry they had showed in the Peloponnese since 317 had paid local dividends so Alexander still controlled strong posts in the peninsula while his father remained active, offering another focus of opposition while enjoying Aetolian hospitality, while almost inevitably the Spartans refused obeisance to any foreign master despite her days of real greatness being long past.

Cassander's response to these political wrinkles in the realm he had so recently won was typical of this busy man. Since eliminating Olympias at Pydna and securing Pella in 315 he had married Thessaloniki, daughter of Philip II, to graft his line to that of the Argeads and, claiming that prerogative of kingship most outstandingly exercised by Alexander, he founded Cassandreia on the site of old Potidaea in the Chalcidice. As the year was winding down he even found the time and inclination to deal with the problem to the south where only Alexander seemed possessed of a force that could stand against him. The new ruler of Macedon, 'after assembling an adequate force, set out from Macedonia', crossed Thessaly before being held up at Thermopylae by the Aetolians, taking up a position at this choke point as they had done so often in the past. It took real fighting but he dug them out in the end and with the road cleared the Macedonians reached Boeotia. There he re-established the city of Thebes in the rich Teneric Plain before his progress took the army through the Cithaeron Mountains across the Megarid and over the Gerania hills before discovering that Alexander's men were well-positioned blocking the isthmus. Temporarily stymied, Cassander showed at his best: backtracking to Megara, he set the local shipwrights to work building not only boats to transport his men but special barges to take the elephants he had with him. It must have been a splendid sight to see the huge beasts trumpeting in concern as their conveyances set sail with the sun shining off the armour of the warriors following their wake in the flotilla, crossing the Saronic Gulf to arrive on the coast of the Argolid at Epidaurus, there disembarking at this ancient port famous for its healing centre at the sanctuary of Asclepius, offspring of Apollo.

They pushed on to the city of Argos. There the municipal leaders were pressured to 'abandon its alliance with Alexander and to join him', and after this promising start he progressed right across the peninsula through Arcadia and into the region of Messene. Cassander managed to enter the town and take control, but it was beyond him to capture the stronghold on Mount Ithome. So it was a precarious presence left behind when he retraced his route back to the Argolid where he was able to negotiate the submission of Hermione, a place on the southern coast near the island of Hydra. Despite this enemy parading around his domain, Alexander felt he did not have the numbers to react, instead keeping safe behind the walls of the fortress Acrocorinth rising rugged and precipitous from the coastal plain. So the fighting season terminated with the main army returning to Macedonia while leaving 'at the end of the Isthmus towards Gerania two thousand soldiers commanded by Molyccus' to try to bottle up Alexander in the peninsula and deny him any opportunity to join his Aetolian allies in interfering in Attica or Boeotia. This force was not incredibly numerous but still sufficient to be able to hold these defensible hills against almost anybody coming against them. The ruler of Macedon might now have felt he had good reason to feel he had solved the problem of the sprig of old Polyperchon who had not been up to contesting the open field with him, particularly as the father looked an even more spent force hiding out in Aetolia with an old Epirot ally.[7] Surely he expected that with Olympias gone and Macedon secure he would inevitably inherit the old ascendency in mainland Greece? Yet it was not going to be that easy; things would soon hang in the balance as Hieronymus' master took a hand.

This intervention was spearheaded by a very significant official named Aristodemus of Miletus who, although he suffered from bad notices[8] as an archetypal sycophant, was one of Antigonus' most dependable agents and closer to his master than many of his weightiest military men. He had been first with the news of Antipater's death in 319 and was years later on hand to profit, if slightly belatedly, as the foremost to report the extraordinary victory of Demetrius at Cypriot Salamis in 306, but now in 314 he was offered the opportunity to flex his military and diplomatic muscles in an independent mission. He was sent to the Peloponnese with 1,000 talents to make friends with Polyperchon and his son and buy a bespoke army with which to ferment a war against Cassander. We know that when he reached Sparta he greased palms and got permission to recruit 8,000 soldiers, most probably at the great mercenary mart of Cape Taenarum at the tip of the modern Mani peninsula. Once established as a local player, Aristodemus approached the family firm then dominating the region. Polyperchon and son were not fantasists. They knew that compared with the big political beasts they were but hyenas who could only feed between the tracks of the great dynasts, so when the newcomer offered the senior man the post of Antigonid commander in the Peloponnese, he bit his hand off. This marriage of convenience was consummated as Polyperchon, prepared to gamble with his son's life to gain the advantages on offer, shipped him over to visit the great ruler of Asia in his headquarters at Old Tyre.

While Hieronymus' master played on a world stage, the Greek audience always remained significant and he took the opportunity of the young man's arrival to advertise his good intentions to this constituency. At an assembly of Macedonian soldiers and civilians this master of propaganda launched a tirade against Cassander as the murderer of Olympias and spinning his reported mistreatment of Alexander's wife Roxana as indicating ambitions for the Macedonian throne. More than that, he had founded a city named for himself near where Olynthus, ancient enemy of Macedonia, had stood before re-establishing Thebes, a place the great Alexander, despite a glorious past hardly less shining than that of Athens, regarded as a nest of traitors who had famously Medized in 480 and twice revolted against Macedonian rule. Indeed he razed it to the ground, leaving it a gutted ruin with the dogs howling, echoing the anguish of their exiled masters who fled from among toppled statues, charred corpses and incinerated houses carrying any valuables that could be saved. The terrifying fate that hung over the band of refugees who survived along the road from the broken city was reinforced by the knowledge that Alexander had announced a specific diktat that Thebes should never be rebuilt. The assembly trumpeted that Cassander must undo these misdeeds and put himself under Antigonus' orders as the proper guardian of the legitimate dynastic line or face destruction. It was also on this occasion that the decree of Greek autonomy was promulgated, posting a clear opposition to Cassander's line that contended the only way to deal with the Greek cities was by the establishing of garrisons, sympathetic oligarchs and tyrants. What this Greek freedom really meant to these Macedonian grandees is moot. Whatever he may have promised for Antigonus, it was surely more about weakening Cassander than any ideology, and his rival understood it as realpolitik. The reality was all about context. Alexander himself, while largely suppressing autonomy on the mainland during the invasion of Achaemenid Anatolia, had not scrupled about mobilizing local Greek support by sponsoring the democratic factions in the Aegean cities where the Persians had previously favoured oligarchs and tyrants.

This fishing in the muddy waters of the Peloponnese by Antigonid strategists was not the only sign of tentacles approaching Macedonian Europe. The old man's nephew Ptolemaeus was progressing through Cappadocia, throwing out Cassander's lieutenants before his army pressed on into Bithynia, making clients out of not just the local king Zipoetes but the key Greek communities in this region around the crossings to Europe. Then this increasingly noteworthy relative marched south into Ionia and Lydia to organize their coastal defences against Seleucus, the exiled satrap of Babylonia, at the time functioning effectively as an admiral in the service of Ptolemy of Egypt. This had been the condition of affairs in 314 when Antigonus moved into Phoenicia and commenced the siege of the mighty maritime centre of Tyre, during which operation his army also conquered down the Levantine coast to Joppa on the way to the Egyptian border. Yet if he had his eyes fixed south, he was far from forgetting his new ally. Polyperchon's son's plans were given the nod and Antigonus, knowing magnificent munificence was key to his appeal, furnished him with 500 talents before returning him to his father. The Grecian mission may not have been the old general's top project at this time that centred on the siege of Tyre and conquest of Phoenicia, but he was putting down a marker of a continuing interest in taking swipes at an enemy who occupied the homeland from which he and the other great power-brokers had sprung.

Ptolemy in Alexandria was stunned into action by this propaganda campaign that threatened to get so many Greek communities onto his enemy's bandwagon and followed suit by publishing his own Greek Decree of Freedom in an effort to mitigate the damage being done to the anti-Antigonid cause. His confederacy had been showing signs of expansion with Asander, the ruler of Caria and various Cypriot potentates joining in and indeed it was at Cyprus that the Lagid fleets concentrated with Seleucus and Menelaus, Ptolemy's effective brother, on hand to lead them. When this council assembled on the island they did not disregard the importance of the armed squabbling transpiring in southern Greece and dispatched an officer called Polycleitus with fifty ships to hold up their end in the crucial peninsula. However, when this new actor took the stage he discovered that there had been a number of meaningful developments since his expedition had been envisaged. The slippery Aristodemus had brought a new dimension to peninsular politics when, with bags full of Antigonid specie, he had not only been able to hire his own considerable mercenary force but had offered steady and considerable financial backing to Polyperchon when he hooked up with him in Aetolia. Despite the bleakness of the news he was receiving, Cassander knew that things still hung in the balance and that he must respond. First he tried to subvert Polyperchon, but this old man had been burned before and showed no signs of biting. So, deciding on direct action where intrigue had failed, he again brought his army down through Thessaly and into Boeotia and after assisting the Thebans to build defensive walls, breezed unopposed across the narrow isthmus, took the port of Cenchraea and ravaged the Corinthian countryside, incinerating all the fields and farms his men could get at.

He stormed two unnamed fortresses and 'dismissed under a truce' the soldiers Alexander had left to defend them, but this was not enough as on his second visit to the Peloponnese Cassander had determined on major conquests. Orchomenus in Arcadia was the next named destination that took his fancy where a faction had invited him to come and take over. Important enough, as with Tegea and Mantinea it had been one of the richest and most powerful regional powers before Megalopolis had been established in the 360s and was extremely defensible, part surrounded by mountains with a 3,000ft-high acropolis that was considered almost the equal of the formidable fortress at Mount Ithome. The fifth columnists who had made contact ensured treachery handed Cassander the city where he left a strong garrison to hold the citadel and, aware of the need to reward his local friends, made no objections to their bloody dispositions when, showing no mercy to those of Alexander's associates who had been taking refuge in a shrine to Artemis and disregarding mores of divine sanctuary, hauled them out and assassinated them on the steps of the temple.

He was now within sight of Messene, the most important place in the south-west and, with Acrocorinth, the most formidable bastion in the peninsula. This had probably been his target from the start but he was going to find imposing his will on the Peloponnese no easier than many others before him and on arriving near the capital found it well-defended by Polyperchon's men. Disinclined to get bogged down in a long siege so far from home, Cassander faded back into Arcadia where he established one of his men as governor of Megalopolis before returning to the security of the Argolid. Here in the summer of 313 he enjoyed himself 'presiding at the Nemean Games', showing the kind of cultural sponsorship that was de rigueur for these Hellenistic dynasts, before withdrawing reasonably well satisfied with his efforts, back to Macedonia. However, the fragility of his achievements was exposed soon enough, as Alexander and Aristodemus emerged from the strongholds where they had weathered the storm and, continuing to boast of their commitment to Greek freedom, began to recruit locals to drive out the garrisons left behind by the Macedonian ruler. The news of the potential threat posed by this family-fostered counterpunch found Cassander disinclined to take up arms again. Frustrated that however often he progressed with his irresistible military through the Peloponnese, it seemed not to make a decisive difference, he turned to underhand methods and, looking where he might divide and rule, dispatched his own trusted agent Prepelaus to try to convince Alexander to dump Antigonus with the promise that he would make him his commander-in-chief in the Peloponnese and back him with Macedonian money. The journey from Pella proved very well worth the candle and a concordat was soon reached: 'Alexander, since he saw that the thing for which he had originally made war against Cassander was being granted to him, made the alliance and was appointed general of the Peloponnesus.'[9]

This dramatic volte face turned out to be of considerable local significance when Polycleitus with his fleet of fifty ships arrived outside Cenchraea where he had been directed by Seleucus. There at this Saronic Gulf port of Alexander's headquarters he found no one in arms to oppose him but in place a welcome haven and instead of discovering enemies to fight he encountered a new friend with apparently no urgent need of reinforcement, so he withdrew from the region. This Lagid admiral's impact had turned out not to have occurred where he had initially been dispatched, yet the reports of the arrival of his fifty warships in the vicinity of the isthmus had persuaded Antigonus that his enemies were prepared to up the ante in the struggle for mainland Greece. So while his main efforts might have been directed to the building of a mighty navy allowed by the conquest of the great maritime cities of Phoenicia, he could not completely disregard the far western front. Some 240 warships were finally assembled; some real monsters, if not quite the giants that Demetrius' megalomania would soon demand, but still warships with 5, 6, 7, 8, 9 and even 10 men working the tiers of oars. The struggle for thalassocracy dominated Antigonus' grand councils and most of the prodigious marine would soon be directed under Dioscurides, another nephew, initially against Ptolemy, the man who had choreographed the coalition that had recently emerged against him, before cruising the Aegean to win over the islands by force or persuasion. Yet in the matter of the Peloponnese it was better safe than sorry; an insurance policy was worth the premium sufficient for him to detach fifty of his own battleships to counter those under Polycleitus still thought to be cruising the waters of the Saronic Gulf.

Recent history had shown that only the most cunning could hope to steer a steady course in the Peloponnesian theatre of war, but here Aristodemus of Miletus had found his natural element, navigating the factional feuding of Greek politics in order to expand his master's portfolio of Hellenic allies before travelling over the Gulf of Corinth to Aetolia where he expected a convivial reception from people who had in virtually all circumstances stood in opposition to whoever ruled at Pella. Such an attitude is made fathomable by the fact that after the Lamian War the Macedonians had registered an intention to accomplish the complete eradication of their communal past by deporting the whole Aetolian population to the desert regions of Asia. He was in the process of successfully persuading the assembled populace that cleaving to the Antigonid party was in their interest when calamitous tidings arrived that Alexander, despite being so sumptuously received by Antigonus not long before, had jumped ship and tied his colours to Cassander's staff. Confident that he now had steady allies on the north shore of the Gulf of Corinth and with his military beefed up with reinforcements from a people always enthusiastic to fight for steady wages, Aristodemus hurried his soldiers back aboard ship and transported them over into the Peloponnese. The returnees arrived in the vicinity of Cyllene and there discovered Alexander in person at the head of some Elean troops laying the port under siege. Aristodemus' timing was good as the people were close to surrendering when his men arrived to be received with open arms by the locals when they raised the siege, even accepting the need for some of his soldiers to stay on to protect them against Alexander and their regional foes from Elis. The majority, however, were soon on the road again heading north-east up into Achaea, targeting the important crossing-point of Patrae where the Gulf of Corinth was near its narrowest point. This defended port was important enough to warrant a considerable garrison, but the intruders were in strength and took the place before moving on Aegium a few miles east down the coast. After a formal siege here, again the defenders surrendered, though unfortunately for his reputation as liberator, Aristodemus' soldiers got out of control: going well beyond the usual victory pillaging, they killed a substantial number of the civilians and burned down many of the town's buildings.

Having established himself on the southern shore of the gulf, Aristodemus, after receiving worrying news from Aetolia, shipped back to those jittery allies in double-quick time, a power visit that it turned out had significant implications elsewhere. At Dyme a few miles west of Patrae and another crossing-point the locals, knowing these potential champions were now only just over a narrow channel, gained the confidence to do for themselves what had been done for their neighbours. These resourceful people trapped the occupying garrison in the citadel by building a strong defensive wall between there and the main part of the town and then from this base 'invested the citadel and made unremitting attacks upon it'. This insurgency was not long in being reported to Alexander, who with Aristodemus' army across the water responded with alacrity, pressing down the road from Sicyon, and arriving at the divided town he swiftly forced his way in before disarming, executing or imprisoning those he found attacking the citadel. This proficient young commander tried to finally settle the place by banishing anybody he considered a troublemaker, but if the victor turning from the picture of his enemies trailing off to an exile's billet felt he had solved this problem he was to be disappointed. This Dyme war still had plenty of legs. Once Alexander had departed, the survivors, after a period required to come to terms with the butchery and recover their nerve, called in what they hoped would be decisive aid from the garrison Aristodemus had left not far away at Aegium. These mercenaries had an immediate impact, surprising the garrison left in the citadel, killing many and dispatching any citizens they could find who had shown any partiality for Alexander.

Yet even now the inhabitants were left little time to celebrate the removal of this hard hand occupation before they received tidings that their erstwhile ruler was not going to let things lie. However, before he could make his presence felt, they found themselves the beneficiaries of what for Polyperchon's son was unfortunate fatality taking a hand. Just as the columns of his men were leaving their billets in Sicyon he was set upon and killed by a group of locals who had wormed their way into his confidence by vociferously upholding his cause among the citizenry. Their leader was one Alexion of Sicyon, an otherwise unreported actor who looked like he would throw the whole Cassandrian party into confusion before the murdered man's spouse took a hand. Her name was Cratesipolis, and she had during their marriage made quite a name for charity among the impecunious in her husband's army: 'She was most highly esteemed by the soldiers for her acts of kindness; for it was her habit to aid those who were in misfortune and to assist many of those who were without resources.'[10] This was the character who used her reputation and considerable ability to fill the power vacuum. 'She possessed, too, skill in practical matters and more daring than one would expect in a woman'[11] to hold together an army that with their leader gone would probably otherwise have fallen apart and sought employment elsewhere. Not that stumping up their salaries was the only problem she faced as local resistance fighters, synchronizing their coup with the assassination, had gathered in arms to rid themselves of oppressors who had been occupying their city for some time. Ordering her husband's officers to deploy their men, she attacked the assembled insurgents and beat them back to their homes with considerable carnage. Now there was no more suggestion of softness when power was wielded by the distaff side than there had been when Olympias took control in Macedonia, as outside Sicyon's walls thirty of those panicked opposition leaders who could not bolt in time were crucified, their bodies left to rot in the sun and Cratesipolis' hold on the city was ensured for some years to come.

A new fighting season brought another nephew of Antigonus called Telesphorus[12] who was dispatched with fifty ships and a 'suitable force of infantry' to maintain his uncle's posture as sponsor of Greek freedom. After landing without opposition and scoring some local success, on approaching the heartland strongholds of the dead Alexander's demesne he found himself bashing his head against a brick wall. There at the great fortified cities of Corinth and Sicyon the widow Cratesipolis and Polyperchon opted to retreat behind their ramparts, imperviously ensconced with plenty of soldiers despite how often Telesphorus' envoys read Antigonus' Greek freedom decree outside the walls. The new family coalition was showing itself still firmly in control at this crucial communications node where the peninsula attached to the mainland and despite a number of abortive assaults the most recent of Antigonus' agents to enter the old Peloponnesian game had to satisfy himself with moving off to try to occupy the Argolid.

Peace feelers may have been put out across the lines in these years, but with the possibility of real compromise remaining illusory Cassander, determined as ever to retain as much of his Greek holdings as possible, mobilized to impose his authority on a crucial barbican that defended access to mainland Greece from the east. Embarking an army on thirty ships he sailed to Oreus, an Antigonid ally at the north end of the long island of Euboea, swatting aside any challenge to his landing and setting up siege works to press hard on the defenders of the town. However, if he was active, so were his opponents as after an ultimatum had been delivered and a number of assaults looked set to produce success, Cassander found his forces surprised by the same man who had so recently been making trouble for him in the Peloponnese. Telesphorus brought 20 ships and 1,000 soldiers while an admiral called Medius arrived from Asia with 100 more warships and together they attacked the blockading vessels with fire pots, burning 4 and causing such consternation among the rest that under cover of this distraction they were able to throw reinforcements into the city. Yet again the Macedonian ruler proved resilient. Gathering reinforcements for his navy from Athens, he attacked Medius' ships lying off the coast, surprising the inattentive sailors. They sank one ship and captured three more with their crews, men unable to find any way off their vessels and escape to their comrades.

This war remained a real concern for Antigonus and despite already having risked so many lives he had the resources to raise the stakes, despite his commitments in Anatolia and the Levant. Having received missions from Aetolia reconfirming their friendship and from Boeotia, incensed by the resuscitation of their old oppressor Thebes, both calling for help, he fed in more troops, this time led by that other active and competent nephew Ptolemaeus who was given a force substantially larger than that which had gone before. Some 5,000 foot and 500 horse were dispatched while Medius' squadron was brought up to 150, all backed up by 10 Rhodian warships manned by some of the best sailors in the world persuaded to join in this effort to liberate their mainland compatriots. Island-hopping across the Aegean, he arrived 'at the harbour of Boeotia known as Bathys "Deep"' on the Euripus near Aulis. Only 3 miles from Chalcis, this Boeotian port on a rocky promontory was where the Greek fleets had gathered under Agamemnon en route to Troy and saw the fateful sacrifice of his eldest daughter Iphigenia as a curtain-raiser to the bloodbath awaiting them in the Troad. Spread around nearby harbours to hold the large numbers of ships,[13] the Antigonid prince was pleasantly surprised to find friends were waiting. Some 2,200 foot and 1,200 horse mobilized by the Boeotian league were on hand and after incorporating these reinforcements he sent for the ships stationed at Oreus to monitor Cassander's siege and gathered everybody in a secure camp a few miles north at well-fortified Salganeus, situated on mainland Boeotia across from the Euboean shore. The newcomers' strategy was hardly new, intending to subvert the enemy garrison at Chalcis after being contacted by citizens vociferous in their affection for these new arrivals still touting their commitment to Greek freedom. The planning for the coup was, however, not kept secret and Cassander, getting word and knowing that Chalcis was his key stronghold on the island, aborted the siege of Oreus and rushed south, concentrating every soldier he could muster. Such a dynamic response ensured a stalemate with Cassander looking out from the town walls and Ptolemaeus occupying the country outside but making no effort to assault or to besiege the place and not even able to ravage the country around as the support of the local land-owning burghers had always been his trump card.

Antigonus, hearing news of how his lieutenants were faring, decided the significant navy he had dispatched west was being wasted, so he ordered Medius to ship them out back to Asia to assist in covering his new project of attacking directly over the Hellespont or the Propontis [Sea of Marmara]. Summer 313 had seen him rolling up the opposition in Anatolia despite an almost catastrophic attempt to rush through the snow-deep Taurus passes in the previous winter and with the potent old warlord personally on hand Asander in Caria threw in the towel, turned over his military to Antigonus and agreed that the Carian Greeks should regain their autonomy. However, this was only a ploy as he soon was intriguing with Ptolemy and Seleucus and calling for them to come to his aid in throwing off the Antigonid yoke. The old king of Asia responded to this double-dealing by sending Medius with a navy and Docimus with an army to liberate the Greek cities. Places with legendary pasts like Miletus were released from bondage before things really heated up as the old man himself arrived on the scene, besieging and capturing Tralles and bringing most of his new navy on to Kaunos, captured despite hold-outs in the citadel only succumbing after numerous assaults. Success here had encouraged the one-eyed dynast to try his luck with one of his most persistent foes and so he opened communication with Cassander himself, but the talks foundered because the Macedonian ruler would not countenance any significant Antigonid influence around the Hellespont which he knew comprised both the door and the key to the eastern marches of his realm. To threaten here was clever policy, as despite his refusal to negotiate, it ensured that if Cassander remained in Euboea. Macedonia itself would be short of its ruler and home army to make a defence, but if he returned to protect the homeland his position in not just Euboea but in all of Greece might crumble under pressure from opponents already entrenched there.

Cassander had confronted this kind of dilemma before and thought he knew the way out. He left his brother Pleistarchus to defend Chalcis, while with the main army he pressed on north to oppose a threat he knew would probably soon be materializing from the direction of Anatolia. This was grand strategic stuff but he did not forget the details. Crossing over to Attica, he first stormed Oropus, a town on the level seashore near the mouth of the Asopus River that had been a bone of contention between Athens and Boeotia for centuries. Having guaranteed this place, he continued on to Thebes to confirm in place a congenial administration while making a truce with the other main Boeotian communities. An officer was left behind with a considerable detachment to offer some military muscle while he departed with the rest of his men, pressing north as fast as possible to cover the hundreds of land miles between him and his threatened border. After days on the road they entered the Vale of Tempe, through this 5-mile steep-sided gash shivered by celestial caprice, passed the Greek cities along the coast of the Thermaic Gulf and nearing the familiar valleys and meadows of Macedonia they discovered that events elsewhere had aborted what had seemed an existential threat. Antigonus had tried to make his crossing to Europe not at the Hellespont, where once Xerxes' engineers had laid massive hawsers to anchor the pontoon bridge which, spanning the channel, would transport his hordes intent on taming the Greeks, but at the Propontis where the Byzantines with a small but efficient navy controlled the crossing. This people, persuaded by representatives of Lysimachus in particular, turned out unco-operative, saving Cassander the need to face his dreadful enemy in battle.

With Cassander on his way, Ptolemaeus found he could terminate the shadow-boxing and really spread his wings on Euboea, first closing in on his original target city of Chalcis. Just his arrival was sufficient to intimidate a garrison whose confidence had been shaken by their leader's departure and who surrendered this very defensible place that dominated the narrowest point of the Euboic channel as well as being a handy base for dominating east-central Greece. This fortress that would be later noted as one of the fetters of Greece was on this occasion left free and ungarrisoned by a conqueror who knew the importance of public relations. Yet the impression of freedom was always complex, so when Antigonus' nephew besieged and captured Oropus, south over the channel on the mainland, after the captive garrison was marched away into captivity he handed the place back to the Boeotians, showing an inclination to meddle in matters of Greek sovereignty that could not have sat well with the model of municipal freedom they were peddling. The need to placate a key local player trumped any local feelings about independence. Then it was back to Euboea moving south along the coast to Eretria and right to the south of the island at Carystus. Here under Mount Oche or along the way there were plenty of people who saw which way the wind was blowing and were eager to make friends with the visitor before he took to the waters again to ship over into Attica.

There had long been heated talk in the gatherings of Athenian Jacobins since Antigonus' Decree of Freedom had been promulgated and now these dissidents took their opportunity to call in Ptolemaeus to rid them of Demetrius of Phalerum who ran the city for Cassander. Soon enough all eyes turned east as his troops were reported disembarking on the seashore and marching hard by the coast road that led past the high tumulus covering the blessed dead of Marathon, warriors from whose heroism two centuries earlier all Athenian freedom had derived. Now Cassander's controller came under massive pressure to trim his course in a new direction from parties resentful of past subservience and, pressed between an army without and a citizenry with no love for his sponsor within, he had little option but to send agents over to Asia and make his peace with Antigonus. Ptolemaeus himself continued on his impressive tour by passing over the Cithaeron Mountains into Boeotia where he entered the new city of Thebes and attacked and took the Cadmea, handing over this legendary citadel and setting the people free. 'After this he advanced into Phocis' where again he drove out the troops left behind by Cassander and was welcomed by locals who happily hitched themselves to the Antigonid cause, before concluding by traversing Locris to return to the Euboean channel not far below the pass at Thermopylae. There at Opus he pressed a siege against an obdurate stronghold where unusually a local leadership stayed impressively loyal to the absent ruler of Macedon.

The tail end of these shenanigans on the western periphery continued past the peace of 311 when the contestants competing for Alexander's leavings took a breath before taking up cudgels again a few years later. During the last fighting season it became clear that Antigonus' nephew Telesphorus had been far from happy to accept a subservient position, particularly when it was to his cousin. He considered his standing had been unreasonably undermined when he saw this new man on the scene arriving with the kind of military resources he had never been granted and, lurking around Corinth, he pondered deeply on his wrongs. Used to being the big fish in a small Peloponnesian pond and far from prepared to just tolerate these slights to his *amour propre*, he took the kind of action that was becoming absolutely typical in these Greek wars. Antigonus' apparent preference for his other nephew was enough of a trigger and, filling his coffers by peddling off his warships, Telesphorus betrayed his uncle's cause by setting up as an independent captain on his own account. He secured himself a base at Elis, where Polyperchon's son Alexander had found ready support before and a place still loyal since the locals had joined the cause when he was still his uncle's man. However, the independent power business turned out sufficiently costly for him to risk his reputation by plundering the 'sacred precinct at Olympia' for the 500 talents needed to keep his soldiers for hire content.

Tipped off in respect of this arrant desertion, Ptolemaeus, worried that his cousin becoming an established nuisance might deal the death blow to any hopes of completely bringing Greece below Thermopylae into the Antigonid fold, reacted immediately. Whether he had taken Opus we don't know, but now his strategy of securing fortresses on the Euboea channel had to be put on hold as the bulk of his army was embarked, leaving only enough to hold what he had won, and he set out for the Peloponnese to hunt down the renegade. Events now are difficult to be sure of, but still his impact was immediate, undoubtedly taking Elis and destroying the citadel that Telesphorus had turned into his stronghold and, finding some of the plunder from Olympia there 'restored the treasure to the god' while organizing compliant locals into a pro-Antigonid government. While this was accomplished, familial attachment proved profound enough that after feelers were put out the cousins were able to make up their differences. This might have seemed a quixotic outcome at first considering how enraged Telesphorus must have been to jump ship in the first place, yet the errant officer definitely did come in from the cold, even showing good faith by handing over the port of Cyllene that was then returned to the control of an Elian administration now even further indebted to Antigonid generosity. This key housekeeping seems to have been sufficient for the season and we hear of no more activity on Ptolemaeus' part until his rollercoaster career took another extraordinary turn, at which time he was still to be found in the Peloponnese.

As the decade turned, Antigonus had been pushed too far, recognizing that his nephews had turned out not totally reliable despite the resources he had lavished on their projects. Not only had Telesphorus tried to turn independent warlord in a region celebrated for the greatest of Hellenic games, but Ptolemaeus himself had eventually turned out a broken reed. In the years of Antigonid pomp he had been given great power and responsibility, not just in command of the main army in the Peloponnese but elsewhere, evinced by the fact that one of his dependants called Phoenix was given the governorship of Phrygia along the Hellespont, one of the wealthiest and most strategic districts in Anatolia. Yet still he was not satisfied, believing he had not been honoured according to his just deserts. This malcontent with plenty of models from the recent past to follow made contact with Cassander, a man who had become an adept over the years at benefiting from the coat-turning of others and now was unlikely to be unmindful of this prince's worth. So he eagerly welcomed a new adherent who had already ordered Phoenix to garrison the strongholds along the Hellespont against Antigonus and leveraged his considerable influence in Bithynia from when he occupied the place in 315. We are not absolutely certain of the timing or the tangled circumstances of this volte face, but it would probably have been 310 or 309 and must have been particularly gratifying for Cassander that this man who had given his generals such a hard time in both Cappadocia and the recent Greek wars was now playing on his team. However, any sense of satisfaction would have taken a knock summarily enough as an extremely effective response was spearheaded by Antigonus' two sons Philip and Demetrius who swiftly re-established control in the key regions of Anatolia, a disappointment compounded when Cassander's new ally came off worst in some intrigues with Ptolemy I of Egypt. Ptolemaeus trusted the man when he should have been full of suspicion, and ended a promising career arrested and forced to drink hemlock. It was after these disappointments with his nephews that Antigonus would turn to those with even closer blood ties, most particularly Demetrius, a son groomed in the great wars against Eumenes and who would step up as a strong right hand in the years ahead.

A pulse of aggression had faded out in late summer 311 after four seasons of savage warfare that included the first of many attempts by the heirs of Alexander to interfere in Macedonian Europe, although what Antigonus' real intentions were in this complicated and impenetrable conflict remain opaque. Did he really have ambitions to establish his control over mainland Greece? It is possible, but more likely his manoeuvrings were about destabilizing the position of his rivals who depended on their standing as hegemons over Macedonian Europe to be able to compete with an antagonist fuelled by the wealth and manpower of Asia. What had been the effect on Cassander's position? How much of his prestige had leeched away in the perception of Greek elites is difficult to be sure of, but certainly the effective authority so satisfactorily imposed by his father no longer existed. Indeed, it is not easy to understand where power really resided at this time. The political map of Greece was a kaleidoscope with various characters carving out personal fiefdoms and leading armies with little loyalty except to their immediate paymaster. Much was shadow-play with little substance, and any autonomy of even great cities like Athens, Corinth, Thebes and Sparta might be noticed in the context of potentates who, if allowing a measure of freedom, might curtail it at almost any time.

Just before the perceived deceleration in the bloody campaigning around the Hellenistic world Hieronymus himself returns to the forefront, something that we have already seen when he was the hero of Eumenes' embassy to Antigonus at Nora and would be noticed several times more in his extraordinary long life. The details recorded of Demetrius' campaigns around Gaza in the autumn of 312 suggest the historian being in the command tent with a number of other big names like Nearchus of Crete, Andronicus of Olynthus and an Antigonid stalwart called Philip left as an advisory panel for the young prince's first independent command. We certainly know he was in Palestine a little later when Antigonus had brought the main army south to bail out his unfortunate offspring and ensure the reversal of his defeat at Gaza at the hands of Ptolemy and one source claims him as a governor of Syria during these years.[14] This move south was a strategic direction that led to a convoluted and curious encounter with the Nabatean Arabs near the site of the 'rose red' city of Petra in an attempt to secure the Antigonids' desert flank prior to an attack on Egypt. There were two major assaults against these largely nomadic people living off herds of sheep, goats and camels and making money as middlemen along the trade route from the spice rich lands described by the Romans as Arabia Felix. The picture we get of them is of a noble wandering people untainted by the dross of civilization with strict rules about not living in permanent habitations,[15] qualities sufficient to allow them not only to defeat two task forces sent against them but also to engineer a frustrating time for the historian himself in the role of revenue man.

The trusted Cardian found himself involved when after their double buffeting at the hands of the Arabs the Antigonids camped by the Dead Sea near a rich region of plentiful palms grown in irrigated country and unique medicinal balsam that provided the local producers with a handsome income. Yet this, they learned while resting by the bitter and foul-smelling waters of the inland sea, was not the real treasure trove: that was the great masses of between 10,000 and 30,000 sq ft of asphalt that on occasions appeared floating and seeming to 'those who see it from a distance just like an island'. It might poison the air with fumes and discolour all the precious metals in its proximity but was extremely valuable stuff, essential for the massive mummification industry in Egypt. Hieronymus was dispatched to fabricate a fleet of boats with which to collect the bitumen, but once afloat he found that his men were attacked. Some 6,000 Arabs had made their own fleet of reed boats, and sailing down on the interlopers sprayed them with arrows to such effect that they drove off Hieronymus with the loss of most of his followers. This was enough to finally convince his master to leave these testy desert people alone, deciding that neither suppressing them nor a new income source was worth the trouble, particularly when news was received of disturbances in Babylon. In fact there is a question mark over this whole episode as the fiasco reported around the Nabateans is not mirrored in Plutarch's sources, which give Demetrius credit for a considerable success in bringing off large herds of valuable animals. A cynical analysis could even imagine the historian mitigating his own failure on the Dead Sea by setting it in the context of a larger Antigonid disappointment with the previous two interventions stirring up these locals to scupper his own plans.

However, if this had been small beer, the bigger picture had seen the return of Seleucus to Babylon, frustration for Antigonus in his projects to cross to Europe from Anatolia and the mixed results of his considerable investment of both resources and family prestige in the Greek war. All this meant that the old ruler was prepared to contemplate a truce later in

311, terminating for at least a few years' intrusion into the Balkan world of a dynast fat with Eastern gold to pay his formidable armies and bang up-to-date navies. This had been the first time that Macedonian Europe had been belaboured and battered by those who fell heir to Alexander's great Asian Empire, but it would turn out to be only one of many. A great man from the generation of Philip, an old man from an old-world, Antigonus perhaps more than most would have felt a compulsion to try to unify the whole Macedonian Empire. Alexander the great conqueror had been dead for more than ten years, but his phantom was present in the disturbed sleep and command tents of so many of his successors. The first rounds of the Diadochi Wars had been in a very real sense the 'funeral games' he had prophesied. The great epic played out on the dusty plains of Iran at Paraitakene and Gabiene may have taken centre stage, the desperate end of Hieronymus' first master and mentor, the consigning of the Cardian marshal who had bested even Craterus in battle to the indignity of being sold out by those grandfathers of treachery the Silver Shields, meant it was hardly surprising that as an historian he focused on this action. Apart from anything else, he was there to see these events that meant his years as a loyal follower of Eumenes came to an end while decades of similar devotion to the Antigonids father, son and grandson began.

Yet if this man who came back from the upper satrapies in their train would have been present at the epic siege of Tyre, seen the building of a mammoth battle fleet, accompanied Antigonus over the Taurus in winter snows and attended Demetrius when his father sent the young prince on his first independent command and even played a personally significant role in the fighting in the Nabatean deserts, he still found time to record the contemporaneous proceedings in mainland Greece. He knew the significance of incidents being played out westward across the Aegean, even if it would be years before he would enter that region himself in the entourage of Demetrius. He understood that these first tremors were portentous, and that the incessant meddling of rich and powerful rulers from Asia was bound to have a very significant impact on the future of Macedonian Europe. In the complex and fragile context of competing rulers, peoples and historic cities that filled up the Balkans, the incumbent Cassander might have held his own, but it had been a rough ride and nothing suggested that years before the truce of 311 had been the worst of it.

Chapter Two

Forging the Fetters

Near the end of the third century envoys from a number of Greek peoples spoke before the Roman senate in an attempt to win support against the perceived threat to their liberties represented by Philip V, king of Macedon. Their contention was 'that so long as Chalcis, Corinth and Demetrias were subject to Macedonia, it was impossible for the Greeks to think of liberty; for Philip himself had spoken the exact truth when he called these places the "fetters of Greece".'[1]

The acropolis of Corinth standing guard a few miles south of the Isthmus was the greatest fortress in the Peloponnese and perhaps the whole of Greece. Certainly there were other very defensible places like Mount Ithome near Messene or the citadel of Argos, but Acrocorinth was strategically critical, sitting foursquare where the Peloponnese was anchored to the mainland. On a bright summer's day in 303 Demetrius, the extraordinary son of Antigonus the One-Eyed, arrived under this eminence, but this had not been his first adventure on the Greek mainland; four years earlier this glamorous prince had arrived in the harbour of Athens at Piraeus.

This was planting the family banner in perhaps the one place that was a more significant and revered Hellenic community than Corinth. Athens had special significance for more than 200 years since it spearheaded the epic struggle against Persia before something over a generation later making its own attempt to impose hegemony over Greece, finally thwarted by a Spartan-led coalition. There had been a comeback in the fourth century, but the rise of Philip II's Macedon had finally relegated the city of Themistocles and Pericles to a place as a second-class power. Yet this cultural powerhouse packed with philosophical schools and dramatists competing for the prizes at the annual City Dionysia, where the entertainments played out in the dramatic shadow of the Acropolis, still held a certain sway, even after Alexander had massively extended

Hellenic influence as far as the Oxus and the Indus. The old powers of mainland Greece could not hold on to their pre-eminent position when the Successor epic played out across the whole of the Eastern Mediterranean and the massive land mass of West Asia, but there were still factors that ensured they were not forgotten by dynasts whose interests were so often consumed by developments around the Nile, Euphrates, Tigris and Halys rivers. There was certainly prestige, to be seen as sponsors of famous Greek communities in Europe or Asia always brought kudos and to bring freedom to the nation that Macedonians aspired to be part of was a rallying cry of many outside of Antipater, Cassander and Lysimachus who articulated more open aspirations to dominate the many Greek communities within their respective bailiwicks. There was another dimension too: these Greeks were militarily important, their populations were the greatest providers, outside of Macedon itself, of trained and effective heavy infantry. Armoured Greek mercenary bands had for centuries been key components of royal armies as far afield as Egypt and Mesopotamia and remained so for the Hellenistic warlords who found Macedonian soldiers difficult to come by and had not yet been able to mobilize their local populations as effective substitutes. To beef out the line of battle or to provide the numerous garrisons to defend and police great new realms of mountains, plains, rivers and cities this had become a central role for the soldiers for hire who congregated at places like Cape Taenarum in the southern Peloponnese.

So it is no surprise that old one-eyed Antigonus, once he had disposed of his main rivals in Anatolia, the Levant, Mesopotamia and upper satrapies, tried to wrap mainland Greece in his fold, instigating the ultimately abortive campaigns detailed by Hieronymus. The peace of 311 meant only a hiatus here as well. The old king never lost sight of the importance of Europe and was eager to encourage his son and heir in his ambitions there. So the year 307 saw pageant and drama as Demetrius led a great armada of 250 warships from Ephesus carrying treasure chests full of 5,000 talents into the port of Athens intent on ousting Cassander's protégé Demetrius of Phalerum who had been in power for a decade. The story is that there was consternation as they arrived because Dionysius, the commander of the Munychia fort at Piraeus, thought the ships that hove into sight during a torrid June day were owned by the ruler of Egypt with whom Cassander had recently made an accord. So it was a real shock to register that it was a hostile Antigonid prince who had appeared and was addressing the Athenian soldiers, who had just rushed to defend the port, from the deck of his great warship. It may have been his honeyed words of freedom and democracy that turned out very acceptable to the defenders of Piraeus or that Demetrius' men 'effecting an entrance along the coast, admitted many of their fellow soldiers within the wall'.[2] Whichever was decisive, the Athenians, disregarding Cassander's garrison who had fled to the safety of the Munychia, dropped their weapons, acclaiming Demetrius in sufficient numbers that the authorities in the city negotiating with his trusted agent Aristodemus of Miletus arranged that the other Demetrius should be hurriedly expelled under safe conduct to an exile's billet in Thebes. The Antigonid liberator declined the proffered honour of immediately entering the city until he had disposed of any occupying forces that threatened the Athenians' freedom. So after surrounding the Munychia with 'a trench and palisade' he marched along the precipitous rock-cut road down the coast to Megara, where another enemy garrison was installed.

While besieging this place, rumour entangled him in a disreputable romance. Cratesipolis, the widow of Polyperchon's son Alexander who was living in Patrae, communicated with the young warrior suggesting a meeting, guaranteeing that he rushed off to encounter this 'famous beauty' whose influence in the area was not to be sniffed at. Unfortunately the rendezvous arranged somewhere between Megara and Patrae was disturbed by a party of enemy soldiers and Demetrius, having travelled with only the lightest of escorts, not for the only time in his life had to flee in a shabby cloak for disguise. This is clearly in part a characteristic anecdote to highlight the flaws in his personality 'through his inability to control his passion he narrowly avoided being ignominiously captured',[3] but there may be something more to it as presumably Cratesipolis, no longer in command at Sicyon and wearying of her diminished status, perhaps saw an opportunity to play the femme fatale and utilize the new power on the scene to win the place back from the officer who was holding it for Ptolemy of Egypt. It could even have been a trap from the start and certainly we don't hear any more of this love interest, but if all this is conjecture what is certain was that after this amorous prank with little sign of repentance he returned to the task at hand and swiftly brought the defenders of Megara to their knees. The takeover was enlivened by an interlude with a sniffy Stilpo, one of the most celebrated philosophers of his day and mentor of the great Stoic Zeno, making a crack about the much-touted Antigonid promises of freedom only really amounting to their soldiers taking away every slave in the place as plunder.

Demetrius was on a roll now, returning to unfinished business at Athens. The Munychia hill above the small eastern harbour of Piraeus reached almost 300ft and was heavily defended, but he soon unloaded his engines and had them pulled from the main port to assault the place before bringing his heavy ships round so that the catapults and ballistas on their decks could bring their weight to bear. The men on the walls were veterans long in the service of Cassander and confident in the strength of their position that can be imagined today looking up the roads that lead from the town centre up the hill. The fortress walls were thick and high, yet still in two days of continuous cacophonic assault the numbers and skills of the attackers began to pay off. The garrison suffered numerous casualties from the stones and bolts that rained down on the ramparts and they just did not have the numbers to replace them, while 'the men of Demetrius were fighting in relays and were continually relieved.'[4] Finally sufficient of the ramparts was cleared to allow the attackers to mount on ladders and force an entry, while the defenders, considering the fight they had put up, had satisfied honour and laid down their arms. The commandant Dionysius, also deeming his duty done, allowed himself to be captured by the attackers who he had failed to keep out.

This military success ensured that Athens' ancestral democratic constitution that had been overturned in 317 was reinstated, the franchise was extended and a guarantee of freedom of speech assured for the lowliest citizen, while statues of Demetrius of Phalerum were torn down and melted to make chamber pots. Those few supporters who had not gone into exile were hauled before the courts, although a disinclination to any real witch hunt was shown when, after being given a scare during this legislative process, the playwright Menander, one of the old ruler's known friends, was acquitted. This is the last occasion when we have any record[5] of Demetrius' cousin Telesphorus who was on his staff and spoke up on the comic playwright's behalf. To point up the difference from the regime he had just eliminated while slighting the Piraeus fortifications, he declared he would not put garrisons in either the city or the harbour and more than this his father was generous, sending 150,000 bushels of grain to feed the people and timber sufficient for them to rebuild a fleet of 100 ships. The symbolism here was pointed as a powerful naval arm had been a *sine qua non* for Athenian political significance on the world stage. The advantage for their benefactor was that the reservoir of mariners and shipwrights who peopled the coast of Attica had the potential to provide a considerable maritime auxiliary for a dynasty with high ambitions to become lords of the seas. Nor were there only gifts of provender and wood: he also ordered the north Aegean islands of Lemnos and Imbros to be handed back to Athenian control, generosity that showed it had not been lost on Antigonus that this new positive connection with Athens would win popular support in those many Ionian communities with links to it as their mother city. Places like Miletus, Ephesus, Priene and many others that in the next few years are noticed sending gift-laden delegates to the Attic capital.

So it was in a flush of newfound freedom that the Athenian radical democrats were eager to show their appreciation of their latest benefactors. They were prepared to stump up money, spending 200 talents to consecrate altars to Antigonus and Demetrius, their two new saviour gods, ordering annual games to honour them and having their portraits woven into the body-length garment with which the statue of the goddess Athena was adorned. Two sacred ships were named for them and most significantly golden statues were set up of them next to the tyrant slayers Harmodius and Aristogeiton[6] whose very names personified the spirit of the independent city. Indeed, the Athenian authorities were the first to bestow the title of monarch on the Antigonids father and son while replacing the eponymous archon with a priest who presided over the new cults, also creating two new tribes bearing their names and even changing the designations of months in their honour. The new government also showed impressive activity and transparency with assembly resolutions being published on wooden tablets or marble stellae, while Demochares, the nephew of the old anti-Macedonian hero Demosthenes, is reported as ensuring that the walls of the city, the port and the long walls between them were repaired and that the monies paid to contractors were published, while law codes were eventually made accessible to all, making recourse to the law possible for less prominent citizens.

Most Athenians swelled with pride at the workings of their re-found democracy. Genuinely appreciative of Antigonid munificence, there would have been few who had problems when decrees honouring individuals and states seemed so frequently to go to Antigonid friends and allies, particularly as home-grown heroes like Lycurgus, another anti-Macedonian posthumously honoured well after his death in 324 for his years of efficiently supervising public finances, were not forgotten. However, the activities of certain characters determined to ingratiate themselves with the new power soon raised eyebrows in a soured atmosphere at the interface between near-regal prerogative and democratic government. The man that the most obnoxious sycophancy was pinned upon was called Stratocles, whose reputation was already damaged from years of 'buffoonery and scurrilous behaviour'. The most notable example came after the defeat of the Athenian fleet at Amorgos during the Lamian War when he paraded round the Ceramicus, the quarter of potters and prostitutes, declaring the fleet had won a great victory and when later sailors brought the genuine intelligence of defeat, his response to the not unreasonable public anger was 'What harm have I done if for two days you have been happy?'[7] Yet he was far from alone in his brazen toadying as another such recommended that when Demetrius entered the town, he should be treated with the same honours as those given to the gods Demeter and Dionysus on their festival days and that envoys to Antigonus or Demetrius should be designated scared deputies rather than ambassadors, while when a matter concerning a consecration of shields at Delphi arose, it was even suggested that the young prince should be treated as an oracle.[8]

Antigonid backing was always going to come at a cost. That natural collaborators, however distasteful, would be given their head was inevitable, but equally that people like them, suckers for the glamour of military power and prepared to go to sickening lengths to massage the ego of the new big man in town, were so conspicuous was bound to arouse resentment. So any Athenians clinging on to shreds of self-respect amid feelings of growing anger and resentment were at least relieved for a while as old Antigonus had work for his son on other fronts in an embattled world. Ptolemy became the prime object of their attention and in 306 Demetrius received written instructions from his father to coordinate his Greek allies to hold the fort so he might embark with his forces on a Cypriot campaign. Eventually achieving such a stunning naval victory that it ensured his family's command of most of the Eastern

Mediterranean for a generation, the battle of Cypriot Salamis not only allowed Antigonus and his son to proclaim themselves monarchs, following the lead of the Athenians, but was the platform for an invasion of Lagid Egypt. An enterprise that not only ended in military failure but ensured that the policy of direct assault was for the moment dumped and instead to tighten the economic screw Demetrius was unleashed in 305 to suppress the Egyptians' maritime partner, the republic of Rhodes.

The absence of Demetrius from Athens, if welcomed by some in these years, had a definite down side: Cassander had not forgotten that the place had been his plaything for a decade and, with their protector gone, he swiftly returned. Despite heroic resistance, the outcome would have inevitably fallen the way of his big battalions except for an old man who remembered that despite his son's capacity for being distracted, Greece was too important to let go. Demetrius had spent two years in a fruitless attack on the island city of Rhodes that had escalated into one of the most famous sieges of ancient times, but his father, though not far off 80, still saw better than his son that this obsession with triumphing over the stalwart islanders might cost them elsewhere. He managed to persuade his famously dutiful offspring that he should give up the enterprise, make peace and turn to the defence of their friends in Attica. So with 330 warships and the veteran army that had been showing such invention and aptitude in the trenches under Rhodes' walls, Demetrius island-hopped across the Aegean to stomp ashore at Aulus across from the island of Euboea. Once there, he was not only sitting nicely on his enemy's line of communications with Macedon but also discovered friendly Aetolian troops dispatched by a people who appreciated having a potent Cassander ensconced in central Greece as little as he did. The new arrival also swiftly persuaded the Boeotians to think better of their dalliance with the enemy and to withdraw their garrisons from the city of Chalcis.

The people at this place had a weightiness of pretention based on Homeric longevity, confidence backed up with chamber tombs evidencing Mycenaean roots, while their later efforts at colonization to the north, east and west had been so significant that the whole of the Chalcidice peninsula had been named for them. An affluence based on trade in fine metal work and pottery had suffered badly at the hands of a brutal Athenian imperialism in the mid-400s when many native land-owners were ousted and settlers planted in an effort to provide a handy granary for the expanding capital of Attica. Still the strength of this fortress, where the narrows famous for reverse tides and dangerous currents had been bridged by a wooden structure since the fifth century, remained formidable indeed and with its naval arsenal fallen into Antigonid hands it would soon take its place as one of the 'Fetters of Greece', but for the moment its acquisition was something of a sideshow with the removal of the enemy from Attica the priority. Not that this took long: Cassander raised the siege and made for Thermopylae once he realized his strategic predicament. However, Demetrius was not about to let the enemy pass unscathed if he could help it and, falling on their line of march, 'he routed Cassander's army' with 6,000 Macedonians surrendering and joining his ranks. Heraclea in Trachis was taken too and once the intruders were driven away from Attica people all around showed great enthusiasm for the new power on the scene. Places as far away as Cenchraea, the port of Corinth on the Saronic Gulf and as nearby as Panactum, one of the forts guarding the mountainous border between Attica and Boeotia, were all liberated from occupying garrisons and control was handed back to the locals.

The designation of archons and consuls[9] suggest the campaign of 303 as the period when Demetrius really began to unpick Macedonian hegemony over mainland Greece. With Cassander's troops no longer immediately threatening when the young king gathered with his generals, there seemed to be a world of opportunities open to this favourite of fortune. So with the Antigonid clarion call of freedom for the Greeks still on their lips, it was decided to deal with the enemy in the Peloponnese, many of whom had been sitting pretty in their southern fiefdoms for years. The choice was made that before attempting an invasion of Macedonia itself, it was necessary to eradicate Prepelaus' power base around the isthmus. This steady officer had persuaded Alexander, son of Polyperchon and a major power in the peninsula, to join Cassander in 315 and after he died had slipped into his shoes, meaning that he was well installed in his stronghold of Acrocorinth when the young Antigonid set his sights on him. There were other players muddying the waters too. A 'very distinguished' Lagid officer called Philip was occupying the important city of Sicyon west along the coastal plan from Corinth and Demetrius, perhaps a little daunted by the sight of Prepelaus' stronghold, decided on this as his initial target. If distinguished, it looks like the man in command at Sicyon had become sloppy and was taken by surprise when Demetrius rapidly pushed his army over the isthmus and arrived unnoticed in advance of the city walls.

The attackers, either by treachery or escalade, got over the defences and the garrison was so taken aback by the arrival of this enemy in their midst that all they could do was hotfoot it to the acropolis to try to hold out there. In fact, this surprise assault had so unnerved all concerned that merely the threat of Demetrius bringing his siege machines onto the ground between the houses and the citadel was enough to force a capitulation, surrender on condition that the defenders' officers and men were set free and ferried back to Alexandria. What Ptolemy's response to this less than impressive performance by his subordinate was when he arrived shamefaced back in Egypt we are not told, but what was certain was that Demetrius was determined to make the most of his good fortune. To make his new acquisition more defensible in the future, he razed the inhabited quarter near the sea and helped the people to relocate inland around the naturally defensible acropolis, renaming the new community Demetrias and revelling in his founder status with the usual trappings of games where athletes competed to be the best and public festivals where the literati no doubt contended in producing the sweetest adulation for the new community founder.

Full of confidence now, Corinth was next on his hit list and, leaving Sicyon behind, Demetrius led his men down the coast road towards the isthmus. Observation from the Acrocorinth atop its shard of mountain is not like from some heights in misty Britain: there under clear blue skies the spectator can see both the Corinthian and Saronic gulfs sparkling in the sun on either hand, the great plain of the Argolid, and even the Temple of Zeus at Nemea can be clearly made out with binoculars. It was the very finest spy point available before the advent of manned flight and, seen from the land running off towards Megara, the magnificent image of the fortress rising behind the columns of the temple of Apollo is second only to the Acropolis at Athens as the signature image of the glory of ancient Greece. Corinth before Athens, Sparta and Thebes had in so many ways been groundbreaking: first to send great fleets, military and commercial across the Hellenic world, first among the wave of colonists in the great movement west up the Adriatic coast and into Magna Graecia, and at the forefront constitutionally by establishing the tyrant Cypselus in the middle of the seventh century. The locals even maintained themselves against Phoenician braggarts as candidates for originators of the sleek and dangerous trireme that belligerently cruised the waters of the ancient world for centuries; a byword for luxury with tales of temple prostitutes to match those of Babylon or Comana Cappadocia and Pontica and ingenuity that would see something like an early railroad to transport ships across the isthmus. The city's very position had ensured significance and the character of her people warranted greatness.

Having arrived in front of this prize, Demetrius again tried a surprise attack in the dead of night, coordinating with friends in the town primed to open a gate in the city walls, groups of his soldiers spilling in, spreading through the sleeping town and down to the harbour. However, with this place it was not the habitations that mattered but the rock-girt citadel. Most of the defenders in the town managed to withdraw in front of the attackers and either reached an outwork called Sisyphium on the slopes leading up the hill or to the fortress itself rising imposing in front of them. Now an amazing picture is painted as the attackers 'brought up engines of war' so that not only heavy projectiles flew but javelins and slingshots pinged off helmets as a task force was dispatched forward to clamber over the rocky ground to reach the enemy defences. This would not have been prime work for pike-armed phalangites, though we know from Alexander's time that some of his elite heavy infantry called the Hypaspists had been just the ticket for this kind of mission. These troops grown out of the monarch's foot guard are something of a mystery, or at least the way they were armed is. Their position alongside the phalanx in Alexander's great battles suggests that they were armed with pelte and pike and this is certainly the case for regiments so designated under the successors, but that Alexander used them to assault walls and attack in difficult terrain has led to a belief that they were closer to a Hellenic hoplite with short spear and larger shield, a sort of troop type clearly shown on the Alexander sarcophagus now housed at the Istanbul Archaeology Museums.

Whatever the units that plunged forward, the defenders of Sisyphium had not had time to properly prepare themselves and were unable to form behind the defensive walls of what was a considerable outpost. So when the attackers arrived they panicked, finding it almost impossible to keep them off the ramparts, ladders allowing the Antigonid scaling parties to roll over those who did put up resistance: pressing them back, chopping and stabbing at anybody who showed the least sign of resistance. Soon the defenders were bolting further up the slopes, trying to gain the heady heights, hordes of men in hardly any sort of order, many having dropped their weapons to allow swifter flight, trying to escape through the gates into the main citadel itself. Hard on their heels came their assailants with the walls so many deemed impregnable looming above them and who, though they had suffered considerable casualties, were determined not to let the advantage they had gained slip away. It was a long rough trail up to the top of the rock that the defenders pressed along followed closely by Demetrius' peltasts and other light troops while the heavier infantry came on behind, pushing and dragging the sheds and rams that they expected to need once they reached the main citadel walls.

The defences of Acrocorinth show to this day as almost impenetrable with the remnants of medieval walls topping the beetling heights and even in the confusion of the enemy onslaught the occupying garrison and those fugitives who had won through the gates surely must have thought they retained the upper hand, finally safe against the mass of enemies pressing up the rugged track winding below them, but it was not to be. 'Then, when the men there fled to those who had occupied Acrocorinth, he intimidated them also and forced them to surrender the citadel; for this king was exceedingly irresistible in his assaults, being particularly skilled in the construction of siege equipment.'[10] Softened by years of largely undisturbed garrison duty, the defenders, it turned out, were not prepared to risk their lives to defend their post; had they been so determined it is impossible to believe that the attackers would have got in so easily and a protracted blockade would have been needed to starve them out. That Prepelaus himself was unable to reach the fortress would not have helped; his presence might have stiffened resolve, but without his leadership the reputation of the city-taker was sufficient to tip the scales. The appearance of impregnability turned out to be deceptive and this of all Demetrius' achievements surely meant that his famed sobriquet was well warranted. There are those who perceived some irony in the epithet Poliorcetes, suggesting it was failure in front of Rhodes that was behind the derisive name. Certainly in the seventeenth century AD there is no doubt it was an accolade to be proud of, as shown when the uncle of the infant Louis XIV, after success at the Siege of Mardyke in the Low Countries, had himself styled Gaston Poliorcetes.

Now another fetter was clamped shut as an Antigonid garrison marched in, though Demetrius assured the locals that this was just to ensure the safety of Corinth while the war with Cassander lasted. In fact it would be many decades before the Antigonids would depart and then only after an extraordinary night-time escalade by Aratus, the hero founder of the Greater Achaean League. Despite the public relations benefits of being seen to free the Greek communities from foreign garrisons, this place was just too important to not militarily occupy and indeed in the fraught and convoluted years to come this strategically vital rock-hewn location remained one of the most crucial Antigonid holdings, whether family fortunes were on the rise or in decline. The remarkable feat of taking the impregnable fortress was not just a minatory statement of intent: it ensured that Prepelaus, Cassander's Peloponnesian proconsul had been disposed of, returning to his master and future responsibilities that would include making a final impact on the war building in Asia. Yet for Demetrius this was just a beginning as his attentions were firmly fixed on securing hegemony over as much of the Peloponnese as he could.

Next on his inventory for conquest was Bura, 40-odd miles west towards Patrae in the hills above the coastal plain. His men stormed in, driving out the garrison and freeing the people, a process repeated at a another town called Scyrus, which was most likely on the road inland into Arcadia, the next stop in the peninsula picaresque. These towns were of little strategic import and no garrison was left behind; the propaganda value of leaving them free from Cassander's bullying and able to govern themselves unhindered outweighed any military down side. Having hopefully convinced the locals that he was not just another Macedonian interloper looking to exploit them he moved on, reaching Arcadian Orchomenus, almost in the centre of the rocky peninsula, where the invaders ravaged the country to pressure Cassander's garrison commander Strombichus into surrendering the town. This man had been put in post by Polyperchon and, having remained in power for some years, had no intention of quietly handing over to this newcomer who was drawing near. So, warned well in advance by the sight of the haze of dust kicked up by the feet of Demetrius' men and with confidence in his solidly-constructed defences, vestiges of which remain to this day, when envoys arrived to demand submission he not only sent them packing but yelled venomous insults at Demetrius from the city walls.

The young Antigonid was not a man to countenance such lèse-majesté and, never inclined to lentitude, he got down to what he loved best: setting up his engines, building siege works and preparing for an assault. His rams smashed at the defences, and catapults and bolt-throwers bombarded the battlements while towers were constructed to land his men on the walls. How long it took we are not told, but the defenders would have sweated as the inevitable occurred and a breach was widened to the point where an escalade could be attempted. Demetrius, deeply annoyed by the enemy jibes, led his assault force with no thought but reaching the man who had so insulted him and, picking through the rubble-strewn breach, his veterans made short work of defending troops whose years of garrison duty had left them soft and out of shape. So as the commander and his officers were dragged before the victor there was no chance of any indulgence being extended: Strombichus and a minimum of eighty others known to be bitter enemies of the Antigonids were crucified outside the battered city walls with their sightless eyes fixed on the picture of 2,000 of their captured mercenaries being registered onto Demetrius' payroll. He had sworn revenge and it had been taken with the hanging bodies left as a sobering sight to any others contemplating resistance. It turned out to be a regional tipping-point: the message of intimidation was clear and the rest of the strongpoints in Arcadia surrendered once the famous besieger fixed his gaze on them and drew near. Realizing that none of their previous sponsors – Cassander, Prepelaus or Polyperchon – could be expected to come to their assistance, terrified defenders slipped away before they might be caught and receive the same treatment as Strombichus.

Two stories have been told about these events and if the tradition from contemporary accounts of Hieronymus is pretty convincing, there was a second that contended[11] Demetrius had bribed the defenders of Corinth, Sicyon and Argos with 100 talents to hand over these places to him. Whichever version is accepted, clearly the young king had acquired not only the crucial southern fetter at Acrocorinth but had established himself in much of Achaea, the Argolid and Arcadia outside of Mantinea. Cassander, Polyperchon and their officers had been dominant here beforehand, but now their influence was almost completely eradicated and militarily it was probably only Sparta who could have mounted any sort of opposition in the Peloponnese, a situation confirmed when

Demetrius resuscitated the old league of Corinth where a 'huge concourse of delegates' proclaimed him *strategos autokrator* just as they had Philip II and Alexander III before him. However, this time the crusade he was touting was not to gain sweet revenge for the Persian trashing of Greece in 480 but to free the Greeks from the heavy hand of Cassander's tutelage. Interestingly, despite supervising an increase in the franchise at Athens, the deeply conservative instincts of these monarchs is emphasized when the clauses from Philip's old league constitution that specifically banned cancellation of debt or land redistribution were retained, despite ongoing pressures of inflation and bad harvests.

The new hegemon soon made it clear that he did not consider his new title some meaningless honorific. Having liberated the Peloponnese, he was determined to dig Cassander out of the rest of the country despite the Macedonian king's armies not being inactive and having 'occupied the passes in advance', blocking Thermopylae and showing every intention of holding on there. After scouts had carefully reconnoitred and reported these developments, Demetrius laid his plans. First he left Athens, ordering his ships and soldiers to gather in massive force at Chalcis, leaving only sufficient men to hold key places like Acrocorinth and the Piraeus. Then once there, after deciding a frontal assault would be too costly, this mercurial man loaded up his army and coasted up the Euboean channel, disembarking at the port of Larissa Cremaste in Phthiotis at the mouth of the Malian Gulf. There was hardly any resistance, and with the citadel taken, the garrison was 'put under guard' and control handed back to the locals. Then spreading out from the disembarkation point they found other communities welcoming, particularly as recently Cassander's officers had been making threats that they would forcibly uproot the locals and transport them into more defensible locations in the area. With the hills of Phthiotis rising to 1,000ft in places on their left, it was easiest to keep to the coast before debouching into the Crocus Field where Philip II had decisively defeated Onomarchos of Phocis in the 350s to establish himself as a power-player in mainland Greece.

Cassander responded to being outflanked by pulling back from Thermopylae and gathering a defence force of almost 30,000 infantry and 2,000 horse, numbers that were sufficient to give even Demetrius pause. Yet he still fielded a larger force than his opponent with 8,000 Macedonian phalangites, 15,000 mercenaries, 25,000 Greek hoplites and another 8,000 light troops and 'freebooters of all sorts'. Such a quantity of soldiers had allowed him to steamroller up the coast road through Antrones and Pteleum, places that controlled the channel north of Euboea and the entrance to the Pagasaean Gulf, before opening the road into Thessaly and scuppering Cassander's well-laid plans to establish a defended position at Phthiotis Thebes. Now, with little other recourse, he gathered together his forces and, taking consolation that many of the enemy would not have been the quality of his own Macedonians, endeavoured to constrain the manoeuvring of his rampant enemy by barricading them in 'when Cassander saw that Demetrius' undertakings were prospering, he first protected Pherae and Thebes with stronger garrisons; and then, after collecting his whole army into one place, he encamped over against Demetrius.'[12]

These Macedonians might not have been quite the digging men that the later Romans were, but they knew the worth of triple palisaded earthworks[13] and could be quite sniffy about ignorant Illyrians who failed to fortify their camp in the face of the enemy.[14] Demetrius' followers clearly showed this when they dug in very securely behind ditches and palisades on the spot where New Halos would sit near a northern outcrop of the Othrys Mountains and where marshes led down to the Pagasaean Gulf. Square with grid-pattern streets on the Hippodamian model and with some fine Hellenistic walls on the south-west, it mirrored the massive camp established in 302 to block any moves from the north and provide a base for an invasion of Macedon. In years to come, fine town houses would cover the plots where soldiers had drawn up their lines of skin tents, flaps opening on wisps of smoke rising from cooking fires and men drinking thirstily from jugs and wine sacks, but as the two kings confronted each other from their defended encampments Cassander could hope that he had for the moment neutered the intruders' threat to Thessaly and Macedonia. It is said that neither side was inclined to break the deadlock because they were both awaiting the outcome of the main campaign in Anatolia where Antigonus had brought up all his military might to confront the confederate strength of Lysimachus, Cassander and Seleucus, whose armies were on the road, aiming for a conjunction near Pontic Heraclea and trusting that together they might have the strength to confront the main Antigonid forces.

It had become a stalemate, a phony war among the low hills and open meadows of south-east Thessaly with both sides parading in front of their camps but never prepared to risk coming to blows. The eyes of both sides were firmly fixed on what was happening in Asia, each knowing that it would be victory or defeat there that would decide the war. Of course the opportunity for taking some pawns in this game of chess were never likely to be overlooked, and Demetrius seemed briefly inclined to take decisive action when a faction at Pherae offered to open the town gates to him. So with men from this place just north of Theban Phthiotis, which Cassander had intended to make the centrepiece of his defensive line, offering a welcome, Demetrius' men slipped into town and in hard fighting drove the enemy garrison out of the citadel, asserting that they had come to free the people from the tyranny of Macedonian rule. However, if this local success looked like the beginning of offensive manoeuvring, it in fact presaged something very different. Fortunately for Cassander, worried about the frangibility of his bulwark, before the invader could make further inroads into his Thessalian holdings he saw them take pause. Couriers had landed on the coast of Thessaly and the word they brought was urgent.

Making their way to the camp, Demetrius was informed that his father needed him and his men to come to his assistance 'as swiftly as possible' for the climactic campaign that would be fought in Anatolia the following year. Always compliant when it came to his father's desires and tipped off that his enemy might be amenable, feelers were put out and emissaries shuttled to and fro, discovering on both sides an inclination to call a ceasefire. Cassander knew that he could not both reinforce a crucial Asian war and defend in Europe against a rampant Demetrius, while the latter recognized that time was pressing to obey the call of an insistent father. In these circumstances, after a deep sigh of relief the ruler of Macedon snapped off the proffered hand and an armistice was not long in the arranging, the only proviso being that it must be acceptable to Antigonus. The young Antigonids' whip hand in these negotiations is apparent as his antagonist even agreed that all the cities of Greece should have their autonomy restored or confirmed; good public relations for a man who intended to come back once the war in Anatolia was completed. All ensuring a war gestated in Europe finally migrated across the Aegean Sea.

Demetrius had in the last decade of the fourth century decisively secured the position of his dynasty on mainland Greece. Great fortresses defended by dependable mercenaries comfortably barracked behind near impenetrable walls would ensure against any buffeting of fortune experienced in the great wide world. Yet this strategy of establishing solid posts was not yet complete. However, the last of the shackles that were intended to keep the Greeks constrained was, unlike the others, not hoary with history. It was a new town only founded in 294 or 293 by Demetrius. Strabo[15] testifies that it was constructed on the sea between Nelia and Pagasae at the head of the gulf and packed with the inhabitants from nearby towns. Nowadays adjacent to the modern community of Volos, the remains of what had been a fortress, royal palace and naval base can still be found, easily capable of housing an army of more than 20,000 men. Lines of streets, house foundations, the 6-mile-long walls and high-status accommodation on the Goritsa Hill ensure that a ghost of the old royal headquarters remains. Not a natural fortress or strategic choke-point, but still it had impressive man-made defences and remained a favoured abode for the Antigonids in Greece for generations, as well as the base for most of their maritime efforts. It was always important, situated at the base of the highland folds that followed the coast from Mount Pelion to the cone of Ossa and onwards to Mount Olympus, in controlling Thessaly and the road to Macedonia from where troops could be sent anywhere inland up to the pass at Tempe. Forces based there could also dominate south along the coast down to the long island of Euboea. So the other bookend of these fetters was put in place: not as formidable as the one menacingly dominating one of the most famous and ancient cities of mainland Greece, but it would soon be designated as command centre for the wide-ranging and disparate realm that was left to Demetrius after his father was defeated and killed in battle at Ipsus, remaining so for his son Antigonus Gonatus and his descendants who so often held court at this favourite residence. Even after the Antigonids won the throne of Macedon, this crucial stronghold remained close to their heart, demonstrating a commitment to retaining their hegemony not only over those neighbouring Thessalian barons in their broad sun hats riding fine cavalry mounts but also their influence over the historic Hellenic heartlands to the south.

Chapter Three

Cassander and Lysimachus

While many of the hard men who split up Alexander's empire would head for Hades leaving dynastic messes behind them, with second or even third wives preferred over their predecessors and younger sons set up against their elders, only the old regent Antipater showed so little family feeling that when he slipped off the mortal coil he did not choose his successor from his family at all. The obvious selection would have been his son Cassander who had for some years acted as his chief lieutenant, but the son's behaviour in this period had not reassured the father that he could be trusted with what he had seen as the raison d'être of his long sojourn in power. Antipater had little faith that he would keep the power seat warm for Alexander's heir, and how right he would prove to be. There is absolutely no reason to believe the gossip that when Antipater sent Cassander to the royal court at Babylon it was with corrosive poison to be administered by another son who was one of Alexander's pages. Such behaviour would go against the decades of loyal service that he had given to the Macedonian royal house and indeed was contrary to every act of that venerable and capable old man. There is little doubt that he revered Philip under whom he reached the greatest heights of power and renown and that this dedication followed down the generations of the Argead dynasty. Even the fact of his venomous dislike of Olympias or that Alexander seemed inclined to replace him as proconsul of Europe with Craterus would not have made such a turnaround credible. Indeed, it was this loyalty to the ruling dynasty that is the only explanation for the extraordinary act of handing power not to a family member but to a man not related to him at all. The chosen officer was Polyperchon who could hardly even have been any kind of close associate as that veteran had spent the last fifteen years in Asia while Antipater ruled west of the Hellespont.

Polyperchon was a character with a lighter side, known for dancing in flashy yellow slippers yet still enough of a military figure that Pyrrhus could laud him, even if only to illustrate that a king's only proper concern was warfare.[1] This man who had led a regiment of Macedonian pikemen across all of Asia was well struck in years, of Philip's generation rather than Alexander's, yet if past his prime he had the crucial quality of commitment to the royal line and could be reasonably expected to survive long enough to allow Alexander's child by Roxana to advance to manhood. Yet lack of parental endorsement had not slowed Cassander down. Soon taking by main force what he had been denied by heredity, he had ousted Polyperchon before disposing of his ally, the recently re-established queen Olympias. So now it was Cassander who became the main European power in situ required to respond to the Antigonid incursions recounted in a previous chapter. That Antipater had shown considerable perspicacity in not designating his son as defender of Philip and Alexander's line was revealed when he not only displayed scant respect for the royal family in his elimination of Alexander's mother but absolutely confirmed this attitude soon after the great Macedonian warlords botched together a transitory peace in 311. The wording of the treaty designated him as caretaker of the old dynasty in Europe until Roxana's son came of age, but when in 309 young Alexander was reaching his middle teens, his response was along very different lines. The young man and his mother had been kept at Amphipolis in no great state and even less freedom for years, but it seems there were those who had not forgotten him. Yet when 'word was being spread throughout Macedonia by certain men that it was fitting to release the boy from custody and give him his father's kingdom'[2] the ruler at Pella ordered Glaucus, the commander of the boy's guard, to poison both him and his mother. All was done far from the public eye with the corpses disposed of surreptitiously and the perpetrators sworn to secrecy.

Not that Cassander was incognizant of the magic of the Argead name, and on coming into his own he had married Alexander's half-sister Thessalonike, a great princess christened for her father's victory at Crocus Field in Thessaly. Only 21 when Alexander died, she had been a dynastic pawn touted about for years before Cassander bagged her in Olympias' entourage when the town of Pydna fell to him in 315 and took her as a wife. A city was founded and named for her where the town of Therma had stood as one of his first acts after properly securing his position in Macedonia, showing he appreciated the benefits of further entwining his name with that of the old royal family. However, along with genuflection to this ancient glamour, bile remained and the final stroke was against Alexander's illegitimate son Heracles, born to a Greco-Persian princess named Barsine. He had last been mentioned at Babylon in 323 when Alexander's boyhood friend, admiral and chronicler Nearchus very briefly suggested him as a candidate for the imperial throne. Around 309 he was plucked from obscurity when the aging but still ambitious Polyperchon saw this last remaining heir of the true royal line as a useful creature and looking like he was inclined to become a kingmaker in his dotage. After eighteen years on the periphery, he had brought him from Pergamum to join an army gathered on the Macedonian border at 'a region of Epirus, also called Tymphaeum'. However, Polyperchon had been living on a small scale too long and the altitude of high politics was much too rarefied and, guessing this, rather than fighting, Cassander decide to subvert the old warrior. The man at Pella had been worried for a time: he was well aware that he was no popular choice as ruler and was much concerned that a youth touched with the glamour of Alexander could win over plenty of people who looked back with great affection to the days of Heracles' father and grandfather. So when he approached Polyperchon's position and camped his army, he was prepared to come up with a good deal:

> As for the king, Cassander tried to show Polyperchon that if the restoration should take place he would do what was ordered by others; but, he said, if Polyperchon joined with him and slew the stripling, he would at once recover what had formerly been granted him throughout Macedonia, and then, after receiving an army, he would be appointed general in the Peloponnesus and would be partner in everything in Cassander's realm.[3]

The old opportunist, apart from estates in Macedonia itself, received 4,000 Macedonian foot and 500 Thessalian horse to set him up in his new Peloponnesian vice-royalty and there was hard cash too, 100 talents if Plutarch's 'discourse on shyness' is to be credited, as payment for strangling the young prince after a dinner party. Egregious conduct that brought to mind a line from Hesiod 'Invite your friend to supper, not your enemy', and that at least earned some little retribution when on marching south Polyperchon found himself blocked by the soldiers of a coalition of Boeotians and Peloponnesians compelling him to give up any hope of reaching his new home and forcing him to winter in Locris not far past Thermopylae.

Antipater's shade must have been horrified at this shedding of royal blood and down the centuries Cassander's reputation has certainly suffered from the stain. There was something deeply personal here: Cassander had since his youth been the very antithesis of Alexander. There is one canard that at the age of 35 he still had to eat standing up because he had not yet killed his first bear, a personal slight that it is utterly impossible to imagine Alexander tolerating. It was not that they were so different; the feeling is that they really did not like each other. Not only was he kept out of the Asian adventure but years later, when he visited Alexander in Mesopotamia near the end of that king's life, Alexander physically assaulted him after he laughed at courtiers prostrating themselves.

However, much of this might have been the vestige of a propaganda war fuelled from a rubbish heap of ideas that included 'The Book on the death and testament of Alexander' fabricated by 317 at the latest, fought alongside the military one by Olympias and Polyperchon. Mendacious or not, Cassander's reputation was affected among those who chronicled the period and this has been freighted into modern times. Distrusted by his father and painted as the butcher of the Argeads, his posterity suffered considerably: 'He destroyed the whole house of Alexander to the bitter end'[4] with his final dropsical days with his body alive with worms, bringing to mind the awful Sulla, and seen as just karma for a sanguine career as exterminator of a rightful royal line. That there was substance to this rivalry is indicated by his determination to undo the great conqueror's most famous act of terror. No episode gave Cassander greater pleasure than his resuscitation of the great city of Thebes as a kick at Alexander, undoing what he had so notoriously perpetrated when he torched the place after a second rebellion in just a year in 335.

Once the refoundation was accomplished, people had quickly returned to the ruined capital of Boeotia to settle in squatter camps around the temples and shrines that Alexander had left standing while they rebuilt their homes and reconstituted the rhythm of communal and political life that meant so much. While the returnees dug in the blackened ruins of the Cadmea they unearthed two statues that must have encouraged people set on what looked like a herculean task. One was of Hermes, noted for mediating between the human and heavenly, and the other, more specifically Theban, was of Epaminondas, the hero of the city's greatest age since legendary times.[5] Nor were all discoveries due to chance: there is mention of someone who returned to recover a fortune in gold he had hidden in a statue before Alexander's troops got to work knocking down the walls, monuments and houses.[6] The dramatic revival of the ancient home of Phoenician Cadmus, where the cursed sons of Oedipus had fought around its seven gates and beloved of Dionysus, had been back in 315 and it had touched the hearts of a few communities who contributed to the rebuilding of its walls and monuments, particularly the likes of Eretria and Melos that themselves had in their pasts experienced annihilation at the hands of respectively Persians and Athenians.

Unsurprisingly at least here among the toilers repopulating the city many loved their sponsor in Pella, a considerable positive for a man whose desire to control the crucial real estate in central Greece remained intense, despite it increasingly bringing him head-to-head with the mighty Antigonids. Not that the Hellenic world was the only region that absorbed Cassander's interest. To his west he needed to worry continually about Epirus, King Glaucus and his Illyrians and the powerful Corinthian colony of Corcyra, though after the civil war ended in 315 he could feel somewhat relaxed about the situation in Olympias' homeland. The ruler Aeacides, who had combined with his countrywomen and Polyperchon, had found himself on the losing side and driven out by his own people, meaning that after leaving Lyciscus as viceroy Cassander might for the moment expect little trouble from that quarter. However, high hopes of stability were soon undermined by the entry of the Aetolians into the Antigonid camp, something that determined him to try to neutralize these enemies in an effort to retain his dominant position in the north-west. Naturally he looked to his Acarnanian allies to bring this about and in 314 moved to utilize the circumstance that these two west Greek powers were already engaged in a spluttering border war.

To turn this tame endeavour into something of decisive moment, Cassander prepared to employ major forces. Heading south through Thessaly and over the Pindus Mountains his army entered the borderland between Acarnania and Aetolia to camp beside a tributary of the Achelous River. Once established, he showed more administration than ambitious campaigning, no doubt aware of the problems of attacking the Aetolians in their own country, a place where Craterus had his difficulties in 321 and a people the rampant Gauls would later find a doughty foe. So despite being present in numbers, instead of invading his enemy's country he convinced the Acarnanians gathered in assembly to relocate those of their people living in small, scattered and unfortified villages to walled towns where they would be able to gather swiftly and effectively when the Aetolians threatened to attack. The most important of these ramparted posts was Stratus in the fertile Achelous River basin, controlling communications east, west, north and south and noted as early as the fifth century as a gathering-place of the Acarnanian federal assemblies. Another that provided a headquarters for the Oeniadae tribe was at Sauria, while the Derians and others removed to Agrinium further towards the east. Nor was it just good strategic advice to relocate to these forts on the Acarnanian-Aetolia march that Cassander offered. He also called Lyciscus down and left troops under him to beef up local defences, while personally further securing this western frontier country by acquiring the alliance of Leucas, the capital of a key island off the west coast.

The Aetolians, it turned out, were not prepared to accept this Cassandrian disposal in their backyard and on his departure with most of his army they mobilized 3,000 warriors to immediately have a go at Agrinium, the nearest of those cities that had just been fortified. Determined on far more than just a border raid, they settled down to a formal siege, much to the consternation of the inhabitants whose co-operation in the Macedonians' plan had been predicated on increased security, not a redoubled threat from their dangerous neighbour. In fact, the outcome was pretty awful for these transplanted folk. Their leaders decided to do a deal, agreeing to surrender if they were allowed to leave unmolested, but the Aetolians' leaders, either with treacherous intent – they were notorious for stooping to such low ruses – or unable to control their men 'pursued hotly' just as the refugees were leaving the town, killing so many that only a small proportion ever got out alive.

If Cassander's efforts just south of the Gulf of Ambracia had in fact turned out far from decisive, further north a period of stability was also wearing out. With Neoptolemus of Epirus gaining maturity about 315, Cassander's man Lyciscus had departed for Acarnania but any assumption of the new reign progressing in security and stability soon proved unfounded as later in the same year news arrived that the Illyrians, Corcyra and other nearby Greek places were preparing to take advantage. In fact Cassander acted first: after leaving Acarnania and visiting Leucas, the Macedonian ruler turned to these other Adriatic concerns. He attacked and captured Apollonia before overrunning the Illyrians and forcing peace on Glaucus. Although by effectively moving around these western waters he had shown he remained in charge, still it was a fragile hegemony and in the next year troubles came in battalions when the exiled king Aeacides reappeared from a sojourn in Aetolia. Dumping out Cassander's puppet, he raised a considerable army from his old adherents, promising they would soon be seconded by his Aetolian friends. The conjunction of what would have been a powerful amalgamation was not allowed due to the presence of another one of Antipater's capable sons. This Philip, famous with his brother Iollas, Alexander's cup-bearer, from the improbable rumour that charged them as the purveyors of the poison that killed the conquering king,[7] was in Acarnania in considerable strength sitting just between the two enemy armies. This prince, whose son would in the future occupy the Macedonian throne for forty-five days, had invaded Aetolia, wreaking havoc far and wide before being distracted by the outbreak in Epirus. Taking up the gage, he found the Epirot enemy frail, dispersing them and forcing their leaders back into exile in Aetolia. Determined to properly clear the decks, he followed up and killed Aeacides in battle, while just his presence forced the Aetolians, after trying to involve those Boeotians upset by Cassander's resurrection of Thebes, to their usual tactic of forsaking their walled towns and taking to the hills.

Glaucus had not been quiet in this opportune time, getting in on the act by taking a swipe at Macedonian-held Apollonia as Corcyra also got involved, ensuring Apollonia and Epidamnus were able to wriggle out from under Macedonian control. Beyond this in 312 a new Epirot royal Alcetas had arisen to cause trouble that despite threats in the east of Greece Cassander could not disregard. Lyciscus was wheeled out again to try to contain the new monarch who was proving unpopular, with many deserting his cause until his more well-liked son Alexander came to his aid. After a ding-dong campaign in which Cassander had almost been required to personally ride to the rescue, peace was imposed on this Alcetas who was reduced to hiding out in a mountain stronghold.

However, this did not turn out to be a staging post on some triumphant road as Cassander, failing to retake Apollonia, had to withdraw to Pella with his tail between his legs, while a force from Corcyra arrived to bundle his men out of Leucas.

Even after massive success in Anatolia, the ruler of Macedon was far from done with these Adriatic concerns. At some stage around the turn of the century he put together a considerable expeditionary force to have another crack at Corcyra. His men had disembarked and established their siege lines with the project seeming near completion when one of the great figures of the western Greek world took a hand. The remorseless tyrant Agathocles had been in power at Syracuse since 317 and now he intervened with a powerful navy, and presumably catching them beached and vulnerable, managed to 'set fire to the entire Macedonian fleet'. The Syracusan, it is reported, was in a position to land and obliterate Cassander's entire force, but well conversant with the vicissitudes of fortune in war was content with what he had already achieved. He set up a trophy to show that not only had he fought and defeated Carthaginians and other barbarians but had now bested the very people who had conquered Asia before returning to his project of expansion in the very south of Italy.

Yet if western worries were always there, at least labours against rulers in places like Epirus, Illyria, Aetolia and Acarnania and contests with the Greek colonists of Apollonia and Epidamnus on the Adriatic littoral always provided opportunities to expand exploitatively against culturally backward and divided polities that did not exist against his great Macedonian rivals or even in the complicated and ancient world of the mainland Hellenes. Still, this was essentially peripheral stuff. It was always the Antigonid menace that had filled most of Cassander's waking thoughts: the threat from the old king and his ambitious son who as an existential foe threatened to undermine his authority and standing where Antipater had ruled with a rod of iron. Through proxies like Polyperchon's son Alexander or his nephews, the one-eyed ruler in Asia had never let him rest, hardly permitting him a moment of peace until the hiatus in 311 allowed breath to be taken. However, the respite had not lasted long and hardly had he been able to enjoy being fitted with his diadem than the younger of these rival monarchs pounced in dramatic fashion. Frequent intervention almost from his accession had confirmed Cassander's interest in the regions south of Thessaly and unsurprisingly his influence was soon felt back in Boeotia once the conflict between successor generals-transformed-into-kings began again. Still, if Demetrius' occupation of Athens had threatened his whole house of cards, he was never going to allow this play to go unanswered. So when the young prince left to go on to smashing success at Salamis in Cyprus, if Cassander realized this might not have been a plus in the larger scheme of things, at least it allowed an opportunity to reassert himself south of the Hot Gates.

Almost ten years since Cassander had resurrected ancient Thebes, he kicked off a four-year war. He had to struggle almost continuously to retain the Greek hegemony his father had held tight for generations and now again his objective was to eradicate as far as possible Antigonid influence there in the very heart of the country, and with many thousands of new Theban adherents cheering his cause, he concentrated all the soldiers at his command. In the first round, if his forces got as far as threatening the long walls of Athens, mainly the year saw fighting round Elateia, a populous place in Phocis that had experienced the trauma of being burned down by the Persians in the invasion of 480. As bustards living along the River Cephissus saw the Macedonian pikemen arriving with their cavalry support the locals, filled with terror, bolted to get behind their city defences preparing for an inevitable siege, but Cassander's men found the task considerably tougher than had been anticipated. Not long after starting their siege works they found themselves faced by a disturbing combination: it was not just local Phocians but strong forces drawn from both resolute Athenians and an army of dangerous Aetolians as well. Olympiodorus, an Athenian with whom we will become familiar later, was in charge and it had been he who had convinced the Aetolians to join the cause after sailing over to their country in person. Such a combination worsted the invaders, giving a reprieve from a Macedonian menace that well warranted the sending of a bronze lion in thanksgiving to Delphi and the honours inscribed both on the Acropolis and in the town hall to the man whose diplomacy had secured the help so crucial to the confederate cause.

Yet this failure was but a prequel and Cassander was soon back with serious intent. The Macedonian ruler pushed hard in 305 with his troops making hay all over Attica, the forts at Phyle and Panactum were systematically reduced and garrisoned and a useful naval base acquired when the island of Salamis, across the narrow straits from the mainland, was won over by a navy sufficiently strong to neutralize the Athenian vessels built from the timber provided by Antigonus. After these preliminaries, proper siege lines were drawn around the city defences and the long walls were packed with refugees from the country 'demes' just as they had been in the early years of the Peloponnesian War. We do not hear of an awful plague on this occasion, but still the danger was no less pressing, fighting was hard and there is a report that Cassander's brother Pleistarchus led an assault through a debris-strewn breach that was only repulsed by a desperate charge of Athenian cavalry.[8] Nor was this the only setback for the attackers as this might well have been the occasion when Olympiodorus raised a local defence force to see off an enemy raiding Eleusis, a place sacred to Athenians where once a year the Great Mystery was revealed to honoured initiates.

Two campaigning seasons had seen Cassander tightening the noose round Athens with high hopes that Demetrius being tied up at Rhodes would give him further time to play with. Attempting to expand this window as far as possible, he sent the islanders 10,000 measures of barley, while Lysimachus chipped in with 'forty thousand of wheat and the same amount of barley' that with aid from other dynasts provided such a fillip to a people long suffering the adept attentions of the besieger of cities that they were emboldened to sally out and burn his siege towers and ballistae. Still, this distraction was bound to be of finite duration, however much Demetrius' reputation was on the line or that he had committed resources enough to build one of the biggest siege machines ever seen. So well before the Athenians had succumbed, Cassander found that he did not just have to deal with a troublesome Greek coalition led by local resistance heroes but that in 304 Demetrius was back, having dusted himself down from setbacks against unyielding islanders and heeding his father's repeated urging, returned to the conflict on the mainland. Not in the least fazed by his failure, he arrived in strength with a fleet of 330 vessels and sufficient soldiers for those in the siege lines around Athens to have found their position becoming increasingly uncomfortable.

The arrival of Demetrius, a self-proclaimed king since his triumph at Salamis, ensured a rethink among many of those previously committed to Cassander's cause. So with local friends falling away, having little hope of relief from his allies in the south and knowing that the Aetolians had joined his enemy, he realized that, outnumbered, he would need to swiftly readjust. He found himself forced to raise the siege of Athens, bundled out of Attica and chased through the Hot Gates of Thermopylae. Once in Thessaly with a moment to pause and lick his wounds, Cassander heard that Demetrius had been welcomed with great enthusiasm by the Athenians. While preparing a defence in depth, Cassander would have learned with little amusement of his antagonist's antics as he lodged himself in Athena's temple on the Acropolis and revelled in his prerogatives of a saviour god, knowing that such behaviour had never slowed down this steamrolling enemy in the past. At least it was with some relief that he realized any threat was not imminent, even if cognizant that the respite was bound to be short-term. When news came in that even the Acrocorinth had fallen and his allies in the Peloponnese were under the cosh, nothing could hide the fact that his enemy was in main force hardly 100 miles south of his Thessalian frontier.

Sitting in his command tent in the year 302, Cassander was as worried as he had ever been since the occasion that Byzantine obduracy had ensured no Antigonid army arrived in Europe to try to finally suppress him after years of proxy conflict. He had been far from inactive as, while still at Cassandreia, he had briefed envoys on the desperate need to get the other Macedonian warlords on board and create the kind of confederacy that might have a chance of stopping the one-eyed monarch who was clearly intent on devouring the whole world. This was after attempting to make peace with Antigonus, an approach that received short shrift, a peremptory demand for surrender from the old man making it clear that he would have to fight whether he wanted to or not. Lysimachus, shrewd and farsighted and now feeling almost as dangerously exposed, responded by immediately meeting with Cassander to plan a common strategy while the other monarchs to whom they put feelers out, being further away, were bound to take longer to respond, though at least when replies arrived they were almost all that could be hoped for, with Ptolemy and Seleucus agreeing to mobilize for war. Antigonus would not back down and with appeasement no longer an option, Cassander understood that he would have to grasp the nettle of all-out war and meet his foe in Asia. The decision to take the conflict to the enemy was made clear when his trusted lieutenant Prepelaus took part of the home army to join Lysimachus in opening an Anatolian front while he remained to try to handle the enemy in Greece. Time showed he had done well to act because Demetrius, returned from the Peloponnese, showed he had lost none of his vaunted energy. The man who had managed to take the Acrocorinth initially looked like he would make short work of the lesser fortresses that would have to be overcome on the road to Pella, but before getting much further than the border of Thessaly the epicentre moved when the opponents of the Antigonids rallied round to push at an edifice that had grown in twenty years to look like the nearest thing to a continuation of the empire Alexander had left leaderless at his death.

The vital ally who had rallied to Cassander in a crisis that would turn the world upside-down had a colourful back story. At Babylon when Alexander died Lysimachus had been a significant enough figure to demand at least a portion in the Imperial division, even if not the very choicest. He received the lands of Thrace, west of the Pontus and north of the Aegean, country that had been incorporated in both Persian and Macedonian empires in the last few hundred years, yet was still very much border territory inhabited by people who, if they frequently fought as auxiliaries for both Greeks and Macedonians, were still derided as barbarians. This hard and capable warrior was not only considered well suited to what would be a very tough assignment, but for Perdiccas his being ensconced in the mountains and valleys of the empires far north had the additional advantage that he might provide for Antipater a significant enough rival that it would tie the old man down while the new regent in the east secured control of all Asia. For Lysimachus, the task he had been assigned proved tough enough. It was open terrain from the Hellespont up to where modern Edirne now stands and if there was high country looming on the left, the north was pretty open up to the Haemus Mountains. Yet this was very far from vacant territory: a people called the Odrysians occupied this region over halfway from the Aegean to the Danube and where east from the Nestus River arable and pastoral acres sustained a significant portion of the Thracians, a people who were claimed to be so numerous and martial that Thucydides considered that they would conquer the world if they ever combined and Pausanias says they outnumbered even the Celts.[9]

The indigenous culture existing there was much influenced by the Black Sea Greeks and Scythians. Partial to tattoos and influenced by Scythian fashions sported by their Getae neighbours, the Thracians loved horse-racing and wine-drinking, particularly at the wakes of their great men, not that this did anything to blunt their warrior prowess. Several decades of Persian penetration under Darius and Xerxes not only considerably affected this melting pot but also made a real impact in terms of state-building. The fifth century saw the emergence of a kingdom that dominated the whole region, but lordly pretensions were stymied by the realm splintering into three sections over 100 years, a circumstance of weakness that allowed Philip II to defeat them separately and intrude Macedonian power into new lands with planted communities like Philippopolis. However, if two of the three kingdoms were virtually vassals of Philip by 352, much remained independent and a monarch named Seuthes III had emerged by 331, maintaining himself in the region even during these imperial Macedonian years, despite the young prince Alexander having campaigned successfully both here and beyond to the waters of the Danube.

When the Macedonians left to tear up the provinces of Achaemenid Persia they did not depart without arranging to hold the province under the overall authority of the regent Antipater, but from what is recoverable, their experience in Thrace had not been easy. First around 333 a governor called Memnon turned traitor and raised a large army among the locals that necessitated Antipater marching out to confront the danger, but the rebel was either well-informed or lucky because before he could deal with them, Antipater was drawn away by news of an upheaval in Greece instigated by Agis, the king of Sparta. So, accepting 'what terms he could', the old regent turned around and retraced his steps down to the Peloponnese. Only a couple of years later Memnon had been replaced by an equally ambitious officer called Zopyrion who, if not treasonous, instigated one of the worst debacles of Alexander's reign when he began a campaign against the city of Olbia, a place halfway between the Crimean Peninsula and the Danube delta. To resist the siege army of 30,000 men the city leaders emancipated slaves, enfranchised foreigners and cancelled debts in an effort to recruit a sufficient defence force, but it was not this that mattered in the end. This intrusion into their back yard had affronted the local Scythians and this dangerous enemy gathered their forces, cut off the invaders, killed the ambitious Zopyrion and quite possibly completely destroyed his army, deeply undermining Macedon's recently-won hegemony of the west Pontic littoral. It was this poor performance that had allowed the national recrudescence that would be the context of Lysimachus' arrival. The Odrysian king Seuthes III had already during this period been a centre of opposition to Macedonian power and Alexander's death was an unexpected fillip to his endeavours. He had been noticed since 331 when he may have been trying to make hay during Memnon's rebellion and since then he had expanded his power base. The future of this independent Thracian kingdom looked promising with sons virtually grown and a new capital founded at Seuthopolis with its impressive valley of royal tombs discovered adjacent to modern-day Kazanlak.

So when a tall, well-built, vigorous warrior then in his 30s looked proprietarily across the Hellespont to the Thracian Chersonese, he had no doubt that he had a considerable job on his hands. One of a generation of Macedonian blue bloods who had risen to prominence during the ten extraordinary years when Alexander of Macedon crossed West Asia like a cyclone, he had travelled from the valley of the Axius, a small world being expanded by the warriors and wiles of Phillip II almost to the Indian Ganges, a cosmos so vast that even those who traversed it could barely comprehend. This man was almost coming home. He had been at the great Durbar at Babylon, convened when Alexander died so great and so young that he became a Heraclean or Dionysian demigod for his own age and provided a legendary space for every generation thereafter. Lysimachus had been one of the players who had begun carving up the empire the young king had conquered; a second-level one certainly, but significant enough to ensure he would not be left out when prizes were distributed. The new ruler would come to power at the hinge of Europe and Asia and ascend in an extraordinary fashion considering his initial paucity of resources, to end decades later touched by tragedy after gaining a not necessarily reliable reputation for being both tight-fisted and particularly hard on the Greek polities that came within his purview. A conclusion perhaps only appropriate after Aristandrus, one of Alexander's soothsayers, had declared when on the occasion of his being accidentally wounded in the head by Alexander's spear as he ran alongside his horse and the conquering king staunched his blood with a diadem: 'That man will be a king, but he will reign with toil and trouble.'[10]

Gossips in Alexander's court claimed that he originally came from Thessaly rather than Macedonia and was not even of noble stock, his father being a peasant recruited near Cranon who rose through the ranks in Philip II's army. Yet another belief that he was born at Pella where his father Agathocles was a significant figure at the Macedonian court suggests a more orthodox background as a young blue blood destined to occupy an honourable place in the entourage of Crown Prince Alexander. Certainly Demetrius, who was always prepared to massage the truth to denigrate his rival, never suggested either that he was a foreigner or came from common stock. In the great Asian campaign as one of the bodyguards he stayed close to the king, but despite his brother Philip being recorded as dying in Alexander's arms after they had fought all day against the Sogdians, for years Lysimachus was not ranked at the top of either the army or civilian administration. Indeed, one of the few mentions of the man is far from wholly creditable as it is mooted that he was key in poisoning Alexander's mind against Callisthenes. This was the great-nephew of Aristotle taken along in Alexander's caravan of savants to chronicle the conquests of his master but, discontented with being just a hagiographer, he became part of a faction unhappy with Alexander for aping Persian ways. He reserved his particular scorn for the practice of proskynesis or prostration and when a former pupil incriminated him when a page's plot against the king's life came to light, he suffered months of imprisonment and torture before an ignominious death, by crucifixion if Ptolemy is believed. Interestingly, Lysimachus also became something of a disciple of Calanus, the Indian guru who attached himself to Alexander's court and prophesied the death of the king at Babylon long before he had planned to go there and on having himself immolated at Susa at the age of 73 years, he left him his fine Nisean horse.

If not one of the greatest men of the court, he had always kept physically close to the king as bodyguard and armour-bearer, even getting between his master and one of the prey during a lion hunt near Samarkand. Nor was this his only experience of these beasts as in Syria he killed one with his own hands after Alexander, for a prank, locked him in the animal's cage. So it is no surprise that on Alexander's death he had sufficient standing to be given a province where it was expected that his particular qualities would be required to quell a boiling of local troubles. The Macedonians were nothing but practical people and there were two provinces pretty near home that needed swift and effective attention. One was Cappadocia where Eumenes was sent, but the other was Thrace and Lysimachus was clearly considered up to the job. He might not have had the glitz and charisma of Perdiccas, Ptolemy, Seleucus or even Pithon, but he was a serious character who could be trusted in a crisis and no sooner did he arrive than he showed that they had not misjudged him.

For the first time in years a major Macedonian figure with significant ambition and military might was on the Thracian scene and whether or not he was technically under the tutelage of the great regent Antipater, in his own bailiwick he was determined to push his prerogatives to the limit, an attitude that ensured there would be tempestuous times ahead for his putative subjects from the moment of his arrival in Europe. To tighten his grip upon the territory he had been assigned, he would have to deal with Seuthes III and one of Alexander's lieutenants leading even a small portion of his conquering army landing on the European shore of Thrace was inevitably a disquieting prospect for that man who had begun to think of himself as once more the main power in most of Thrace. He might be happy to appropriate the good things of Hellenistic life but he would not tolerate direct rule being forced down his throat, so in 323 when Lysimachus led his army north from the Hellespont Seuthes was left in no doubt of the menace. His domain, bounded by strategically vital hills and good for both cattle-rearing and arable production, was well worth fighting for and that the Odrysians were determined to not be neutered was a given. So, appreciating the advent of a bullying interloper, the king prepared his defence. Tremors were being felt in a way they had not been for many years since Macedonian interest had been directed into Asia, but the question was whether the aftershock would leave Seuthes or his antagonist sitting atop the rubble and what would the ripples mean to the peoples living roundabout?

The campaign saw the Thracians in arms in considerable numbers. Scouting around for all the friends he could muster, Seuthes had raised 20,000 infantry and 8,000 cavalry fit for duty to face only 4,000 foot and 2,000 horse on the invaders' side. Yet they were 'superior to them in the quality of his troops' and after fighting that was bloody and of long duration, it told. On the level country of the Thracian plain near the Chersonese, veteran phalanxists had the advantage. Thousands of Thracians fell on the end of long Macedonian spears or were ridden over by practised troopers, but in falling they took plenty of their adversaries with them and on returning to his camp Lysimachus found that even if his men's hearts were gladdened by victory their numbers were sadly depleted. So if the details of the fighting are pretty much a closed book it is still clear that he ended the favourite of Ares with the Thracians withdrawing and leaving the field to their foe. Yet if the Macedonian relished this first triumph in independent command, it was not long before it became clear that he had only so far won the first round. He had hoped to execute a brisk war of conquest but accepting defeat easily was never the way of the Odrysian leadership, so after recouping their strength they came straight back in the same fighting season.

For Lysimachus there was no going back either: he doubled down on his efforts to win the country he had been bequeathed. 'Both sides withdrew from the locality and busied themselves with greater preparations for the final conflict.' However, in a second round of fighting the defenders seem to have done little better and by the end of this encounter, for which we do not even have the numbers involved, Lysimachus had established himself, pushing back his enemy from the borders they had hoped to defend. Yet to see him as immediately being in full control of what had been Macedonian Thrace is certainly an error if the archaeological evidence at Seuthopolis and elsewhere is given credence and far more probable is that Seuthes ended by accepting some sort of vassal status. Whatever arrangements were made allowed peace for a decade, during which time Lysimachus by and large retained cordial relations with his technical superior Antipater, a closeness shown when he was chosen as husband for his daughter Nicaea after that inconvenient woman was repudiated by Perdiccas. That he failed to help Antipater in the Lamian War or indeed involve himself in the first successor conflict was no indication of any sort of antipathy, just showing that he had plenty on his plate establishing himself in a still hostile province. The relationship he had had with the father continued once the son had secured his position in Macedonia, a collaboration that if not immutable had an affable trajectory as mutual interest held the two European dynasts in sympathy. It was a matter of money too. Now that Cassander had control of the Macedonian mines and mints, he could coin money not just for himself but for Lysimachus as well, allowing the Thracian ruler to fund future military adventures in a way he had not been able to before. Thus he could play a significant part in the coalition that Antigonid success had raised up against itself when in 315 with Cassander, Ptolemy and Seleucus he signed a letter to the one-eyed ruler of Asia demanding that he disgorge some of the land he had won in his recent wars.

That Lysimachus had claimed Hellespontine Phrygia as his portion, handy to round out his control of the key crossings from Asia to Europe, ended as hardly significant as Antigonus sparked a new confrontation by the complete rejection of all demands. That this would not have come as any great surprise may be true, but what might have been less expected was that it would not be that long before Lysimachus would be required to respond to a menacing Antigonid agenda. Initially much of the fighting took place in Phoenicia and the east Mediterranean that hardly involved him at all, but when the terrestrial juggernaut, now boosted by top-quality maritime auxiliaries from Tyre and Sidon, switched his attention to the cluster of rivals on his north-west border, things changed. Antigonus' main target was undoubtedly Cassander, but to protect the Thracian flank of any advance Lysimachus needed to be distracted. So in the year 313 the governor of Thrace found himself in a 'sea of troubles' as enemy gold greased the wheels of discontent among the Pontic Greek cities and was probably instrumental in bringing barbarian neighbours on board as well, while Antigonus prepared to commit his own forces in a two-pronged intervention.

Little enough is really known about Lysimachus' relationship with the Greek cities of the Pontic littoral, just hints deriving from a partial Hieronymus. Arguments have been made about his curtailing autonomy based on the lack of city coinage or much in the way of inscriptions detailing democratic endeavour and it is certainly possible that his initial high hopes of co-operation as their protector against barbarian neighbours meeting with the usual backstabbing, faction bickering and opportunistic double-dealing typical of the political classes in such places led to frustration. What though did the Greeks in general make of him? Certainly there is a feeling that, like his associate Cassander, the Hellenic communities within his reach feared the power of this monarch, despite sometimes coming with their begging bowls when times were hard and harvests thin. Yet this was typical of the confusing, contradictory nature of the relationship that had developed when Greek polities found their world dominated by great monarchs. Saviour gods were not only heard of at Athens: there was a cult to Lysimachus established at Cassandreia and the founding or renaming of towns for the king or his queens is again suggestive of sacerdotal significance. To accept at face value his reputation as an oppressive tyrant is too easy; it would be extraordinary if his relations with the Pontic Greeks, just like his relations with those in Greece itself and Anatolia, were not complex and convoluted, landing anywhere along a continuum between hated oppressor to saintly sponsor depending on circumstances. Yet we do possess the reported activity in 313 that illustrates a reality of interaction and what is clear is that there were certainly factions within the Pontic communities that resented what they saw as the oppression of his rule, particularly where he had left troops as garrisons when he had firmed up and extended his influence in this region crucial for controlling the Pontic grain routes. However, there is contradictory evidence that some places retained real autonomy, with the likes of Odessus maintaining a war fleet during Lysimachus' time. Yet even if it had mostly been a charm offensive in respect of these Greek places while he was campaigning against Seuthes, a different side of his personality stuck down the ages.

With Antigonid interference as a catalyst, insurrection erupted as the people of Callantia, situated just north of the present-day Romanian-Bulgarian border, got the ball rolling in combination with Odessus and others reaching as far north as the Istrians, living almost at the Danube delta. These freedom-fighters, after driving out their garrisons, had no delusions about how Lysimachus would respond and looked round in desperation for friends and found nearby Thracians and Scythians amenable to their approaches. Soon the confederation of Greek rebels and barbarian auxiliaries found themselves confronting an enemy who wasted no time in responding to this affront. Acting energetically to tackle a dangerous combination, Lysimachus drove over the Haemus range and, well before the inhabitants expected him, dropped down into the flat country round Odessus. Caught in the middle of celebrating their new-found freedom and having paid little attention to providing for a siege, they were promptly scared into capitulation by their swift-heeled suzerain. The Istrians also finally proved less than eager to lay down their lives for liberty and once they had given up their arms, Lysimachus set his sights on suppressing the originators of revolution based at Callantia. However, before he could deal them a similar blow, he found himself threatened by their barbarian confederates, though even these turned out less of a danger than might have been imagined. The Thracians, like the Greeks, were deeply disturbed by the speed of his response. They had come in numbers, but an aggressive battlefield posture 'induced them to change sides', so eventually it was only the Scythians having crossed the Danube and descended into Thrace who posed his men any authentic test. Yet even the storm of arrows released by these caracoling horsemen and their infantry supports could not slow down the veteran pikemen and charging lancers of the Macedonian military. The terrain may not have allowed the nomads to utilize the kind of feigned retreats and flexible defence that so often undid their enemies and, caught in hand-to-hand combat, many were slaughtered and the rest unceremoniously chased back to their own country, all of which left the city of Callantia dreadfully exposed to an advancing army that had been fed on nothing but success in this campaigning season. Fields around were stripped wholly bare, and siege lines were opened as Lysimachus, settling into his headquarters tent, prepared to be as patient as was required to take a place so instrumental in instigating the uprising.

For a moment it seemed that Lysimachus might have the leisure to indulge in the luxury of vengeance against these ringleaders of rebellion, but not for long as it was soon clear that the emergency was far from over. Suddenly, from a local brawl he found himself involved in a world war. That Thrace was ruled by an ally of his great foe in Europe had not escaped Antigonus' notice and the king of Asia had the resources not just to confront major enemies like Cassander and Ptolemy but had plenty to spare to trouble lesser fry. When the welcome word arrived at his Anatolian headquarters that the Greeks had acted against Lysimachus, he activated his plans, and intending to pin his enemy to the western rim of the Pontic Sea he ordered a two-pronged assault into this northern war zone. 'That the general Lycon with the fleet had sailed through into the Pontus, and that Pausanias with a considerable number of soldiers was in camp at a place called Hieron.'[11] All was far from lost, but that Lysimachus was deeply worried by these developments is not in doubt. This was the first time he had had to face the full might of the greatest power of the Macedonian world and he could not have been sure that his allies would offer sufficient distraction for him to survive the experience. Certainly for the moment he had to do what he could for himself. He had exerted such labours to suppress Callantia that even with this new danger he was not prepared to give up the prize and left a holding force to mask the town as he turned to face the new and greater menace. Withdrawing most of his best men from the siege lines, he turned to the south, rushing to oppose what had developed into an even greater problem once Seuthes, never dependable, decided to throw in his lot with the Antigonids. So the first blood spilt in this Lysimachus against Antigonid war was Thracian, as the Odrysian king was discovered defending the passes over the Haemus Mountains that separated Lysimachus from the invading army under Pausanias. Battle was joined and a long and desperate struggle began. As in the fights years before, the Thracians showed considerable endurance before their brave defence collapsed in blood and, despite sustaining considerable casualties, Lysimachus' army crashed on through.

However, the losses incurred turned out to be worthwhile because with these guard forces gone the Antigonids were exposed and surprised by Lysimachus' sudden arrival. Even being encamped near a holy site in difficult terrain did not help them and, ever resourceful, he captured the place by assault, while Pausanias was killed and not a few of his soldiers turned their coats to join his army or stumped up hard cash to purchase their freedom. Nothing more was heard of the expedition headed by Lycon, although it is possible this intervention really mattered and that by batting aside any opposition found in the Hellespont or Bosporus the Antigonids reached Callantia, relieving the siege, explaining why the citizens remained free, requiring Lysimachus to undertake another campaign against them in 309. Even if there is confusion over the details, the ruler of Thrace was surely pleased with these outcomes and had further cause for satisfaction by playing his part in thwarting Antigonus' attempt to ship his army over into Europe to directly confront Cassander. His influence over the nearby polities after his string of recent successes was well illustrated as the campaigning season drew to a close. His garrisons directly blocked the Hellespont crossings, so Antigonus, intending to cross by the Bosporus, arrived at the Asian shore hoping once there to win the co-operation of the locals. Intent on bringing all his might to bear against Cassander, he approached the Byzantines but unfortunately for his plans just as his own ambassadors were nearing the town they found themselves forestalled by agents of Lysimachus greasing the diplomatic wheels with all the influence and specie he could bring to bear. These persuasive men won the day and with winter not far off the putative invader found himself stymied. To try to assault the town would mean concentrating most of his naval and military might and he just would not have the time in that fighting season. So instead he 'distributed his soldiers among the cities for the winter' in Asia rather than Thrace, which would have functioned so much better as a springboard for a campaign aimed at the heart of Macedonia in the following year. By that time his son Demetrius had stumbled in battle against Ptolemy at Gaza, meaning he had little option but to go and pull his son's irons out of the fire, so ensuring the enterprise of Europe was shelved, for what in the end turned out to be forever.

This war in which Lysimachus had played his part had been especially frustrating for Antigonus as he discovered he could not finally suppress his rivals in either Macedonia, Egypt or even Mesopotamia, particularly now that this confederacy of enemies included the ruler of Thrace whose realm sat solidly where Europe linked to Asia. By 311 Antigonus, battered by wars on multiple fronts, decided he needed to come to terms and if the likes of Cassander, Seleucus and Ptolemy felt relief at the lifting of existential pressure that the Antigonids had on different occasions exerted against them for Lysimachus, it must have had a special thrill. A sequence of successes had for the first time projected him from the periphery almost into the centre of things. The details of the peace of 311 are difficult: intentions and even terms are opaque, yet if there was confusion over who was getting what, particularly in Asia, clearly there was a recognition that Cassander should hold Europe until Alexander's son by Roxana came of age, while Ptolemy and Lysimachus were confirmed in the position of all they currently controlled and Greek autonomy was guaranteed. However, much of this was cant as all the participants were aware that it was merely a truce they were signing, but at least for Lysimachus it signified a real change, years of secure and developing government ensured any early feelings of inferiority in respect of the other Macedonian rulers had receded. He had seen off threats from the greatest of them and was now a valued ally, wooed by his peers as a crucial asset in the dangerous post-Alexander world. If on entering his satrapy there had been a suggestion that he was technically subservient to Antipater, that had been a long time ago and now he was a warlord in his own right who dominated most of Thrace and the Chersonese and had no real rival in the wheat-rich world of the Pontic Sea; a transformation from small fry to one of the major powers of the Diadochi world.

Such a man was not going to allow his peers to outstrip him in reputation and distinction so it is hardly astonishing that when they began to build up great megalopolises to house their imperial courts, he too decided to demonstrate his status in this traditional way and in 309 he began to mark out a new capital at Lysimachia. The land at the head of the Gulf of Saros by a crystal sea at the neck of the Thracian Chersonese was surveyed and inhabitants from nearby communities either enticed or forced to up sticks and move to the new foundation. Not long after this city-building in 306/7 Lysimachus took another step that saw him tie a royal diadem around his brow to match those taken by his peers since Cassander's disposal of the last of Alexander's line had left no obstacle to each claiming regal legitimacy over their spear-won lands. Royal trappings could be shown off at a city named for him, particularly with the peace dividend available after the treaties concluded in 311, while his marrying into the Odrysian royal line around 312 suggests a cementing of arrangements with previously troublesome vassals. However, if good times were rolling for this new big beast in the Hellenistic jungle, he was never going to be able to keep completely aloof from problematic entanglements in a wider world where conflict was so prevalent. The Antigonids had not gone away and any increase in their already dangerously powerful realm was bound to be troubling to a ruler who had so recently been at hot war with them. So when Antigonus' son descended on the crucial trading entrepôt and important maritime power that was Rhodes it sent shivers down Lysimachus' spine as much as it did Ptolemy who was the city's closest ally and had himself just survived an assault on his own kingdom led by Antigonus on land and Demetrius by sea. So during the Rhodians' trial between 305 and 304 he did what he could to sustain the brave islanders: supplies were dispatched to go with what Cassander and Ptolemy sent to feed the starving citizens, assistance commemorated by a statue raised to him in the city along with others who gave the islanders crucial succour.

The gradual re-forming of the anti-Antigonid coalition that occurred as the century petered out can first be observed with the circulation of letters by Ptolemy informing his peers of failure of the attack on Egypt in 306 and that he intended to have himself acclaimed king the following year. However, the ignition button was most significantly pressed when Demetrius, determined to realize some compensation for his failure at

Rhodes, arrived to mount an all-out assault against Cassander's position in mainland Greece. That Lysimachus' attachment to Cassander had a history that went way back is indicated from the time the latter was competing with Polyperchon for Antipater's inheritance when he assassinated the enemy admiral Cleitus when he fell into his hands after a defeat near the Hellespont in 317. Since then there had been little antagonism and not infrequently they worked in tandem against rivals who endangered their standing in the lands of Macedonian Europe. Now, near the end of the century, the relationship showed impressively robust, even though it would demand a commitment from the ruler of Thrace like never before as he was pulled into a wide world of conflict. It was he and Cassander who were the core in 302 and it was Lysimachus who took the lead as he prepared to utilize all his resources and risk his whole kingdom by taking the fight to Antigonus in Asia. Agents were sent to Ptolemy and Seleucus to activate these rulers already committed to the cause, but for the moment it was the two men from Europe who carried the burden.

Lysimachus showed as a risk-taker in this war in a way he had not done before. There was no question that he was taking the lead, even if well seconded by Cassander's man Prepelaus. Nor did he forget the importance of diplomacy, marrying the ruler of Heraclea whose country on the south shore of the Pontic Sea would end up being crucial as the campaign rolled out. This Amastris now brought as dowry access to a key winter base for the confederate army facing Antigonus that functioned as a staging post for the receipt of reinforcements from Europe and a rendezvous point for the army of elephants and chariots on top of the usual infantry and cavalry that Seleucus had marched in heroic style from the upper satrapies of Asia. It was not just his logistical decision-making that was apparent but his military flair as well, withdrawing in good order away from Antigonus' greatly superior army and utilizing sophisticated fieldworks to run out the campaigning season of 302 until winter weather called an end to any fighting. The aging but irrepressible Antigonus' initial reaction to the confederates' incursion into his rich Anatolian holdings had been stunning, almost turning what had begun so well into a disaster. Putting the great festival to celebrate the founding of his capitol of Antigonea on hold, he had acted at breakneck speed, landing with a huge army right on Lysimachus' doorstep in Phrygia. Outnumbered, he sensibly decided that discretion was the better part of valour and fell back to encamp behind stout defences manned with numerous catapults. His enemy tried to starve him out, but under the cover of a fortuitously stormy night Lysimachus slipped away and for a season the confederates were saved as brutal winter rains and impassable mud brought a hiatus in fighting, allowing him to take up winter quarters in the well-supplied country of Salonia south of Pontic Heraclea.

The next year, which turned out climactic, commenced with troubles as the confederates lost men through desertion or drowned in the Black Sea while Demetrius, arriving from Greece and disembarking at Ephesus, retook many places along the Aegean and around the Asian shore across from Byzantium. Then the appearance of Seleucus' army permitted the confederates to face the new campaigning season of 301 with renewed confidence, allowing the showdown at Ipsus that ended as an overwhelming victory with Lysimachus commanding his own men alongside those of Cassander and Seleucus. Old Antigonus, fighting to the end, died on the battlefield as a distraught Demetrius was unable to come to his aid because the cavalry he had led to triumph on the Antigonid right were kept away from the main battle by the terrifying smell of a cordon of 300 of Seleucus' elephants. Two great regional imperial disposals at Babylon and then Triparadisus had solved nothing in the Macedonian world, and the question was whether the bloody decision arrived at in central Anatolia would produce more permanent results? For his part Lysimachus was gifted Anatolia to the Taurus. This country could fill his coffers in a way that his Thracian holdings were never able to do. There were minerals in the Troad and Lydia, Croesus' riches had been proverbially based on gold mined in Mount Tmolus and the rivers like the Meander and Hermus watered fine grain-producing country, while olives and wine grew in abundance outside the high plateau. Now even the grandest had to take Lysimachus seriously; no longer reduced to picking up scraps on the barbarian periphery, he had taken the lead and had been rewarded with the richest pickings. However, if the gains of Ipsus were potentially game-changing they still had to be harvested, and many of the key places along the Aegean coast of Anatolia remained either garrisoned by troops loyal to Demetrius or still adhering to the Antigonid cause. The young Antigonid king was holding on to a still extensive realm and a well-articulated inclination to push back ensured that Lysimachus continued in alliance with Cassander.

On more equal terms with other monarchs, being richer with horizons widening, Lysimachus indulged in diplomatic manoeuvrings and is discovered making contacts in Greece, particularly at Athens where his friend the poet and playwright Philippides is honoured for making sure the Athenians who died fighting at Ipsus received proper funerary rites and that any citizens taken prisoner were ransomed. More important were the machinations in which the great powers tried to make sense of what had been thrown up in the air at Ipsus. Lysimachus' preparedness to dally with Ptolemy was shown in 299 when he married his daughter Arsinoe hoping for advantage from good relations with a man who had the ships to challenge Demetrius and whose confrontation with him over Cyprus and Phoenicia could be expected to cause sufficient of a distraction to allow the retaking of more of the Antigonid-held towns along the Aegean's Asian shoreline. Great cities soon came under his control and the hugely impressive walls built at Ephesus and Carian Heraclea showed he was prepared to invest his new-found wealth in the infrastructure of these new dependants. Yet none of this seemed enough to make them love him, whether the perception of Lysimachus as a ruler was calibrated by the Pontic Greeks or by the views of their Ionian cousins long used to interpreting imperial governance since even before Achaemenid times, it seems that if they understood him as a great man, few thought him likable.

If the complicated world of great Hellenic metropolises led to frustration, perhaps this was part explanation for Lysimachus directing his interest much further north in the 290s. It is his interaction with the warrior Getae living around the Danube delta that gives us some real detail in those years directly after Ipsus, when darkness falls with the failure of Diodorus except in rare fragments. It is now we hear of his son Agathocles turning into a willing apprentice. A chip off the old block, he rapidly proved as competent as his father and perhaps a little more personable as well. A keen student of his forebears' political and military practice, he must have seemed to many the very assurance of continuity with none having any idea of the fatality waiting down the years. It was in the northern war he began to take up independent commands after his father had decided that the country of the Getae was ripe for the plucking.

The exact sequence that drew this man, who had been happily establishing his court in Lysimachia and exploiting his vast new domain in Anatolia over almost a decade of power, into a different world of Bosporan kings and nomad warlords is unclear. Involvement in the world of the great grasslands of the Pontic steppe had been forced on him in the crisis of 313, but now events suggest that attraction in this direction was a consistent strand in his career. One such contact was made after Eumelos, battling to gain the throne of the Bosporus kingdom, overthrew his elder brother after a series of campaigns round the Maeotic Lake. Eventually emerging triumphant, he beefed up his military with Greek mercenaries as well as long-time Sarmatian allies and strengthened his fleet to boost trade revenues and deal with the perennial scourge of piracy. This king from the north intended to make a mark in the wider world and wooed the Pontic Greek cities, especially Sinope and Byzantium, key trading places for a man with plenty of corn to sell. In this charm offensive he was even prepared to risk getting on the wrong side of a ruler whose earlier success against the Scythians was bound to have reverberated round the region, being prepared to give sanctuary to 1,000 refugees that Lysimachus had driven out of Callantia when he had returned in 309 to deal with a people who he perceived as behind so much of his trouble along the Black Sea shore.

It was the Getae, however, that were Lysimachus' main concern. Fighting on this front sometime in the 290s saw Agathocles, his eldest son and strong right arm captured. This young man had been taking on more and more responsibility since his father's kingdom had expanded after Ipsus as it was not possible to be everywhere to guard a realm stretching from south of the Danube right down to the Taurus Mountains. The captors of the prince resisted the desire to take out their bile against their belligerent and troublesome neighbours by killing him or demanding an exorbitant ransom. Instead, as apparently they had little hope of winning the war they had so long been fighting, they loaded him with gifts and sent him home in the hope that the father would, affected by their munificence, return 'that part of their territory which Lysimachus had seized'. Little did they know the man who hardly skipped a beat in pressing the war; in fact his enemies' beneficence seemed to inspire even greater efforts and 292, the next campaign that is noticed, saw him personally taking charge, intent on finishing off the enemy by invading the Getic heartland along both banks of the lower Danube. It was a difficult task as these nomads provided hardly any conventional targets for the invaders to aim at, forts, palaces and towns were few and far between and Lysimachus found himself deeply frustrated as he followed a will o' the wisp enemy. Like Darius before him and many later, after crossing the great river he found himself in flat and marshy country where his enemy were in their element. Groups of horse archers galloping in effortless choreography encircled the heavily-armed soldiers in the invaders' caravan, while other columns cut off their supply lines. These remorseless steppe warriors generated a fatal rain of arrows, eventually compelling Lysimachus to halt and dig his army into an entrenched camp.

The invaders behind their ramparts were soon hard-pressed for food, with it rapidly becoming clear that even if temporarily safe from their gadfly tormentors, the reality was that they were trapped. Starvation or surrender appeared the unhappy options before them as many on the king's staff urged him to flee, to escape with just an escort the seemingly ineluctable fate of death or capture that was bound to be the lot of the rest of them. Lysimachus' refusal to desert his army may have been more to do with the dangers of such a plan deep in hostile country as it was any sentiment of loyalty, but once decided, the only possible recourse was negotiations. With few cards to play, the intruders, confused and humiliated, were forced to the indignity of virtually unconditional surrender, handing themselves over into the hands of a foe they disparaged as abhorrent barbarians. Yet once again they found that at the hands of these people they reviled they were treated with a consideration they hardly deserved. King Dromichaetes of the Getae faced down his understandably vengeful warriors, determined that Lysimachus and his men should suffer the condign punishment warranted by the ravishing of their homeland. This ruler might not hold absolute power, but gathered with his own army and their captives at a place called Helis he claimed the foresight that were Lysimachus to be executed, other kings, possibly more to be feared than their predecessor, would assume his authority. If on the contrary he was treated well and released with his men there would be a chance that they would get back the lands they had lost in the past year's fighting and with them a peace that ensured they would not have to stand forever on the defensive against these invaders from the south. It was a remarkable example of clemency, even more so in that it was the second time this policy had been tried. Indeed, the very improbability of the people being convinced of trying this again after what had happened when Agathocles was released suggests we are getting repetition here and that the capture of the father and son occurred together on just one occasion.

The story continues with a banquet where the captives were set on furniture embellished with spoils from their own camp while the hosts sat on straw beds and when the food was brought in, the Getae were served camp fare on wooden plates and horn cups while Lysimachus and his followers received 'a prodigal array of all kinds of viands' laid out on a table service of gold and silver. All to prove the obvious: why would people with so much want to attack those who had so little and lived in such an inhospitable land? We do not need to believe this wonderful stuff about the blow-out, it is such a trope, yet still the facts suggest that something of a sea change in attitude occurred after these events. Despite the crushing weight of humiliation that he must have felt, Lysimachus had finally learned his lesson so that peace could descend on the steppe country for a while, a circumstance reinforced by the marriage of Dromichaetes to Lysimachus' daughter and the dispatch of one of his sons by Amastris as a hostage to the court of his new son-in-law.

There is little doubt that Lysimachus' attention being pulled elsewhere played its part in establishing a more peaceful Pontic country. Occupying lands beyond the Danube paled into insignificance next to the dangers and opportunities in the great Hellenistic world of populous cities, opulent temples and rich trade routes. While a daughter might go to a barbarian monarch, his eldest son's matrimonial prospects were brighter, being wed to Lysandra, daughter of Ptolemy of Egypt and his queen Eurydice. Friends were needed in a universe where Demetrius was looking dangerous again. This Antigonid had already allied with the great power in Asia and was bullying Pleistarchus who had received Cilicia as his portion in the territorial disposition after Ipsus, but finally he still relied upon one dependable man in these fractured and kaleidoscopic times and Cassander felt the same: 'It was his invariable custom when facing the most alarming situations to call on Lysimachus for assistance, both because of his personal character and because his kingdom lay next to Macedonia.'[12] The problem was that the years were passing and as the 290s progressed, one of these two was coming to the end of his days.

Chapter Four

Demetrius Rex

If the two great regional carve-ups at Babylon and Triparadisus had solved nothing, the bloody denouement at Ipsus in 301 was almost immediately understood as a game-changer. King Antigonus, a man so old he was almost a contemporary of Alexander's father and so powerful that no single other ruler could have hoped to contend with him, was dead and the destiny of his demesne that stretched from the Hellespont to the Euphrates and beyond was bound to be up for grabs. This had not been a minor affair like Gaza in 312 where in hardly a campaigning season the defeated Demetrius had bounced back to confront Ptolemy again or some complication in Mesopotamia around the same time where Seleucus regained a local ascendency which, even if portentous for the future, had little immediate impact. It had been a conclusive event and the military might of Macedonian Europe directed by the kings from Pella and Lysimachia had been decisive, with these two emerging to relish in their triumph over an Imperial family who for a decade and a half had looked like the only candidate capable of consolidating the whole empire that Alexander had left as the prize for funeral games that commenced by the river of Babylon before covering regions inhabited by men from the Adriatic Sea to the Indus River. It had not been these two alone. Seleucus had done his bit after an epic march from the borders of Afghanistan with elephants and chariots in tow and, if Plutarch can be believed, the great beasts from India had been critical in keeping Demetrius from returning after a dramatic and victorious cavalry charge to save a father who fell in the centre where the masses of infantry contested the field. There it had been the heavy warriors of the phalanx, provided by Cassander and Lysimachus, that were the core of the victorious army and without which no Hellenistic military could take the field with any hope of success.

Yet for all that had changed, after the awful butchery perpetrated in clouds of dust on a plain in the centre of Anatolia, King Demetrius remained alive and free. Scarred he might be, but resisting any excess

of despair and accompanied by a young and fiery Pyrrhus, whose name
will soon figure gloriously in our story, he had made his way to Ephesus
where he joined up with a fleet that remained stoutly loyal to the man
who had led them to such triumph at Salamis only five years earlier.
Nor was this by any means all that was left to him: the Antigonid realm
that remained loyal still stretched from strongholds in Greece to the
great Aegean cities of Anatolia, down to the maritime communities of
Phoenicia as well as over to Cyprus, with plenty of members from the
league of islanders in between. However, as the rump of the Antigonid
leadership assessed their new situation, news arrived of another body blow
both to their power and prestige. The wheels of the Athenian democracy
had not ground slowly at all, as almost in a heartbeat they abandoned
the cause of men they had six short years before hailed as saviour gods.
The tension between the monarchic and democratic principles had
inevitably caused problems during Demetrius' sojourn in Greece with his
behaviour when headquartered in the Parthenon under the disapproving
gaze of Athena's huge ivory and gold-plated statue fashioned by the great
Phidias lovingly detailed for our censure.[1] Should we actually believe that
Demetrius turned his accommodation in Athena's temple into a brothel?
Probably not, but that he allowed himself to be treated like a god and
was a sucker for much of the sycophantic stuff Stratocles is claimed
to have orchestrated, very possibly yes. The idea of great dynasts and
warriors joining the demigods went deep and the kind of success these
Macedonian warlords achieved is very likely to have gone to their heads
just in the way it is suggested it did with Alexander himself. Certainly
there was exaggeration, particularly as some of the most salacious reports
probably originated from the playwright Philippides who, as a friend of
Lysimachus, hated Demetrius with a vengeance.

When the reports of Ipsus hit the streets in early autumn there had
been enough people oppressed by all too human resentment of Demetrius'
ascendency to provoke joy in many hearts. In the years since he had arrived
offering freedom and autonomy on the end of his sword, they had learned
what this really meant with sufficient resentment engendered to ensure
that the Antigonid honeymoon was a long time over. Now excitement
about the possibility of getting out from under was palpable, it could
almost be tasted. These Athenians were far from always truly admirable
but still there was an impressive core, a desire for real sovereignty that

meant the likes of Stratocles were bound to be under threat once it was clear his sponsor was no longer the foremost ruler of the Hellenistic world. The administration would have been careful; the first news could be unreliable but eventually repeated reports from credible folk, traders first, then perhaps Athenian soldiers who had fought in the battle and emissaries from the other powers. When the evidence was overwhelming, all those except the few totally committed to Demetrius acted. The assembly was convened and the posture of the majority was clear when they voted never to allow another king to enter through the city gates again. In the past an Athenian need to get rid of anybody too powerful, too popular or too grand had contrived the mechanism of ostracism and the sentiment remained. The Antigonid king was just too much in every way for many and they wanted him gone.

How the king's wife, the sister of Pyrrhus, felt at this turn of events can be imagined as stuffy civic officials arrived to unceremoniously arrange for her departure. They might have been polite enough, organizing an escort for her as far as Megara, but for both her and her husband it was a slap in the face. Perhaps of more moment for Demetrius based at Ephesus was what would happen to that part of his fleet and treasury still in the city. He was far from prepared to write off these vital resources, nor indeed to accept as any kind of fait accompli being ejected from where he had lorded for so many years. The man who had lived in deified state in the Parthenon was in no mood to accept this as just another aspect of the fall-out of the great battle in Anatolia. However, for the moment the young Antigonid, regretting no doubt that he had not at least left a garrison in the Piraeus, realized he was in no position to make demands but would have to negotiate. A meeting took place somewhere in the Cyclades where the defeated king was able to restrain any resentment at his treatment and the Athenian envoys, who did not want this still formidable man as an enemy, not only agreed to hand over his ships but also to remain neutral in a situation where Demetrius would be bound to try to reassert control in the other places in Greece that had repudiated his hegemony. Neither side was playing straight here. Demetrius had far from given up his designs in Attica, and the Athenians soon showed their concept of neutrality was very elastic indeed where their self-interest was concerned. Within two years a delegation had been dispatched to formalize relations with Cassander, while the Athenians' attachment to

Lysimachus was highlighted when the playwright Philippides facilitated a considerable gift of grain from the Thracian monarch. Yet immediately Demetrius, having at least had the ships that were moored at the Piraeus returned, including thirteen of one of the deadliest, most up-to-date warships, moved in considerable might to his great stronghold of Corinth.

While most of the evidence we have about events in Greece relates to what happened in Athens – after all, it had been Demetrius' headquarters for so many years in the 310s as well as being a key cultural centre of the Hellenic world – this does not mean that strains did not surface elsewhere. He discovered 'everywhere his garrisons were being expelled from the towns in which he had stationed them and the whole region was going over to his enemies.'[2] It is only possible to interpret this to mean places in the Peloponnese that he had taken from Cassander's officers now returned to the adherence of a king whose armies had played such a part in the victory at Ipsus. What is extraordinary is that instead of taking action against this pressing threat, Demetrius scratched a different itch that had become unbearable. He decided to take a swipe at Lysimachus. The bitterness between these two was proverbial and best expressed by the derogatory nickname that he gave to his rival. Not that this name-calling was so unusual in the group of rival Macedonian aristocrats who ruled the world as the Antigonid described Seleucus as 'master of the elephants', but designating Lysimachus 'the treasurer' was scarifying indeed. It not only highlighted a perceived parsimony, damning him as a tightwad who did not properly reward his followers, it also cast aspersions on his manhood as this was a post frequently occupied by eunuchs.

So, leaving Pyrrhus of Epirus to hold tight in Greece, he took most of his navy and as many soldiers as he could spare from his garrisons and sailed along the eastern coast towards the Hellespont. There was some fighting near Lampsacus,[3] situated on the southern shore as the straits broaden out into the Propontis, where Lysimachus decided he had to massacre 5,000 of his Autariatae mercenaries because Demetrius had captured their baggage and he was afraid they would go over to his enemy just as the Silver Shields had done a deal with Antigonus to betray Eumenes after the Battle of Gabiene. Once ashore on the Thracian Chersonese, Demetrius had the satisfaction of not only plundering the heartland of his hated rival and utilizing the spoils he had won to sustain his men, but was able to threaten the city of Lysimachia as well. That he could terrify the inhabitants of the capital and throw the court itself into confusion must have been of huge satisfaction, highlighting as it did that despite Ipsus, his enemies could still not begin to confront him at sea. That none of the Thracian king's old allies showed any inclination to come to his aid must have been a delight, though if he was conscious of it the general opinion that after Ipsus, with the gains made in Anatolia, Lysimachus was now 'more to be feared' than Demetrius would have been much less gratifying.

If one monarch had been left dishevelled and anxious in his capital, another had been establishing a headquarters that would end as a very much greater city than Lysimachia. On the left bank of the Orontes River below the soaring crest of Mount Silpios, where there was a spring whose waters it was claimed brought back memories for Alexander of his mother's milk and with beautiful Daphne to the south, a chequerboard foundation had emerged, orientated to get the best of each season's winds and shade. Originally peopled with the denizens of Antigonus' old capital of Antigonia, many of whom had themselves been incomers from Athens, these now enjoyed the bounties of nature from land and sea while providing a node for caravan routes from the interior. All of this should have been enough, but there were omens too, with eagles flying off with sacrificial meat and co-operatively dropping it on the site of the new city of Antioch. It was in the direction of this foundation of Seleucus that Demetrius discovered opportunities in a new century.

Hardly a year after Ipsus, not content with just setting his personal enemies' assets in ashes, he also determined to look for new friends in an altered world. Seleucus had found himself heir to considerable new regions after the Antigonid realm crumbled, but with fresh advantage came new dangers. He found himself not only with Lysimachus, still allied to Cassander, as a neighbour but that the latter's brother Pleistarchus as his reward for leading the Macedonian troops at Ipsus was now ensconced in strategic Cilicia, no distance from his own Syrian border. So his western frontier was abutted by rulers who no longer had need of him now that Antigonus was overthrown and apart from this, some of the most prime real estate that had come his way as part of victory had been annexed by another ex-ally. Coele-Syria had been occupied by Ptolemy and despite any post-Ipsus settlement he was hanging on to it and as Lysimachus and Cassander both hoped to remain on good terms with him, as a naval counterweight to Demetrius, Seleucus could have little expectation of receiving anything but more grief from their direction. Such circumstances meant that Demetrius soon discovered envoys at his court from the new master of anti-Taurine Asia asking for an alliance that he hoped would be cemented by marriage between the two families. So it was settled that the man who provided the elephants that had been so crucial in destroying his father in battle would befriend the loser of that climactic encounter and faintly the sound of old Antigonus turning in his grave must have been heard as Demetrius led his daughter Stratonice on board his great flagship to transport her to a new husband waiting at his western headquarters in Syria.

It turned out to be a happy and lucrative cruise, particularly when they alighted on the coast of Cilicia where the mint new ruler found himself in no position to make any military defence against the intruder and instead went to Seleucus to complain of his putative father-in-law's incursions. In his absence Demetrius dashed to the town of Cyinda where 1,200 talents was still being banked from his father's time and after loading the treasure on his ships and leaving a garrison to hold this key stronghold, sailed on to Rhosus where he had arranged to meet with Seleucus. After travelling miles around the Amanos Mountains from his just-founded capital to reach this seaport on the Gulf of Issus, Seleucus had come in sufficient style to treat his visitor and his followers to a sumptuous feast in his camp on the coast. The Antigonid, not to be outdone, reciprocated this hospitality the next day on his own element when both monarchs foregathered on the deck of the great thirteener he had so recently received back from the Athenians. The laid-back pair seemed happy to enjoy themselves where they could and the image transmitted is that 'the two rulers conversed at leisure and spent the whole day in one another's company without either guards or arms.'[4]

If nothing very stable proceeded from this junketing, one by-blow would have a major impact on Macedonian Europe. Seleucus had over this period made friends not only with Demetrius but with the royal tenant at Alexandria too and, acting as intermediary, he managed the trick of reconciling him to Demetrius, the same man who had invaded his country hardly five years before and the one power who had a navy that could compare favourably with his own. Part of these arrangements involved Pyrrhus of Epirus travelling to Egypt as a hostage for the surety of Demetrius' good intentions. The new Seleucid-Antigonid pact in fact had little internal logic and began to show signs of fraying almost as soon as it had been established when the former began pressing to have not only Cilicia but then Tyre and Sidon handed over to him. Demetrius would never have countenanced this and rejected his son-in-law's representation, although with a new project filling his thoughts, he would have welcomed a settled situation on this front. That he had allowed his trusted lieutenant in Greece to depart for Alexandria in no sense meant that he had forgotten his European ambitions. Much had happened at Athens since they had ejected their saviour god from his palace in the Parthenon and keeping the flame of autonomy and democracy alive in a complex world was never going to prove easy. So events in 298 showed as famine had driven the people hard despite some hand-outs from the likes of Lysimachus and after something like a civil war, only discovered from an *Oxyrhynchus Papyri*, the leaders of the city's mercenaries took control. Yet this coup by a character called Lachares was far from complete as Piraeus was detached from municipal authority in spring 297 when news of Cassander's death spread abroad, and a party of resistance against the impious tyrant who had filched the gold sheeting from Athena's great statue to pay his mercenaries had established a base there. So when Demetrius decided again to target the city he might reasonably have expected to encounter only a ragged and divided defence.

From the time of his matrimonial excursion east the exact whereabouts of the Antigonid king is something of a mystery, but he may well have based himself in Cilicia. This country was provided with good timber to repair and build his warships and was not far from Phoenicia that was home to some of his most expert mariners and their craft, and it is difficult to place an incident when he is reported clashing with Lysimachus at Soli in Cilicia[5] at any other time. His presence to some extent might also explain why Seleucus, worried by his continued proximity, had decided to cosy up to Ptolemy despite bitter contention over ownership of Coele-Syria. Wherever he had been, 296 or 295 saw him move to re-establish himself where he had so recently cavorted with the goddess Athena. Initially his efforts were attended by unfortunate results. An attempt to surprise the Athenians started well enough until 'along the coast of Attica' his armada was hit by a terrific storm; screaming wind and rain lashed low-lying galleys for hours until vessels just not made for these conditions broke apart and foundered. The havoc-wrecked fleet was almost smashed to pieces with thousands of soldiers and sailors perishing, though numbers could only be conjectured from the litter of oars, spars and bloated corpses. What was not in doubt was that Demetrius' arms might have been considerably diminished, his military personnel shaved to such an extent that if the whole enterprise was not chasteningly aborted, all he could achieve with curtailed resources was to try to overrun the outlying forts and undefended villages in the Attic countryside. Yet despite this incapacity to make decisive headway around the city itself, while his officers were busy rebuilding his navy, the ever-active man decided to try to regain ground further south.

This was the dashing Demetrius all over. Gathering the remnants of his army at Corinth, he resolved to pounce on the other defensive horn of the Peloponnese, Mount Ithome above Messene. This very defensible place appealed as a meaningful challenge to the great besieger and soon his engines in spectacular demonstration were closing in and an assault was prepared with himself at the head. However, before he could mount the walls, Demetrius suffered an awful wound when a catapult bolt penetrated through his jaw far into his mouth. When his followers saw their dazzling leader felled with a 2-metre-long lance in his head they must have believed him dead and themselves left rudderless, but it turned out not at all the case. Somehow he not only survived this terrible wound but recuperated in a remarkably short time, an almost miraculous recovery that perhaps explains why a number of places that had overturned Antigonid rule returned to the fold, though there is little evidence regarding whether he actually took Messene in the end.

The irrepressible man now revisited his earlier undertaking. Returning to the fighting in Attica, it was the usual stuff to begin with, trashing the countryside and driving the farmers and their families inside the city walls while his soldiers overran the forts at Eleusis and Rhamnus, the latter north of Marathon with its sanctuary to the goddess Nemesis above the sea looking out over to Euboea. These two places positioned him strategically both west and north-east of the city while he clearly still had sufficient warships left to institute a blockade. This policy, with Demetrius paying attention to detail, turned out particularly effective when disincentives were viciously enforced after a grain ship bound for Athens was captured by his captains who had the pilot and owner hung from their own masts. With potential importers frightened off, the suffering city experienced one last wellspring of hope when a fleet of 150 ships from Alexandria was sighted 'off the coast of Aegina' looking set to break Demetrius' cordon, but by now the weather-beaten vestige of his navy had been reinforced with the reserves from the Peloponnese, Cyprus and no doubt his Phoenician strongholds where for months from sun-up to sun-down the air had rung with the clamour of hammers and saws, filling their slipways with replacement warships. His naval establishment had managed to scrape together a fleet of 300 vessels, enough to see off the danger without even a fight, so 'Ptolemy's ships hoisted sail, abandoned the city and made their escape',[6] cutting their losses and scurrying for home at the sight of the Saronic Gulf black with Antigonid shipping.

Initially the Athenians, snug behind their walls, had shown brave, skating over the implication of even these setbacks and decreeing death for anybody passing a resolution to treat with Demetrius, but it soon became clear that the long walls were in poor shape and the city was easily cut off by experienced engineers, many of whom had served apprenticeships under the great besieger himself. When the strength of these forces became clear, consternation swept the citizen body as the forebodings that had gripped the more realistic proved well-grounded. How bad things soon got for a people ruined by war is well illustrated by an ominous story of a father and son living in the city. These two, sitting despondent in their house and having no expectation except death, noticed a dead mouse falling out of their ceiling and despite hardly having any energy left they still fell to fighting over this morsel of food. Alarmingly, even initiates of Epicurus could not be sustained by their philosophy and their leader is reported keeping tabs on his store of beans and doling out a meagre ration to his disciples each day. Finally, with famine biting hard, collaborators came out of the woodwork pointing out that there was no alternative to sending envoys to their tormentors.

During this period, before the city fell, the rapacious tyrant Lachares left the scene initiating some wonderful stories by Polyaenus about him escaping to Boeotia disguised as a slave with a blackened face, carrying a basket of illicit gold hidden beneath stinking faeces. Not that this was the end of his adventures that included hiding in the sewers at Thebes for days to escape when it fell to Demetrius and similarly lurking in a pit at Sestus and escaping disguised as a female mourner when that town was taken. An exile's billet at Lysimachus' court eventually lay in store for this man who had absconded from Athens before a surrender was arranged in April 295 or 294 when the Athenians opened their gates again to their old saviour god. It must have been with huge trepidation that the crowds, racked with dreadful imaginings, moved along nervous streets to gather in the theatre to hear what their new ruler had to say. Their concerns would not have been alleviated as they saw the back and sides of the auditorium surrounded by menacing armed men but when after what must have seemed a perilously long time Demetrius entered with all the drama of a practised actor it was to everybody's relief that his tenor was gentle and friendly. Their city was not going to be sacked, their citizens would not suffer mass execution or exile, but if his words said forgiveness and trust, not all his actions did. He might promise 100,000 bushels of wheat so the people could eat again, but he also posted garrisons of his soldiers in not just the Munychia at Piraeus but at the fort on a Hill of the Muses just across south-west from the Acropolis where the long walls joined the defences of Athens itself and the Philopappos Monument now stands. It was clear that it was no longer the votes of the assembly that really counted; no longer formal debates at the hollowed-out auditorium of the Pnyx across the valley from the mighty Acropolis rock where key decisions would be arrived at. Once again the one voice that mattered was that of Demetrius and next time he left town he would leave enough of his hard and efficient mercenaries to ensure that it stayed so.

This time, however, there was no question of gadding about in impious debauchery in the confines of Athena's quarters; the conqueror was determined to reinforce his earlier success in the south. Having suppressed probably the most celebrated of the cities of Greece, he determined to deal with the next most illustrious. Sparta was the only power in the Peloponnese that had the resources and will to really contest his hegemony of the peninsula, so he resolved to try to eliminate them as a threat. In this campaign to quash the hallowed old place, Demetrius again showed genuine elan and flair, intending to arrive in their midst like a thunderbolt. Marching hard from the isthmus, he encountered at the familiar battlefield of Mantinea the Spartan army under Archidamus IV, nephew of Agis III, the king who had died in battle fighting Antipater at Megalopolis in 331. Between the fifth and third centuries there were four or five significant encounters in the country around this town involving

Spartans, Thebans, Athenians, Achaeans and plenty more. Sitting foursquare at the head of what is now the plain of Tripoli in north-east Arcadia, it was well situated to defend against those attacking south towards Tegea and Sparta or to oppose incursions over the mountains north-east into the Argolid.

This time it was a rout and Demetrius pursued the beaten enemy over the Parnon hills and into Laconia itself. Now Sparta was in danger and fine words about the city needing no defences because her soldiers were her walls must have rung very hollow; still, they were the only option available and while the invader drew his army up in the Eurotas valley outside the precincts of town, the locals prepared to put their faith in the warriors of ancient tradition. Yet the venerated place had changed, the numbers of full Spartan citizen fighters had been declining for years and if a form of the Agoge military education still existed it was non-citizen, periochae warriors and even unfree helots that filled out most of the ranks on their side. The Spartan hoplite army had shown an incapacity to face proper Macedonian-style phalangites back when King Agis had been defeated and it could hardly be different now with the number of veterans Demetrius was fielding against them. They were overthrown again with 200 killed and 500 captured when the day's fighting ended, with the odds now looking like ancient Sparta, the home of Leonidas, would finally fall to outside invaders as it had never done before, not even after defeats by the great Theban commander Epaminondas.

Yet the legendary home of Helen and Menelaus was not destined to fall; something intervened that had long been the great business of so many of Alexander's successors, the throne of Macedon itself. Cassander had passed away in his bed sometime in 297, apparently rotting from the inside as appropriate penalty for his treatment of Alexander's family, while his eldest son Philip was crowned without challenge in a smooth-as-silk succession. However, the best-laid plans of this competent dynast determined to embed his family on the Macedonian throne were scuppered by lethal fate. Philip, who must have still been a young man, after four months on the throne succumbed to a wasting disease while campaigning near Elateia in Phocis. With this child of Cassander's queen Thessalonike dead, there were two more left: Antipater who was around 16 years of age and Alexander even younger. Despite the youth of these claimants, their line had such legitimacy that the Macedonians did not consider looking outside the family but acclaimed both as kings, expecting that their highly-respected mother and half-sister of the great Alexander would hold the reins until they reached maturity. However, an apprehensive court and political establishment found that dividing the realm did not guarantee stability. The claim is that Thessalonike favoured Alexander and was determined not to see him disinherited, despite Antipater's prerogatives as the elder son. Indeed, she ensured that in the division Alexander took the west part of the country that included the capital and the most prime real estate while Antipater, who was married to Lysimachus' daughter, was given the eastern portion of the kingdom that abutted the Thracian realm of his father-in-law. Like Cassander, when he was not given what he felt was his due on his father's death, he kicked. The east was not without its attractions, it was where the mineral mines were and significant cities like Amphipolis and Philippi, but it was not enough: he wanted the lot and was prepared to act.

The arrangement had lasted a couple of years when by 294 Antipater, having probably now come of age, showed restive under his mother's tutelage. Having only received a share of an inheritance he regarded as all his own and convinced she preferred her younger son, he moved against an authority whose partiality meant danger for himself. This desperate prince showed himself astonishingly ruthless when, before being packed off to his allotted division, he had his mother murdered and claimed the whole kingdom for himself. We know nothing of the details of the conspiracy. Antipater would no doubt have tried to canvass support among the court elite before taking such desperate and decisive action, but the indisputable facts are that he killed his mother. Whether it was by assassin's knife or subtle poison we have no way of knowing, but the murderer compounded this awful disposal by driving out his brother while the capital was riven with clamour and uproar.

Matricide was an horrific crime in the face of men and gods and the perpetrator did not long easily enjoy the benefits of his crime. Macedonia with two minors as kings from the start must have looked like easy pickings to anybody with a claim and an army to enforce it, and if this was not bad enough this dysfunctional family did not help themselves. Self-destructive divisiveness was apparent from Cassander's death and before three years were out all hell had broken loose. If it was no surprise that the murderer faced retribution for his profane and bloody act, the nemesis who would make him pay had already been noticed in the past few years. He was a young prince last remarked kicking his heels in pampered exile in the great palace of Ptolemy in Alexandria who, sent by Demetrius as hostage, had made himself friends at the highest level, enjoying sufficient favour that he was wed to Antigone, the child of Ptolemy's queen and the king's stepdaughter. In the web-close world of Macedonian politics, having well-disposed placemen was an inclination of all the great power-players and Ptolemy had always kept some skin in the game in mainland Greece. His officers had not long since controlled important cities in the Peloponnese and he would soon risk his navy to try to bring succour to Athens in her hour of need. If this would finally be abortive the inclination was always there and not long before this he had made a move to establish a confederate in a different part of the mainland. In 297–96 Lagid troops and ships had brought Pyrrhus back to his homeland intent on restabilizing him on a throne from which he had been twice ejected, first in 317 when only 2 years old and later in 302 when Cassander had driven him out.

That this coup was accomplished just after Cassander had died was no coincidence, as Ptolemy would not have risked the displeasure of this steady ally by interfering so near Macedonia while he was still alive. The restoration had initially involved a compromise that saw Pyrrhus ruling in tandem with Neoptolemus who had come to the throne when he had last been kicked out. This cousin was the grandson of Philip and Olympias and nephew of Alexander the Great, but this pedigree did little to secure his future. In his 30s by this time, he had been around for a sufficient period to alienate many of his subjects by his violent and tyrannical temper; indeed it was only this reality, indicated by local uprisings, that ensured he agreed to the power-sharing arrangement in the first place. However, his position was inherently weak with many of the warrior class preferring the sole rule of the well-reputed young soldier Pyrrhus from the start. Only months after the new king's arrival the dual monarchy was dissolved and that the removal of Neoptolemus is so reminiscent of what would soon happen between Demetrius and another ineffectual king does not mean it is not accurate. Interfamilial bloodletting was just as common a phenomenon in these mountain cantons as in the greater courts to the east. The incident occurred at the ancient Molossian capital 5 miles up the valley north-west from modern-day Ioannina where in

2,000 years Ali Pasha would nest on a mounting pile of glistening treasure and enemy bones. Passaron was more than a century old by this time and already a tradition of a springtime swapping of oaths to maintain laws and customs between the prostates of the assembled people and their kings had been established. Here the co-rulers staged a lethal gavotte: after the formal ceremonial in front of an audience of representatives of the people, when sacrifices to Zeus were being performed, there was a banquet riven by bickering over gifts of oxen and amorous intrigues that encouraged friends of Neoptolemus to approach an apparently disaffected member of Pyrrhus' entourage to poison his master. In fact this wine-bearer, if disgruntled, was still loyal and warned the intended victim, who encouraged him to appear to co-operate to entrap his co-ruler. A buoyant Neoptolemus even bragged of his murderous intentions when in his cups which determined Pyrrhus on a pre-emptive strike, doing away with him at another banquet where Neoptolemus had imprudently failed to retain a sufficient bodyguard and which he had only attended so as not to raise suspicions about his own intentions.

So by 295 Pyrrhus was securely in the driving seat in his mountain kingdom. Still in his early 20s, he was determined to make a splash; after all, had not the great Antigonus the One-Eyed said of him that he would become the greatest general of all if he lived long enough. Now Alexander, the worried younger brother of the murderous Antipater, showing spirit even in the absence of his mother's support, cast around to find helpers in his dispossessed predicament. He was married to a daughter of Ptolemy of Egypt, but that ruler was just not proximate enough to make a difference so he considered nearer neighbours who might lend a hand. He first looked south where a great king with a reputation and army looked well-placed to provide assistance, but the response of Demetrius was insufficiently punctual for a prince on the run and who was afraid that if he didn't get a powerful backer immediately he would end up like his mother. We do not hear that Antipater had actually set the dogs on him, but it would be reasonable to assume that once he had established himself, his first priority would be to extinguish this fraternal inconvenience. So next Alexander turned to Pyrrhus, who received missives from his menaced neighbour with considerable interest. He did not have his hands full at that moment and could take up the dispossessed prince's cause with alacrity, although to enter a relationship with this young man, who seemed to have few of the rugged qualities of his father and none of the charisma of his mother, would only be done with a considerable shopping list. He demanded and received great chunks of upper Macedonia as well as Acarnania, Amphilochia and Ambracia so his Epirot people, eagerly appreciative of the benefits of these arrangements with the Macedonian prince, happily mobilized and, having occupied the newly-bequeathed territories, pressed forward to drive Antipater out of Pella.

There Pyrrhus found he was pushing at an open door as his foe had squandered any possibility of support from most of the Macedonian people by his awful act of matricide, so the bloody-handed prince fled east without a fight, hoping to find succour in the direction of the kingdom ruled by his father-in-law. Alexander was swiftly established in the capital, a switch that was probably made easier by the fact that these had been his lands when the country was divided under Thessalonike. How far Pyrrhus' protégé's remit stretched is unclear, although as the Epirot army did not press on in hot pursuit of his brother it is reasonable to assume that Antipater held on in the east of the country where there might have been some sort of administration at least nominally committed to his cause. To be able to do much more would surely have been impossible as Lysimachus, heavily involved in a Getic war or busy in Anatolia could not spare the military support he would have needed to take on Alexander and his Epirot backer. Yet with the future of Antipater's rump realm in the balance, Lysimachus at least tried what he could to help his son-in-law by diplomacy, aiming to neutralize Pyrrhus by intrigue if he could not do so militarily. He was bound to see the benefits of midwifing an accommodation between Cassander's sons as soon as possible to avoid Demetrius having an excuse to intervene and to influence Pyrrhus in favour of such an agreement he proposed a sweetener of 300 talents while forwarding a letter, purporting to be from Ptolemy, urging Pyrrhus to press Alexander to come to terms with his brother. It was probably easy enough to counterfeit missives from another Macedonian chancery and the benefits could be considerable as the Epirot king's relationship with the man who had put him on his throne was famously close. His christening his first-born son Ptolemy and naming a new town built 'on the peninsula of Epirus' to control the entrance to the Ambracian Gulf near modern-day Preveza, Berenice after the Egyptian queen was perhaps a reflection of real affection rather than just genuflection in the direction of an important backer. However, the ploy failed to work as the bluff was called as a forgery when the message began 'king Ptolemy to king Pyrrhus greetings' rather than the usual 'the father to the son greetings' that Ptolemy perennially used in all his communications with the Epirot ruler. Yet despite this duplicity Pyrrhus was looking to deal, needing peace to digest his considerable gains, so when Lysimachus, Alexander and he met to confirm a peace he was not looking for trouble, even when according to one account a sacrificial ram fell dead of its own accord, causing the diviner to warn of the death of one of the three participants. It is even possible that when the religious rigmarole went wrong, it may have given a convenient excuse to slide out of a commitment to Alexander that was becoming dangerous with another predator clearly on the move.

Pyrrhus had with apparently little trouble massively increased the size and potential of his realm and now the imperative was to consolidate this Greater Epirus, and to be on hand to exploit these new opportunities he returned to Epirus in autumn 294. His had been a meagre, stony terrain with few natural resources, certainly set in magnificent mountain country but without the means to sustain much but marginal hardscrabble agriculture with the only real wealth being in cattle. Pyrrhus himself was claimed as being adept at stock-rearing and a particularly tall specimen of steer was named after him. The kingdom of Epirus was itself a complicated entity of no venerable age and seems to have been unusual in combining both federal and monarchical principles that emerged after an admixture of Greeks arrived early to mingle with an indigenous folk before being overrun by Illyrians who, going by many of the names, provided much of the ruling aristocracy as the country emerged into history. This was an elite who became rapidly Hellenized, particularly under the influence of Corinthian colonies along the coast and on the island of Corcyra lying just over the water. The resulting amalgam of peoples was organized into tribes of which by far the most significant were the Molossians and who by the late fourth century had become the dominant force in a local Epirot alliance. This was not a place of cities, much more of clans, villages and cantons, although there was a popular assembly based on the people in arms gathering to make key decisions about war and peace, a republican strain exemplified by the annual covenant that took place at Passaron, that on occasions could considerably constrain the power of the monarchs. As so often in such pre-modern entities, the personality of the incumbent often played a decisive part in this play of interests and Pyrrhus soon showed that in a world of great Hellenistic monarchs this was the role, rather than anything like a constitutional monarch, that he intended to play. Yet even for him, with an agenda of near-constant adventure, achievement would always be the litmus paper when it came to testing domestic support.

Now he had provided success in spades, intervention in the wider Balkan world had won a massive increase in real estate that would ensure that at least for a few years his creation of a Greater Epirus would turn a country that had previously been a backwater into a real player on the world stage. From an impoverished boondocks comprising small villages and a sparse population where small-scale stock-rearing was all most of its people could aspire to, it became the political powerhouse of the Balkan peninsula. The newly-secured Macedonian cantons of Tymphaea and Parauaea that ran along Mount Boius and Mount Tymphe west of Orestis and Elimea acted as a convenient defensive barrier, while the Aous River running north-west to south-east through both regions provided a useful corridor leading into the Pindus range and over into Thessaly. Yet if these places were essentially more of the same kind of territory that made up the Epirot core – indeed much of it had been Epirot country before Philip II incorporated it into his expanding Macedonia – the other additions of Acarnania, Amphilochia and Ambracia were something different. These places had long been part of the Greek world where proper towns and cities flourished, so it is no surprise that when it was decided to found a new capital, it was to these new provinces he looked.

He intended a centrepiece for his new kingdom to be inaugurated where an already established wealthy and civilized population could provide a suitable home for his court and he found this in the old Corinthian colony of Ambracia that Philip of Macedon had taken over in the 330s and had now fallen into his lap. The commissioning of a new capital joyously proclaimed that Greater Epirus had now arrived as one of the heavyweights in the Hellenistic world and little time passed before he registered this in stone, extending the acropolis defences and much more. Little enough remains now at modern Arta, just some samples of defensive walls, temples and a theatre, but Pyrrhus still remains the local hero, although there is something very disappointing in the modern characterless equestrian statue completely devoid of the man's boiling energy. Yet at the time Ambracia was a showcase for the new country fully entering the world of urbane Greeks and attempting to obliterate their lingering reputation as barbarian pastoralists who followed their herds in nomadic transhumance rather than putting down proper metropolitan roots like the condescending Greeks who had so long looked down on them as riff-raff. Come to power through familial bloodletting, Pyrrhus intended to give his countrymen from the western margins a future of greatness on a world stage that Alexander's conquests had so recently expanded.

Marriage was often the diplomatic strategy of choice for these dynasts and the new king of Epirus now looked like a very good connection to many, particularly in the western Greek world where these Balkan players had long looked like potentially useful allies. This latest addition to the panoply of Hellenistic kings was looking particularly hot stuff so that Agathocles, a well-established strongman at Syracuse in Sicily, was not only happy to give his daughter Lanassa to win a new friend but even prepared to hand over the island of Corcyra as a dowry, perhaps with Leucas thrown in too. The former place was not just an economic dynamo but was well-placed to act as not just a defensive barbican to protect against any threat from the Adriatic side but, as had been shown in the past, a good jumping-off place for those interested in making waves in the Italian world. Hellenistic kings might boast Greek pedigrees and refinement, but their barbarian roots were never more illustrated than in their marital histories: plenty of women was their motto and Pyrrhus was bent on acquiring a bevy of useful ones, marrying around this time a daughter of the king of Paeonia, while also wedding into the family of the Illyrian monarch Bardylis whose people were, if not kept on board, forever threatening to burst out in plundering energy from the mountains beyond the Apsus River.

Yet on the new stage he was strutting there was no disregarding his old constituency. His Molossians craved reassurance that was amply given by their warrior king who had more than a little of the barbarian warlord about him. There was nothing very subtle about their big, bone-mouthed boy[7] who recalled an antique world of heroes that was more Homeric than Periclean. Pyrrhus might have been intent on bequeathing a future sprung from symposiums decorously fuelled by watered wine and dialectic debate in the agora, but still he knew his countrymen well, that the people at the core of his kingdom were closer to the god Pan, with the ingrained wildness of shepherds lashing slingshot at bare-teeth wolves, natural warriors rather than philosophers. If he did not let them down in offering warfare and profitable rapine aplenty, there would also have been expectations in respect of national prestige and reputation and there he did not fail either.

Crossing many high ridges east from the Adriatic coast to reach below Mount Tomaros, an ancient traveller would have found himself at possibly the oldest Greek oracle, sacred to the king of the gods, situated in the lands of the Molossians and though well off the beaten track, for most of the big names in the Hellenic world it still retained a kudos hardly less considerable than that of Delphi. There are claims it had originally been devoted to the mother goddess before she was supplanted by Zeus. Swampy Dodona was also associated with Achelous, a water deity and a holy spring where the rustling of oak or beech leaves and the whistling of wind chimes was interpreted by the priests and priestesses of the sacred grove to advise those who came looking for enlightenment. Its roots were maintained to reach back to Egypt[8] from a date in the second millennium BC, it is referenced in the *Iliad*[9] and it was said that Jason's boat the *Argos* had prophetic gifts because the oak from which it was made came from Dodona. Artifacts from Mycenaean times confirm this antiquity, while inscriptions from the sixth century show an increasing reputation among the southern Greeks from the 650s. There was no more ancient or potent place for Pyrrhus to pray for his country's future and he did a lot more than carry out the appropriate ritual here, spending mightily to refurbish the sanctuary, to make it fit to be Greater Epirus' spiritual centre. Here his masons worked on a theatre dramatically sited against a mountain backdrop that would eventually seat 18,000 people, a monument worthy of the eminence to which the young monarch aspired. The oracle itself and the temple to Zeus were beautified and an infrastructure added to allow the holding of those festivals of athletics, music and drama that were at the core of being Hellenes.

While the favourite of Dodona had just started enjoying the fruits of his enterprise, two threads of news had been reaching Demetrius' camp outside Sparta in the summer of 294. The first was the depressing indication that vital parts of his realm were under threat, with many strongholds on the Aegean coast of Asia feeling the gravitational pull of wealth and power represented by the menacing proximity of Lysimachus, while Ptolemy had descended on Cyprus, which had been solid for the Antigonids since his triumph there in 306. However, with this discouraging intelligence came an invitation to exploit opportunities opening to the north. Alexander's cry for help dispatched some time before instigated an appearance in arms that was going to spell even further trouble for the fragile arrangements that had fallen out in the wake of the death of that long-standing man Cassander. His youngest son had had a brutal introduction to the world of power politics, yet he remained a tyro who worried deeply when he heard news that Demetrius, having left the Peloponnese, had marched through central Greece and was approaching his borders. He had good cause to be concerned about this second dynast arriving hotfoot purporting to answer his call for help. The bill he had disbursed to the last man who had brought such a calling card had amounted to much of his western provinces and nothing in Demetrius' reputation would suggest his charges would be cheaper. With Pyrrhus gone and his reign hardly started, he could not but worry about the contacts that could be forged between the new arrival's entourage and key Macedonian bigwigs if he was allowed to cross the border. So in these circumstances where a charismatic rival was bound to have attractions for any but his closest friends, he had little option but to try to keep his now redundant and deeply unwelcome visitor out of the country. He rushed with what state his just found administration could conjure down the road to the border town of Dium. This city sacred to the Macedonians, strategically placed to both defend the homeland and allow access to the world of Greece to the south, lay a few miles from the sea, squatting under snow-capped Mount Olympus that rose over 8,000ft high with boars roaming its wild and forested ravines.

Here the young king, still raw from his bruising dealings with Pyrrhus, hoped to emerge better in negotiations with the second wolf he had asked to help him get his share of the family flock from his brother Antipater. The air was electric with intrigue and distrust as Alexander prepared a banquet in one of Dium's civic buildings for his guests, though the jittery Antigonid, fearful of putting himself in the other's power, declined the invitation to the dinner party, suggesting they leave for Larissa in Thessaly to celebrate their new-found friendship there. Getting his problematic new friend further away from Macedonia was just what the incumbent had desired in the first place, so he readily agreed and it was after everybody foregathered at that Thessalian city, after threading the route between Mount Olympus and the sea, where the dramatic events fell out that led to a sensational change in the dynastic arrangements in Philip and Alexander's old realm. The story is that Alexander prepared to attend what was intended as a parting celebration without an effective bodyguard, wishing to reassure Demetrius that he never intended him harm, whatever rumours had been circulating at Dium. It was a fatal move as his host had hard men armed and ready guarding the door to the banqueting hall. These knew what to do and needed only the prompting of Demetrius putting down his wine cup and leaving his couch. Then while exiting the room, he spoke softly to their officer, saying 'Kill him who follows me.' So Alexander, shadowing his host, fell beneath the swords of these killers. With slick ruthlessness Demetrius had disposed of a novice contestant on the chess board of Hellenistic power-play and now he intended to take over the unfortunate young man's possessions. After partial despoliation by Pyrrhus, the Antigonid had come with a sucker punch.

The meeting with the members of the Macedonians' court with the dead body of their monarch at their feet ought to have been difficult, but for Demetrius it was not. He was confident he had the whip hand and intended to play it for all it was worth. Most of the officials and courtiers would have been terrified, spending the intervening night contemplating a future that looked bleak indeed considering what they had just seen happen to their leader. Yet if he found no opposition here, the key was how he would be received when he pushed north over the border and onto the road to Pella. In fact, as autumn shadows lengthened in 294 he found few problems, being smoothly acclaimed as king[10] after a cursory explanation to the swiftly-mustered Macedonian army assembly that as Alexander had tried to kill him, he had no option but to instigate his removal. The reality was that he was now really the only game in town and even the grandest of Pella's society were content to accept his accession as a fait accompli, particularly as he freighted considerable credibility as the husband of the venerated Antipater's daughter Phila and that he was accompanied by his son Antigonus Gonatus, an heir with Antipatrid blood running in his veins did not hurt. The pleasure the great adventurer must have felt at taking control of the country where his family had originated must have been considerable; a kind of high point the family's fortunes had not reached since the terrible day at Ipsus. Decked out in the purple and gold both he and Pyrrhus favoured, he would have enjoyed sitting in golden splendour in the royal halls that like the abodes of the elite generally were becoming grander, with large peristyle courts and two-storeyed colonnades where the occupants perambulated along fine pebble mosaics in a capital that had been enormously aggrandized by followers of Alexander returning home with pockets full of eastern gold. Finally sitting on the national throne, it might not be the richest or even the mightiest of the great successor kingdoms, but it had the kudos. If there was such a thing as seniority in this world, there was no question that it was held by the occupant of the royal seat of Macedon. The cherry on top was that Lysimachus, tied up in his Gepid wars, could neither oppose his power grab nor indeed even protect his protégé Antipater who soon found himself bundled out of his portion of the kingdom by Demetrius' officers.

Yet there can be no question that Demetrius' joy was not unadulterated as word kept arriving from far-flung parts of his old domain that his patrimony was continuing to crumble at the edges. The crucial island of Cyprus had finally succumbed to years of consistent pressure by the Lagid navy and only Salamis town itself was holding out where his mother and some of his children had been living since he had transferred them there from Cilicia for safety soon after Ipsus. More than this, Cilicia, that he had so recently filched from Cassander's brother, had in his absence been taken over by Seleucus, a place rich enough and the key to controlling what was the most direct route west through the Taurus Mountain passes. The slippery ruler of inner Asia might have married Demetrius' daughter, but self-interest was the mantra of an aging king who wanted to package up a well-protected realm to hand onto his son. He had already made Antiochus ruler of the eastern divisions of his realm and would soon add a wife to the deal.[11] Worst of all, the hated man Lysimachus had been successfully rounding out his control of the Greek cities on the west Anatolian coast and it would not be long before even the metropolis Miletus would be lost to the Sea King who had just become monarch of Macedonia.

Demetrius now found himself firmly tied to dry land with all the concomitant advantages and problems. He might now rule a major kingdom with a military population and tax base to be exploited, but he also had to deal with potentially threatening neighbours, particularly as an old friend now emerged in a new guise. Pyrrhus had been his comrade and chief lieutenant in the years after Ipsus and later had been useful as a high-ranking hostage from the Antigonid court to Alexandria. Family ties had bound them too after Demetrius had married Deidamia, sister of the Epirot king, a considerable coup at the time to be matched with this woman who had once been betrothed to Alexander the Great's son. However, on being thrown out of Athens in 301 she had only briefly joined Demetrius in Cilicia before dying around 300 after producing a son who seems to have spent his life in Egypt.[12] Now that this family connection was sundered, reality had forced a different interface as two powerful kings eyeballed each other across a dangerous border. Particularly with his prestige now directly at stake, the man on the Macedonian side was bound to harbour revanchist intentions against a ruler who had clipped off so much of the western part of his new realm from a predecessor's weak hands. Fear of the new man at Pella was undoubtedly part of what pushed Pyrrhus into the arms of the Aetolians, only one of many peoples who had deep concerns about the new Macedonian incumbent. Demetrius had striven to achieve hegemony over the Greeks even under his old guise as Antigonid Sea King; how much more might this project be expected to be developed when he was emboldened by the possession of the resources of the northern kingdom that under Philip, Alexander and Antipater had kept so many of the Hellenic communities in an iron grip? If the stranglehold had slipped a little under Cassander and his sons, this was a situation that was unlikely to be acceptable to the latest man in power at Pella. So the applause that greeted Demetrius sitting down on the Macedonian throne had been very far from unanimous. The new king had all sorts of glamour, recalling to some the greatest Macedonian conqueror of them all, even if by now he was well into his 40s, ten years older than Alexander when he died, but this certainly did not cut any ice with two peoples who were deeply worried that the man who already controlled Attica, Chalcis, Megara, Corinth, much of the Peloponnese and the coast around Demetrias was now also master of Macedon and suzerain of Thessaly. He was handsome and gracious but also powerful and menacing to the Boeotians who, like the Aetolians, saw what looked like a man who had once been a friend and ally now in a position to put the real squeeze on them.

The upshot was a kings' war fought in the cattle-rearing plains of Boeotia. Demetrius had friends there in the recent past, so inevitably there was something personal about the conflict. The Thebans were supporters of the Antigonid cause from 304 and it seems likely that the city received not a little largesse from the greatest kings of the world in that time to match contributions made by Lysimachus and Cassander to the rebuilding of the city that Alexander had razed to the ground. So he would have been happy with any range of relations except that of the Boeotians turning into active enemies and that is what looked like was happening when another one of the period's dangerous and bloody men took a hand. This was Cleonymus, a member of the Agiad family of royal Spartans who had last been heard of as one of those condottieri who not infrequently made war for the Tarentines against their Italian neighbours, but by 293 he had returned to Sparta and been dispatched to Thebes to encourage the inhabitants to declare against a man his countrymen claimed as the common enemy of all Greeks. His arrival with an army coincided with a domestic movement led by Pisis of Thespiae who had persuaded a significant enough proportion of the political elite that the new king of Macedon was a real danger to their interests.

Demetrius' policy in Greece had been buoyant even before he found himself able to access the armed might of Macedonia, so his future plans there were unlikely to be any less bold whatever had happened at Thebes. So as 293 wore on he did what he did best. Orders were dispatched to his officers to bring up the siege train while the main army marched south to settle down in front of the city's defences. By the time they arrived Cleonymus had decided he had not come to Boeotia to be trapped like a fish in a dragnet, so before the lines of circumvallation were completed he resolved to move. The Thebans must have been angered by the decision to scuttle back to the Peloponnese as they had only challenged the might of Macedon because of the promise of Spartan muscle, even though history should have given them warning as when Cleonymus had intervened in Greek Italy he had shown very little consideration for the allies when his own welfare was involved. Or it might have been that with no other local powers rallying round conciliatory heads had won out once the besieger of cities had arrived in awful might and main and if this had been the case it is no surprise that it was thought advisable for the Spartans to exit while the locals tried to talk their way out of the trouble they had landed themselves in. The Laconians were able to slip away before the siege lines were completed and with their embarrassing presence removed, Pisis of Thespiae directed envoys to see what terms might be had from the Macedonian king threatening their homes.

With few bargaining chips the only possible upshot was surrender and the many people holed up behind the defensive walls must have worried about what their futures would be at the hands of a man who they had challenged so soon after he had taken over at Pella. Many must have expected hard-hand occupation by an enemy who was bound to have resented the trouble they had given him just when he would have wanted to concentrate on digging in on the Macedonian throne. Yet far from the only time in his career they discovered Demetrius in mellow mood, pleased by the promptness of their submission. Though he imposed fines on the Boeotian cities and installed garrisons, when the ringleader of resistance was brought before him he was not only treated 'courteously' and suffered them to go free but Pisis was even established as polemarch in his home town of Thespiae. Not that all his administrative adjustment in the Boeotia showed such sensitivity to local sentiment as Hieronymus of Cardia, the old Antigonid family retainer, was left as regional governor with command of the soldiers Demetrius left behind, a new controller who showed far more than just cursory interest in his new charges as the reports of local legends and Theban foundation myths channelled through Diodorus indicate.[13]

These garrison troops deducted from the Macedonian army roster were not numerous because the new king had immediately after his Theban triumph spotted an exploitable opportunity for which he needed all the men he could get. Intelligence had arrived from his agents in Thrace of a perfect opening that had arisen now his hated rival Lysimachus had just been captured in arms while campaigning against the Getae. This was the rival who he blamed for the ruin of his family's earlier fortunes and against whom he directed his bile whenever he was able in the years after Ipsus. From as soon as he had been able to recuperate his strength, he had struck at him, but that maritime razzia against the Chersonese and north-west Anatolia in 300 had far from sated his wrath. He wanted more, a feeling only compounded when news filtered in that his enemy's officers were continuing their irresistible pressure against what remained of Antigonid holdings among the Asiatic Greek cities. Calculating that his enemy's realm must be vulnerable if not virtually undefended with the main army defeated and the leadership shackled in a Getic hut, he set his army in the direction of Thrace. It was a long, gruelling road trip from Boeotia to the Thracian border, particularly as he would have needed to stop off at Pella to raise men to flesh out the dust-covered regiments that he had just rushed across Thessaly and passed north through the Vale of Tempe. A journey of well over 300 miles would have taken several weeks and much to Demetrius chagrin, he found on arrival that he had not been quite quick enough. Instead of finding an easy prey when his army approached enemy territory, he received grim tidings, whether from spies embedded in enemy country or travellers on the road, that completely scotched his plans. The Getae, instead of killing or dragging off their royal prisoner as could have reasonably been expected, had let him go and the word was that Lysimachus and his men were already on their way home. Such an extraordinarily charitable disposal may well have been influenced by the threat of a powerful newcomer taking over in Thrace if the captive king and his army were illuminated. Better a weakened Lysimachus than a triumphant Demetrius may have been the thinking at Gepid headquarters.

Now suddenly his nerve failed him. It was not just that Demetrius' intended quarry was no longer a headless target whose military could be expected to be tattered and terrified, not only was Lysimachus and his talented son Agathocles on the way back to confront him at the head of their main army; it appears probable at the same time he discovered the arrangements he had left in place in Boeotia had fallen apart. When the independent-minded people there, oppressed by his dominance and never reconciled to being a client state of Macedon, realized not only that most of the occupying forces had left and were a long way away but were also probably embroiled with a powerful enemy, they took action. There hardly seemed any of the usual factionalism between supporters of a quisling regime and those struggling for autonomy; it was in unison that the Thebans took shields and spears down from their walls and gathered in the agora. Their task would have seemed daunting with the citadel situated on a 700-yard-long plateau flanked on three sides by steep slopes and gullies, but they poured out from the north and east where the residential and civic districts were situated and surprising the few men Hieronymus had on hand ejected the garrison from the Cadmea.

Fires in front and behind demanded a radical rethink and in Demetrius' command tent they felt they had little option but to turn around and trail the army back over the same route it had just travelled. In central Greece the Boeotian independence fighters were experiencing the confidence born of initial success in so almost effortlessly dumping out Hieronymus and his garrison, so when Demetrius' son Antigonus Gonatus, needing little time to find his feet, arrived hotfoot from Demetrias to fight these fires in his bailiwick they were prepared to risk the gamble of battle in the open. However, with no Spartan help they were not up to the challenge and were swatted aside, despite the fact that the army led against them could not have been large, just the men the young Antigonid could scrape together to make a quick response. They were veterans and this made the difference; there was no 'sacred band' now, nor a fifty-deep phalanx led by Epaminondas to maintain the Theban cause, so the rebels went down in defeat and by the time Demetrius hove in sight with the main army the defenders were well contained within the ramparts of Thebes, with his son in charge of the open country. Now the defenders peered anxiously down from their battlements as the great besieger began to unload into the tapestry of fields below the walls those prefabricated Heliopolises, battering rams, tortoises and ballistas he loved so well.

Before he could properly settle down into the familiar routine of a siege, a new actor provided a different dimension to this Boeotian war. Pyrrhus, for one, settling in his new court at Ambracia, saw plenty to worry about at this turn of events to his south-east with Demetrius not only ensconced at Pella but also looking set to re-impose himself on most of central Greece. Opposition to this potentially dominant power was bound to gravitate around this young king who understood it could surely only be a matter of time before he demanded the return of those territories that Cassander's son Alexander had ceded after he had provided the muscle to tear the throne from the grasp of his matricidal brother. Revanchist dreaming was almost inevitable, not just because Demetrius could be expected to stretch his prerogative as far as it would go but also there were bound to be important men in Pella who were far from happy, having lost property and influence in the transfer of territory. These would soon be found to be whispering in the ear of a very suggestible monarch once he was free of his current entanglements, circumstances that meant no past intimacy was likely to save the newly-expanded Epirot state from unwanted Macedonian attention. To forestall this menace, he had little choice but to do something for the brave Theban defenders who were looking, despite their best efforts, like they would soon succumb to the endeavours of the army surrounding their walls. The Epirot levy was called out and mercenary regiments hired in preparation to take the road over the Pindus Mountains and down into Thessaly. Encountering no opposition on the march, they pressed further south towards Thermopylae where at the historic Hot Gates they would be well positioned to block the Antigonid army's lines of supply.

Even by Pyrrhus' standards this was risky stuff, preparing to rush down to Thermopylae to confront an enemy with such huge military resources at his disposal, but if distracting Demetrius had been the aim it made sense and if chancy it certainly worked. This dynamic commander showed himself completely unprepared to accept what he knew was a dangerous opponent emerging from an unexpected quarter and disrupting his communications with his key northern bases, not just Pella but Demetrias as well. So leaving his son to hold the fort again, he led the best of his army to confront this new and present threat. However, the stormy Epirot petrel had not come for a stand-up fight this time, even with the advantage of holding the defensible pass. Everybody had long been aware of the way around taken by Xerxes in the past going the other way and it was no interest of his to endanger the scarce resources that were his Epirot warriors, trapped between the sea and the mountains, just to offer succour to the Thebans. He had created a diversion that he had intended from the start, so when plumes of dust showed Demetrius' army approaching in intimidating numbers he pulled back. The Macedonians followed him back through the open fields of Thessaly into Dolopia, until the tail of the invader's army was finally discovered climbing back into the Pindus Mountains from where they had so recently debouched. However much he smelled blood and was tempted, there could be no exhilarating chase into Athamania to bring the intruder to bay; he had other priorities. So leaving 10,000 infantry and 1,000 horse to keep garrison in Thessaly and with his annoyance with his old lieutenant somewhat ameliorated, the Macedonian king could return to the delights of the real set-piece siege at Thebes.

Now he was in his element and his signature move of deploying of a giant Heliopolis was soon under way. Iron-clad with multiple storeys, it was monstrous and awe-inspiring seen through the shimmering heat even if moving at a snail's pace, though surely the claim that it only travelled two furlongs in two months is absurd. It had wheels and if it moved at all it must have gone faster than a few metres a day. This juggernaut, pushed by great teams of sweating and stooping men, who looked like they were prostrating themselves to an enormous deity, crossed the filled-in defensive ditches and finally reached the walls. With these preliminaries over and the lumbering monster in place, the order for the assault was given. Thebes, however, turned out to be a hard nut to crack: if walls were brought down, others were built inside them from the rubble of broken houses, reminding Demetrius of what had occurred at Rhodes ten years earlier. Missiles fell like rain, clattering on the shields and helmets of the assault troops as they moved up to the walls and the men crossing the bridge of the Heliopolis onto the ramparts found themselves faced with men fighting with the courage of desperation. Attacking a city was always the most dangerous of enterprises for most soldiers, desperate fighting often, unlike in a battle in the open, without the comfort of a comrade by one's side, no shield of a neighbour to keep off the unseen blow of an enemy appearing against an unprotected flank. Demetrius' men fell in droves as exasperation led to him being so careless with his men's lives that it even caused comment from his own son. Yet he was not a commander to expose his men to hazards he would not face himself, and the result was that as he rushed forward at the head of his men he received a catapult bolt through the neck.

Not quite Alexandrine in his propensity to getting wounded in battle, his body already showed numerous scars even before this latest mishap. Unsurprisingly the wound, if not grievous, was extremely painful and must have laid the king up for at least a few days, even if it did not stop the siege being pressed. There are no details but eventually the bloodied men of the besieging army forced their way in, sections of the walls were secured and defence was no longer tenable as the Thebans, hungry and filthy after their ordeal but still with shields showing and weapons held firm, expected the worst: to be overrun and slaughtered with no mercy shown, even to their wives and children. It was all too reminiscent of Alexander; he too had suppressed the place once and on his departure they had rebelled again and suffered for it. Then it had been destroyed, wiped from the map, and Alexander's reputation among the Greeks never recovered from that stain. Now Demetrius, apart from being a very different man, was not just visiting a post station on his way to far-off Asia and any reputation for exterminatory savagery, while it might have a short-term shock effect, could not finally help in re-establishing Macedonian hegemony among the Hellenes. He wanted no comparisons made with Xerxes burning Athens to the ground; suzerainty might be won by terror, but to be effective in the long run at least some hearts and minds needed to be gained. So all we hear is that after the Thebans finally agreed to surrender, ten key rebels were executed and another small group banished, while fourteen principals from the Boeotians who had been involved suffered death while the rest were pardoned, though the faithful Hieronymus was reinstated and a strong garrison reinstalled.

The autumn season of 290 was looking promising for the Antigonid monarch sitting happily in his new headquarters of Pella; the achievements in Boeotia had been considerable and few other obvious enemies seemed to be lurking, although concerns about his fellow grasping opportunist Pyrrhus were bound to remain, particularly as now the personal entered the picture. It was at about this time that Demetrius was approached by representatives from a woman of considerable interest called Lanassa who had been married to the Epirot king, bringing him the strategic island of Corcyra as her dowry. This daughter of Agathocles, tyrant of Syracuse in Sicily, had been incensed when she found she had to share the matrimonial bed with a barbarian princess (parvenu snobbery was the worst, as plenty of people claimed her father had originally been a tanner) and so departed for the island before touting herself to the new king of Macedon well-known for his susceptibility to marrying property. Once the nuptials were formalized, the transfer of Corcyra was completed when the bridegroom came with a fleet to not only consummate the liaison but most crucially to take over an outpost that would be very useful for pressuring Epirus from the west, a coup that was augmented on the cruise back to Athens when he also conquered the island of Leucas that up to that point had been in Pyrrhus' possession.

It went without saying that antipathy for a rival already enhanced by the fact that he had once been an ally was now reinforced by the whisperings of an embittered ex, ensuring that remaining easy neighbours was never going to be likely. Yet despite being prepared to scoop up both his wife and his territory, Demetrius showed a disinclination to directly attack the Epirot king in his mountain stronghold. The problem was that any Macedonian army that he tried to lead against him would include many who had considerable respect and affection for this enemy associated by both blood and reputation with the line of Alexander the Great himself. If he was not able to depend on the best of his soldiers in carrying out an Epirot war, in the end his solution was typically aggressive and energetic. He decided to strike at a different enemy, taking on his antagonists' Greek allies carried no such dangers and he had a *casus belli* that would give some legitimacy to his enterprise. The Aetolians had for some time controlled the roads to the sacred community of Delphi and recently they had refused to allow the Athenians to make the trip to celebrate the Pythian games. This beef resulted in Demetrius being forced to organize the celebrations at Athens and now, conveniently unearthed, this transgression allowed him to claim pious intent as he prepared to penalize them, an enterprise that had the added advantage of keeping his mercenaries occupied and if Aetolia was still not particularly wealthy, any harvest of loot could contribute to his war chest.

So when the cereal crops were ready for harvesting as spring turned to early summer 289 he marched with plenty of motivation but no warning, striking at Pyrrhus' neighbour and ally. Pushing south, through the Vale of Tempe into Thessaly where, having crossed that country's open plains, he entered the Campylus valley, rugged fir-dotted country leading under looming Mount Tymphrestus, towards the Agraei, a people living under Aetolian rule to the north of their core territory. Overrunning that country, he pushed further on into Ophiona where resistance was patchy at best from a people with limited military resources and who could only try to delay Demetrius' expeditionary force by ambushes and other techniques of *petite guerre* (guerrilla warfare) with such men as they found rallying to the colours. Unsettling news of what was happening to the south was not long in reaching Ambracia and Pyrrhus was never likely to fail to respond to the desperate howls of anguish emanating from his closest allies. Now proceedings turned into something of a showpiece, the first big war for some time between Hellenistic kings. Not since Ipsus had there been this kind of manoeuvring by considerable armies under famous kings that would end in bloody confrontation.

As it turned out, the crucial encounter when it occurred was not between Demetrius and Pyrrhus and their main armies but with the Epirot king and the man who had been left to keep the Aetolians in check. What Demetrius' strategic intentions had been from the beginning, whether to divide the Epirot and Aetolian forces from each other or draw his enemy out from his very defensible kingdom is not clear, but if it was the latter he succeeded. What else he had achieved by his intervention in Aetolia is uncertain. The invaders' exact route is hard to locate with any precision and we do not know if the country had been subdued to any significant degree; certainly there is no evidence that the core round Lake Trichonis with the sacred city of Thermum was occupied, something that would not have been easy anyway for an invader coming from the north. Yet whatever he had accomplished, assuming that Pyrrhus would be marching to his allies' aid, the Antigonid king decided to turn north with the intention of intercepting him, leaving an officer called Pantauchus with an army of occupation to keep the lid on Aetolian resistance in the territory he had subjugated.

Demetrius may have taken the thoroughfare up the wide valley leading to Amphilochian Argos which was definitely the easiest until it reached those sections that were choked in against the east side of the Ambracian Gulf. Yet if this section of the route was very defensible, sometimes gaining the appellation the Thermopylae of west Greece, the itinerary had the advantage that once past this obstacle, the wide plain surrounding the new Epirot capital would be out in front. Whichever the road taken, while Demetrius was on his way Pyrrhus had reacted, realizing the word of his enemy's approach was not just scaremongering, he mobilized every warrior he had on hand intent on facing off the menace of a man who not so long before had been his mentor and friend. Pressing south and east to confront the invader, he managed to miss his target and the two armies passed each other on the way, something that would be little of a surprise to anyone familiar with this part of Greece where folds of mountains running north-south from Aetolia up into Amphilochia mean there are a number of routes that might be utilized.

What the Antigonid monarch did when he reached Epirus is a closed book. We hear of no town being taken, only a significant reaving of the fertile lowlands around Ambracia and perhaps raids deeper into the old Molossian heartland. However, we certainly do have intelligence on what occurred after Pyrrhus, marching through a region of hills and forests, had entered Aetolia, indeed it turned out to be one of the highlights of a life that was as eventful as any in the ancient world. The drama revolved around the man Pantauchus, the scion of a famous military family whose father who had commanded a warship in Nearchus' fleet in Indian waters in 325 with a brother who may have been satrap of Bactria. A sort of goliath, physically huge, strong and regarded as the most courageous man in the Antigonid army, this character had been left with a large detachment of 10,000 men when his commander set out on his march north and when his scouts reported the approach of an Epirot army he swept out to deal with the danger. The exact location of the encounter is unknown, but it was certainly somewhere in north Aetolia in a valley where two such considerable armies might spread out over the summer-parched earth to face off.

If we know the number of the Antigonids, we are far less clear about Pyrrhus' army moving into their proper ranks in the shimmering heat. Though marching swiftly with only those troops he had on hand and expecting to flesh out his numbers with Aetolian auxiliaries, it is improbable that he had been able to field many more than his opponent. Indeed, if he had Pantauchus he would probably not have accepted combat, but instead retreated to the many defensible positions available in rocky Aetolia. As a prequel, peltasts and other light infantry would have skirmished on the rougher ground, while the opposing phalanxes deployed to face each other; each side with the five front ranks of pike heads showing levelled with the rest held upright to deflect missiles, and as there was almost certainly little room on the flanks for cavalry, both commanders led from the front of their infantry line. The conflict was remarkable for its intensity and brutality, with leaders from both sides displaying great courage and daring. Pantauchus was a hulking swell renowned for his size and warrior skills, so it was no wonder that as the battle wore on he made every attempt to seek out the enemy chief to confront him in personal combat. In the midst of the fighting he yelled out a challenge and the brave and reckless monarch, whose lexicon would have included no more appalling word than coward, was not backward in responding. As their comrades on both sides held back to allow a space sufficiently unencumbered by mutilated corpses for the duelling pair, the two commanders without formality had at each other.

The first pass involved their spears, throwing them like Homeric heroes; indeed the suggestion is that the Epirot king very much had his legendary ancestor Achilles in mind when the match occurred. After they had deflected their opponent's throw with their shields, it turned into close combat with swords. These two were skilful duellers with targeting swords, hacking at the muscles at the back of the other's thigh or between helmet and shield or shield and greaves. Then it was first blood to the Antigonid general, feinting one way as Pyrrhus raised his shield and managing to strike him a savage blow. Yet despite the initial advantage going to Pantauchus, his enemy remained a tough and determined opponent and when they fell apart for a second time, those viewing the fight saw that the Macedonian strongman had been wounded twice, in the thigh and along the neck. Now the tables were clearly shown to be turned as the Epirot rushed forward, forcing his foe first backwards and then 'on to the ground'. However, the downed hero was far from defenceless and with his shield he warded off the rain of blows from his antagonist, allowing time for his friends to act. Aides and bodyguards ran to the fallen man and as his adversary, himself almost blinded by sweat running into his eyes after the efforts of this terrible contest, drew breath they were able to drag their commander away to the safety of the Macedonian lines.

Any inclination to disbelieve the details of this encounter should be tempered by the fact that there is no question that such Homeric activity had definitely come back into fashion in the era of Philip, Alexander and the Diadochi. For centuries the Greeks had seen the man standing his ground in the ranks of the phalanx as the height of heroism, epitomized by the Spartan pattern, but since Marathon, Plataea and Leuctra there had been a change. It was part Alexander as the great model of hero commander leading from the front, but something more as well that saw Eumenes tilting with his great enemy Neoptolemus and two septuagenarians claimed as coming to blows a decade after Pantauchus and Pyrrhus met in battle. This was a world of warlords and to cut the mustard it definitely helped to be able to hold one's own in hand-to-hand combat. This had always been the Macedonian way and now it was the rule for those who held ambitions to reign in the world their people had conquered.

Ancient battles were always about the psychological edge and there is no doubt that the sight of Pyrrhus bloody but triumphant as his opponent was dragged like a rag doll back into the protection of his army was crucial.

The two sides soon violently reconnected through the swirling dust of battle as paeans were shouted while pipes whistled and trumpets blared with the earth rocking under the pressure of thousands and thousands of booted, sandaled or naked feet. The shields and other arms of both sides were no longer as bright and polished as when they had begun: now the front rank's protection was battered, sarissas were bent or broken, while swords were gouged and dented where they had made contact with those of their foemen. Veterans on both sides were proficient and skilled locked in a pinning push of pike, but one group, drained by devitalizing tension, had seen their talisman downed and the triumph of a hero who even enemies found they could not help but admire. In such circumstances it is no surprise that the fighting was not long in the balance. Some watching their leader fall knew the battle was lost immediately and if the rest fought on for a time, they did not last long. The particulars we have suggest a devastating imbalance in casualties with considerable numbers of Macedonians killed and wounded and 5,000 or half the original army captured. We are not told, but it is reasonable to assume that these men who surrendered were mercenaries, most of whom would have immediately changed sides, so that Pyrrhus' legendary valour and fighting ability not only proved crucial for the battle's outcome but resulted in a considerable addition to his military rostra, more than compensating for any losses his men might have suffered in the fighting. It is therefore highly appropriate that it was on this occasion 'when the Epirots gave him the title "the Eagle"', with the king responding to the accolade by declaring it was his compatriots-in-arms that gave him wings.[14]

Word of this extraordinary turn of events reached Demetrius while he was involved in wrecking the country surrounding Ambracia and he realized at once that he might soon find himself with Pyrrhus and his victorious army, heavily bolstered by Aetolian reinforcements, coming in behind him from the south while the rest of the Epirot national army mobilized to his front. Such an unattractive prospect ensured a rethink and saw the invasion army turn in its tracks to return to Macedonia by the quickest route. In his time in enemy country Demetrius' men 'had wrought great destruction', behaviour that Pyrrhus considered unprovoked, undertaken without reason or warning and that alone would have warranted payback, but beyond this the issue of Corcyra and Leucas still rankled. So after the Epirot king marched back home, his brows decked with triumphant wreaths donated by his thankful Aetolian allies, he was possessed of two particular reasons to desire to wreak his revenge on his Antigonid enemy. Not only had this old comrade trashed his homeland, he had also filched his wife and made himself master of her island dowry. Nor did he have to wait long to scratch this itch. As the summer of 289 waned, tidings seeped through to Ambracia that the Macedonian king had fallen seriously ill. Resentment still palpable, he lost no time in determining to hit back. Resolving to attack while his opponent was unprepared, he probably came through the Pelium pass into upper Macedonia, though only in raiding strength. Yet if his initial intention had been just plunder, when he experienced little opposition and even a considerable welcome from many of the local bigwigs in the upper cantons the sweep of his ambitions expanded. Ruthless and bold, how far would he be prepared to go? Strategy was always open to evolution and he may have been considering more than just a raid as he pressed on over fir-dotted slopes and through productive valleys all the way to Edessa, the gateway to the lowlands round Pella where Demetrius might be expected to have his strongest support and plenty of armed men on which to call.

What the king of Macedonia was suffering from is unclear, but if initially debilitating, his condition was not of long duration and soon enough he was capable of directing his senior generals to mobilize the home army and construct a successful defence. When the intruders got wind of the magnitude of this response, any hopes of driving out Demetrius or occupying the whole country were swiftly discarded, so when Pyrrhus' lookouts came in with reports of myriad troops tramping the road west from Pella to Edessa for the invading monarch, it was enough. No longer interested in any perilous gamble, he gave orders to pack up their tents, gather their booty and retrace their steps back home. However, his men were slapdash and dilatory, allowing the forward units of the Antigonid army to catch them on the march and the officers in charge, familiar with the country, made them pay. Horsemen and light troops fell on the rear of the train and considerable losses were sustained, even if it seems there was never any danger of the army being cut off and eliminated. Yet it was still a tattered outfit that re-crossed the border and began to recruit reinforcements to ensure they would be prepared if Demetrius arrived with a bristling response to the recent invasion of his kingdom. However, it turned out that the mercurial monarch of Macedon was disinclined to concentrate his efforts on punishing his refractory neighbour. He had other things on his mind, and to embark on these projects he needed peace, particularly as winter was closing the passes and would make any penetration of Epirus very chancy. So envoys were dispatched, riding through the sharp autumn winds whistling through the lofty terrain that separated the two countries. Negotiations at Pyrrhus' camp were no doubt fairly perfunctory because it seems that not much more than a guarantee of the status quo was the upshot. Whether Corcyra was on the agenda we do not know, but there is certainly no strong evidence that the island was disgorged by Demetrius at this time.

Chapter Five

Now an Old Man Moves

Ipsus had been the defining contest of the successor age, when Antigonus the 80-year-old one-eyed master of war had fallen to a great combination of Macedonian kings. Yet despite a roller-coaster career that had seen his son Demetrius ascend the throne at Pella, the heir of the Antigonid name always dreamed of greater things and had never truly accepted the decision come to in the wastes of Phrygia. His exile from the golden land where money was invented, that had annually produced thousands of talents for Antigonus' treasury and where he had spent his youth at his father's court remained intolerable for this proud spirit. Now decked out in a diadem of white and purple silk, as he surveyed an Imperial capital shining with the booty of half the world and saw the corridors of the palace and the streets of the town occupied by people wearing rich purple or saffron raiment brought back from eastern campaigns, it seemed possible he at last disposed of the wealth required to try to reverse the verdict of 301. Equally the presence about him of hypaspist guards, some tall men with weather-beaten and scarred visages, veterans of many wars, others younger and more decorative and the open spaces occupied with squadrons of companion cavalry wheeling and caracoling suggested he also had the military muscle. These horsemen had always been the prestige arm and horse-rearing a kingly pastime shown by the presence of royal studs near Pella and other major towns with beasts amply fed by plentiful alpine summer pastures and good riparian grass. From well before Philip, the breeding of tough strong cavalry horses had been under way and a significant part of the loot from that king's Balkan campaigns was horseflesh from Thrace and Illyria and even steppe stock, when he brought back tens of thousands of mares after defeating the king of Scythia.[1] After Alexander, even good blood from the finest Asian herds like the famous Niseans would have made their way back with those returning from the great conquests. Even later and less belligerent rulers like Antigonus Gonatus still kept up the interest with a cavalry stud at Sicyon near Corinth to supply the armies with which he hoped to dominate the Peloponnese.

With these warriors at their back any ruler would contemplate expansion so it is no surprise that Demetrius dreamed of empire. In his mind the logic was glaring that Antigonid entitlement did not just run to his Macedonian and Greek possessions but to the places in Asia his father ruled over as well. To him it was destiny: this man was born to greatness and that so many of the West Asian Greek metropolis had so recently been his fiefdoms made it personal as well, particularly in taking them back from his hated rival Lysimachus. He had been plotting to crush the life out of the ruler of Thrace since soon after the Battle of Ipsus and now he wanted full payback for that disaster. No wonder this character in whom some claimed they saw a new Alexander, with a track record of triumphs enough, was drawn to his own Asian adventure: a springboard back to where he had grown up when his father virtually ruled the world.

Showing a remarkable sweep of ambition and with the decision taken to reopen this war, the wheels of his aspiration ground slowly but mightily, the size of the enterprise being signalled by ordering the laying-down of keels for 500 vessels. Shipwrights in Piraeus, Corinth, Chalcis and even at Pella rubbed their hands together as they prepared the contracts for payment by a king to whom it seemed money was no object: 'Their beauty did not at all detract from their fighting qualities, nor did the magnificence of their equipment make them less operational.'[2] Demetrius travelled widely to personally supervise these efforts that were intended not only to create a massive fleet but one that included ships 'of 15 or 16 banks of oars'. No very precise details are given on the military as opposed to naval preparations made except that 98,000 foot and 12,000 horse were to be raised, surely including national levy phalangites, high-born cavalry and the thousands of mercenaries which every revenue stream was exploited to fund. The talk in all of the kingdom and Greece as well was that Demetrius was planning to commit the largest army the Macedonians had ever put in the field and that in Europe no enterprise had been equipped on such a lavish scale since Alexander left to assail the Persian Empire.

However, in any polity, royal decrees required at least some sympathy from a reasonable proportion of the inhabitants and what soon became clear was that neither in the capital nor the regions did this necessarily exist. Political convulsions had been very far from unknown in Macedonia in the generation past, as could be attested by several descendants of the old regent Antipater, and this kind of stuff is contagious. Dependable solidity in any polity usually reinforces itself and the same is true of the opposite, and in the time between the death of Cassander and Demetrius' arrival, stability had been a commodity badly lacking. If there had been enthusiasm at the beginning of the reign, in nearly seven years attitudes had clearly evolved, a negative mood that might have been encouraged by the fact that Demetrius had not spent much of his reign at Pella entrenching his dynasty in hearts and minds. Unlike Philip and Alexander, there is no sign that he left a trusty viceroy when he departed for the battlefields of Boeotia, Epirus, Attica or Thrace. There is no sign of an Antipater figure in these years to knit domestic interests together; indeed, the most likely candidate for this role was the dependable Antigonus Gonatus, a son noted for upright virtue but who is commonly reported remaining in charge of the family's Greek holdings. It may be that as his adventuring never took him so far from Macedonia it did not appear necessary, but this was a miscalculation that ensured the good governance expected by the Macedonian people was not always consistently available.

Certainly the son of Antigonus the One-Eyed delighted in the high life of acclaim and grandeur, his presence accompanied by all the trappings of great power that blurred the lines and put him halfway between man and god. He had hobnobbed with a goddess in Athens and now in his new surroundings he still showed an unprecedented inclination to excessive display: 'He possessed an elaborate wardrobe of hats and cloaks, broad-brimmed hats with double mitres and robes of purple interwoven with gold, while his feet were clad in the richest purple felt embroidered with gold.'[3] Flouncing around in extravagant garb may not have been untypical of many wealthy rulers. Demetrius, like Alexander, was noted for his celebrity armourer, but he went further, ordering an exquisite robe decorated with heavenly bodies that was so grand that no Macedonian king after him 'presumed to wear it'. Suppliants would be expected to enter his gorgeous presence almost as they would an oriental potentate, and if we do not hear of Alexander-like demands for proskynesis, many may well have thought this was not far away. The man showed absolutely no reluctance to alarm the gentry, men who were born in a rugged landscape cut off from neighbours by mountain ranges, an independent, dauntless people whose antecedents had come to maturity in a tribal monarchy. Having recently become world conquerors, their sense of self-importance had hardly declined and such people had expectations very different from those living under the rule of an Eastern king of kings. Particularly many of the infantry levy hailed from the mountain cantons, rough pastoralists used to almost a camaraderie with community leaders. So even if Demetrius did not quite put on the airs of a Xerxes or a Darius, still this most recent ruler was far from approachable. It is impossible to judge how much this would have affected his popularity, but even Alexander himself had suffered when he tried this kind of high-toned potentate stuff on his Macedonian followers deep in the heart of Persia's upper satrapies.

It is always difficult to know how much credit to give to the moral tales of Plutarch. For him, Demetrius' behaviour was an exemplar of how not to do things, so how much was reality of the king tossing petitions off a bridge and into the River Axius because it was a bother to read them is difficult to tell. Certainly even the suggestion of such derisory dealings with supplicants would be bound to cause considerable upset; responding to such petitions was, after all, one of the core activities of any ancient ruler. Yet were the Macedonian elite really offended by the fact that some poor woman got short shrift? Probably not, although it was not good public relations that allowed this kind of picture to get painted and certainly while the pious might have worried about hubristic extravagance, it was hard-headed and interested reasoning on the part of both the powerful and those in the ranks of the phalanx that really made the difference. There is also something else that is hinted at. Demetrius always had winning personal qualities, naturally gregarious and convivial, even if in a grandiloquent way, that would have gone a long way to making him loved by many of the rich and the powerful with whom he came in contact, but after the illness he suffered that encouraged Pyrrhus to raid the country, this seems to have changed. While his eventual success in repelling the intruder ought to have considerably strengthened his hand, in fact gossips gave it out that Demetrius' illness had brought about a significant personality change, that after his recovery he was never as bonhomous as he had been in the past. This may have been important in eroding any reservoir of goodwill that the son-in-law of the great Antipater might have accrued since ascending the throne. So from this time evaluation of his judgement became less clouded by personal sentiment and his popularity, possibly already eroded by a cavalier attitude to royal responsibilities, took a further downward spiral.

Demetrius' ambition was worryingly extravagant for even his imperial people, contemplating a reach that might not be sustainable. Equally he was proposing to lead them to fight against a figure who struck a far more congenial chord with many of them than he did himself. After all, Lysimachus was a Macedonian of Alexander's generation with all the glamour and legitimacy this implied and had for generations past been a solid and enduring presence over the Thracian frontier. Long on good terms with Cassander, proximity would have ensured interaction at an elite level between the two kingdoms, with intermarriage and guest friendship the pattern of years only recently ruptured by the personal rancour between Demetrius and the Thracian monarch. Macedonian grandees may have evolved as their place in the world changed and the nature of their empire developed, but if they had adjusted to a grander, statelier sort of monarch, on the other hand they would have become even more determined to ensure that the status and wealth they had acquired would not be threatened. They had been familiar with the history and personality of their king for some time and could hardly claim ignorance about intentions he had never been disinclined to broadcast. The imperial designs of previous great Macedonian kings had paid off in spades, but now when it came to subsidizing these ambitions in Asia it was different. Their memories of the Antigonid line were not the rosy ones of Philip and Alexander and the Anatolian revanchist agenda just did not resonate across the board, with many feeling that this latest pulse of aggrandizing foreign adventure could only end in ruin. They resented having to open their purses to fund incredibly expensive imperial projects, navies especially were ruinously costly to underwrite and the shipyards at Piraeus, Corinth, Chaklis and Pella must have seemed like bottomless pits down which the revenues of Macedon poured unceasingly. If the existence of his projects was not startling, when it came to this meretricious man demanding payment it was different and any of his councillors who harped on about the cost was met with stern disinterest. Demetrius' standing was bound to suffer when demands were made on the pockets of the rich and on the declining working population who tilled their fields. The prevalent response of many was that this latest endeavour in the field of foreign adventure was too much and likely to end in calamity.

The rumours of Demetrius' preparations had been eddying around the throne rooms at Lysimachia, Antioch and Alexandria for many months; the business was just too serious to ignore and ensured that anxieties had hardened into threatening reality. The size of the forces being fashioned may have been inflated by our sources, but there was no hiding the forests of masts showing in the key Antigonid ports and the reaction of the other Hellenistic monarchs indicates that they considered the menace real enough. Since the turn of the new century the years had seen the great Hellenistic potentates indulging in diplomatic gavottes often involving Demetrius as makeweight, to bolster those who saw themselves as isolated and vulnerable to neighbours ganging up against them. Now it was his preparations that seemed to suggest a danger that there was no ignoring, no matter how involved they might be elsewhere. Lysimachus, Seleucus and Ptolemy were hardly boon companions; in fact they were deep-dyed rivals over many crucial matters, but now the stories coming out of Macedonia and Greece gave them all such pause that for the moment other matters were shelved. Even if it was perfectly true that the dangerous Antigonid might not impact their immediate interest, they could not be sure of his intentions and that he was so proactive they always found alarming. So despite the power they could wield, they were deeply concerned. All signed up and policies were soon concerted by treaty to try to neutralize the peril represented by the military preparations taking place in Macedonian Europe. Unfortunately, apart from Lysimachus, these great powers were not proximate enough to deter any intended offensive and the king of Thrace, always aware of the Getic threat that had been shown so dangerously in the 290s, feared he would not on his own be able to handle the forces the ruler of Macedon could draw from among his subjects and allies. The only other dynast who might rectify this imbalance had considerable credibility as a mighty warrior, but regrettably had lately signed a treaty of peace with Demetrius. Whatever the recent events, Pyrrhus was bound to be central to any plan to stop the Antigonid menace at source. He needed to be wooed, to be persuaded to take his part, and missions with letters were dispatched from the courts of all three kings to Ambracia approaching a man unable to resist the flattering appeal of all these monarchs, particularly including, as they did, his old well-wisher Ptolemy of Egypt.

There were plenty of buttons to press in these personal missives to ensure he did not skulk in his tent while others acted. First was the fact that a Demetrius whose Asian adventure was a success would ensure that Epirus had a far more powerful neighbour on its eastern border. After this stick there was a carrot: that Pyrrhus could expand again at the expense of a defeated power that would not have the resources to stand against the weight of the confederacy he was being urged to join. Whether the throne of Macedon was offered is not clear, but it is surely likely that his old friend Ptolemy would have suggested such an outcome and Lysimachus in the circumstances would have hardly barred a possibility that must weigh so much with the man they wanted on their side. Pyrrhus, as it turned out, was still irritated with Demetrius: the issue of queen Lanassa and Corcyra continued to sting and this, combined with pure realpolitik, swung the issue. There is little doubt he also worried that if the triple alliance dealt with his neighbour without his assistance, he could hardly expect them to be generous in any subsequent settlement, though there may have been those among his councillors at Ambracia arguing the advantage in staying out, to allow the other rulers to damage each other in great campaigns that might leave Epirus well-placed to pick up the pieces. Whatever was at the back of his mind, his policy was clear: he would join but not show his hand until the other kings had committed themselves by irrevocable action and it is noticeable that when the coalition moved, he was nowhere near the forefront.

Demetrius surely must have heard of these communications, but even his agents nosing about had not discovered the extent of the plot being synchronized against this marked man and it seems the measures taken by the coalition when they came were a real shock. Delayed though action had been when the combination of kings pounced in the spring of 288, much would hang on the result. Ptolemy sent a considerable fleet to Greece, hoping those factions in opposition to the Antigonids that flourished in so many cities might rise in revolt. So the first indication of trouble was when a Lagid fleet hove in sight over the horizon to threaten important strongholds like Corinth, Chalcis and Piraeus. Along with this maritime endeavour another old man acted too and he was in a position to do a great deal more than imperil the Greek coastline. The lord of Thrace and Anatolia might be into his 70s by now, but the opportunity had arisen to do down the man he hated most in the world, so he moved in main force to ensure that Demetrius could never complete his preparations for the invasion of Asia. A day's march out of Lysimachia as the coast road turns west the royal army coalesced around a core of royal phalangites, hoplites from the Greek towns on the Black Sea would have arrived and thousands of those Thracians the king had ruled so long. Most of these would have been the familiar peltasts with small crescent-shaped shields, javelins and animal skins to protect their heads, but there would have been bronze-bound cavaliers from the local aristocracy as well, and perhaps even some Getae, old enemies hired to earn civilization's trinkets, riding wiry ponies and wielding lances and deadly composite bows. All soon assembled and advanced promptly, barrelling westwards along the road down past the ancient town of Neapolis (modern-day Kavala), which offered harbour facilities for the tree- and mineral-rich lands around Philippi.

In the face of this menace, Demetrius might have looked like he was sitting solid with a projected fleet of 500 ships and army of more than 100,000 soldiers, but this was an occasion when appearances were manifestly deceptive. His life had been a roller-coaster, but if this showed resilience it also worried those of his retainers concerned about going down with a ship that had previously shown such a tendency to sink. From being a fugitive from a stricken field on the downswing to an Imperial highpoint on the up, all might be exciting enough but not necessary appealing to people looking for stability to enjoy the fruits on offer at the high table of prevalent power. He was dispatching specie wrung from his subjects to fund the armaments and supervising the organizing of a complex commissariat, making the arrangements for his Asian undertaking, when news arrived of his enemy's movements, that far from sitting still to be attacked they had taken the initiative. As rumours of his enemy's activities hardened into foreboding certainty, he perhaps realized that publicly sneering at Lysimachus had not been such a good idea, but any regrets did not stop him rushing back to draw a line, to defend his realm against the intruder. Initially those willing him to fail kept their council and his people showed solid as he called out the levy that in combination with the veterans he had brought up from Greece looked like they might give him the edge. The road the defenders travelled in the direction of Thrace led north of the Chalcedonian peninsula and Demetrius hustled hard, eager to reach the mineral-rich mining country west of Philippi, to plug the road and ensure the region did not fall into his rival's hands.

The Antigonid prince was always bold and, hoping to catch his enemy before he could take up too strong a position, he pushed his men hard, intending to strike at the earliest opportunity. The convergence of the two opposing armies occurred somewhere near Amphipolis where the Pangaion Mountains fall down to the sea. This was rugged country of stark ridges dotted with brushwood, but somewhere along the coast or in the valley of the Strymón Lysimachus found room to draw up his infantry phalanx with Thracian peltasts in support and cavalry on the wings. Once formed, they found themselves facing an army that looked pretty similar in make-up showing menacingly on the hazed horizon in front of them, advertised by the sound of thousands and thousands of infantrymen's trudging feet and high-stepping horses of the cavalry. There were more proper Macedonian phalangites in the opposing throng confronting them with brightly-coloured shields emblazoned with representations of sunbursts, gorgons' heads, Zeus with a sceptre, goats, eagles, bulls, snakes or Heracles' club and wearing high-plumed helmets to give the impression of stature with the type and number of attachments indicating authority.[4] The bravest wore gold crowns wreathed around their helmets, while officers sported precious rings, bracelets, gorgets and perhaps even sashes adopted from the Persians as a token of rank. The most senior men gloried in the finest outfits. Zoilus of Cyprus is famous for providing Demetrius with a corselet proof against catapult bolts, requisite enough considering his propensity for getting hit, while plenty of others commissioned distinctive outfits so that they could be recognized in the heat of battle. Banners raised, this infantry surged to the attack, while on the usually decisive right wing Demetrius would have fielded companion cavaliers in considerable numbers, trotting horsemen fanning out across the plain seated on gorgeous leopard, lion and tiger pelts or panther-skin shabraques (saddlecloths) sacred to Dionysus, all following rigid cloth standards also borrowed from the Persians. A new generation of blue-blood knights who had grown to manhood since so many of their fathers had gone to leave their bones on the battlefields of Asia, and the same was true of his Thessalian cavaliers, heirs of the men who had usually held the left wing tight under Parmenion when Alexander won his great victories against the Persians.

We have no information about how the combat played out, only that it was stubbornly fought, hardly surprising as many of the combatants involved on both sides would have honed their skills in the great campaigns of the earlier Diadochi Wars. There is no indication as to how many casualties were sustained or if a tactical tour de force decided the day; all that is known is that Lysimachus was knocked back and Demetrius, full of confidence, was preparing his advantage when at that moment messengers arrived that rocked his plans to their foundations. Everything that had started so well began to go wrong and he found to his horror that Pyrrhus had stabbed him in the back. Mobilizing his host as soon as he was confident that his allies were primed to go and that Lysimachus had drawn Demetrius towards the Thracian border he had made his move, force-marching from the west through the mountain cantons of Macedonia and discovering little opposition along the way. Pyrrhus had done his homework and it was a smooth advance with the country stripped of its fighting men of military age, most of whom were off defending the eastern border, so the Epirot invaders were able to debouch north of the Bermion Mountains, probably not far from Edessa, an important station on the main road east to Pella that once had been the country's capital. However, instead of keeping to the route to the capital, he turned south and took another way leading to Beroea, a place hardly 10 miles distant from the old royal centre of Aigai. The reason for this change of direction is not reported, but it is reasonable to assume that in not following his instincts to head directly towards where he knew his enemy was contending with his ally, Pyrrhus had good reasons. It may well be that he intended to hedge his bets, hoping that in the triangular contest he had entered his best interest would be served by allowing the other two players to exhaust themselves in bruising battle, leaving him then to pick up the pieces. This policy had its own risks as if one of the other two showed decisively victorious, they might then turn on him in dangerous strength, but then any course was bound to be fraught with danger and at least this policy ensured he would keep his own army out of harm's way for the moment.

Whatever the Eagle king's calculations, his activities occasioned a highly dramatic outcome. A probably ad hoc strategy had metamorphosed into a dazzlingly coordinated onslaught. Having failed to completely counter the menace of one rival and now having had to contend with the ambition of another, Demetrius, cursing this latest foe who had failed to hold to a compact made only months earlier, had to readjust completely. Exasperated at being forced to let Lysimachus off the hook, he nonetheless gave orders for his men to terminate their pursuit, to reorder their formations, turn back west and retrace their steps. Yet when word of the situation at home reached his men, 'the whole camp resounded with tears and lamentations'. The loyalty of the key men, the phalangites and companions, was torn: they had fought Lysimachus but had not been happy about it and now it looked like they would have to fight on another front against another man who many considered almost as legitimate a chief as Demetrius. Lysimachus had been one of Alexander's marshals and Pyrrhus was his close kin with Olympias' blood flowing in his veins and with this in mind, some started cursing their leader and openly declaring that they should not be involved in this bloodletting but should return to their farms and families, while some even slipped away to discover where Lysimachus' army was encamped to enrol in his battered but still surviving command. In his headquarters tent, Demetrius had faced making desperate choices. It was agonizingly frustrating but absolutely clear that had he continued to attack Lysimachus where he was grimly holding his position he would be courting disaster; that too many of his followers would have refused to confront this fellow Macedonian. So with little option he had decided to turn against the other threat, hoping to pander to normal Macedonians' chauvinism, that he could at least paint this policy as being about defending their homeland against alien intruders. Initially the ploy seemed to have worked as the soldiers settled down and, obeying their officers, followed on as they were led west, past the head of the Thermaic Gulf, over the green and brooding waters of the Axius River and into the valley of the Haliacmon where the most recent news placed the Epirot army.

The new enemy Demetrius was about to face had had a dream when his army camped before turning south to Beroea: he saw Alexander the Great himself lying sick on a couch but offering nonetheless to help him and when asked how this could be accomplished: '"With my name!" replied Alexander and, mounting a horse from Nisean, he seemed to show Pyrrhus the way.'[5] With encouragement from this ghostly talisman of Macedonian glory, the Epirot ruler was optimistic when Demetrius' army trailed out of the water meadows to confront him and he had good cause because as soon as the Macedonians were again settled in their defended quarters, groups of soldiers began gathering together whispering that a future with a great warrior like Pyrrhus might have considerable advantages over the dangers of adhering to the unpredictable Antigonid. This was particularly so when locals from Beroea who entered the camp to visit friends and family enrolled in the national army, informed them that those of their comrades who had been captured had been treated with 'kindness and consideration'. Among these visitors slipping through the gates or over the palisades were Epirot agents disguised as Macedonians, well tutored in highlighting their sponsor's qualities as a soldier's general, reminding their listeners that he was the man they remembered from the Homeric contest with Pantauchus a few years earlier. They no doubt boosted him as a commander who shared the hardships of campaigning with his men, in contrast to the overbearing and unapproachable Demetrius who was leading them to disaster, caught between the two artfully fashioned pincers comprising the armies led by Lysimachus and Pyrrhus.

The mechanism is opaque, but the camps must have been close together as after some time small parties of Macedonians began deserting until the tipping-point arrived when Pyrrhus himself approached the camp, hoping to finally induce the whole army to change allegiance. It did not go smoothly to begin with as he had taken off his helmet so the Macedonians might recognize him. His appearance made little impression until some of those who had already transferred sides explained to him that many who did not know his face would be as familiar with his famous high crest and goat-horned headpiece, referencing the god Pan, as their forebears had been with Alexander's colourful military cloak. So it was a fully accoutred monarch who finally welcomed the men transferring covertly in driblets until the 'climate of disorder and sedition spread through the whole camp'. Yet if the feeling among Demetrius' men was rapidly turning, there were still loyalists and some of these now hurried to the headquarters tent and persuaded the guard to admit them to tip off their commander that they had seen their men slipping out of camp to join the enemy. Feeling a tremor of alarm at this news, he traversed the tent lines and was soon convinced that all was lost and that the only hope was to try to escape, so borrowing a soldier's cloak in place of his stately robes and a typical kausia (flat hat or cap) worn low to hide his face, the king of Macedonia slipped out of the back of the royal pavilion to find a horse and make his getaway, while in his wake his rival received the acclamation of the whole army.

The encampment from which Demetrius had turned tail and fled became a scene of riot as his luxurious tent and those of his officers who had fled with him were looted by his old soldiers, many of whom were now sporting oak leaf sprigs in homage to the sacred tree of Dodona so associated with Pyrrhus and Epirus. As the Macedonians acclaimed a new leader, the old one rode hard for the Chalcidice and the city of Cassandreia, having in a blaze of hours lost a kingdom he had held for seven years. There in the palace he found his wife Phila who was feeling the shock of despoliation keenly, worn down by the vicissitudes of fortune that formed the normal life of the spouse of Demetrius Poliorcetes. She would have hardly expected a faithful husband, and multiple marriages and other philandering would not have been a problem, but this highly-respected matron found life no longer supportable with a man whose ineptitude had brought her to the current pass. This daughter of Antipater took poison to ease her way out of a life no longer supportable, but her husband, it turned out, was far from in a similar mood. Unstable though he was, Demetrius, looking to salvage something from the wreck, was always the comeback kid; he had self-confidence in abundance and a record for bouncing back that was extraordinary.

Throughout his life Demetrius had surfed the waves of fortune with extraordinary sang-froid and he was not about to change now, whatever the odds against him. Amid the seeming ruin of all his hopes he held his nerve and joined his son Antigonus Gonatus at Demetrias and was soon indicating he had far from totally shelved the great Imperial project of reclaiming the old Antigonid possessions in Anatolia. Losing his Macedonian crown had at least one immediate consolation: his relationship with many in Greece had considerably improved. He was no longer perceived as the personification of threat that perennially showed from north of the Vale of Tempe since the days of Philip II but in fact as a potential counterweight to the new men in power in the northern kingdom. This showed when he toured much of the country 'as a private citizen', eschewing any royal pomp in an effort to escape from that reputation of high-toned grandiosity that had so worked against him with the people of Macedonia. At Thebes he was well received and these people were rewarded for their loyalty by having their ancestral constitution restored and other places, which were now seeing him as a potential protector against Pyrrhus or Lysimachus, also reaffirmed their adherence to the Antigonid cause. It may have been more than two decades since his great triumphs at Salamis and Athens, but memories of the golden victorious prince who built some of the biggest siege engines and warships ever seen still lingered.

Yet it was far from all auspicious in the world south of Thermopylae. In Athens the impact of Demetrius' rise to Macedonian pre-eminence seven years earlier had been instructive. His long and glamorous shadow was absent, and that he no longer strutted around the halls of the Parthenon in Athena's raiment must have been a relief to any citizens with even a modicum of self-respect, but there was much that was less palatable. Though Athens may have hoped to enjoy a particularly favoured vassalage, Demetrius still had the knack of offending a constituency which had forgotten how he had freed them from being Cassander's puppet long ago. On one occasion he apparently kept a delegation from the city waiting two years, something that could not have been agreeable to people who had expected their recent guest would, when king of Macedonia, show them preferential treatment. Yet it was more than discourtesy: he was shameless in his manipulation of city life, though no longer on the spot, he was determined to keep his proxies firmly in control. Stratocles was still there, an old sycophant from the high days of 307 and paying heed to Theophrastus, head of peripatetic schools, exiles like the oligarch Deinarch of Corinth had been brought back to engineer a Big Tent coalition that might keep sufficient people happy. The council of 600 was re-formed and when Demetrius wanted greater reassurance as he left for the north, to ensure the citizenry remained firmly under his thumb, he countenanced the rigging of the lottery and bending of hallowed conventions in a manner that was particularly repugnant to people whose constitution was their pride and joy.

To ensure that his local protégés were kept in power, regulations were bent mercilessly, as suggested by evidence that the office of eponymous archon was held by the same man for both the years 294–293 and 293–292 in direct contravention of a law forbidding such a repeat incumbency, while registrars of the council were reintroduced that had last been heard of under the oligarchy of 321–318. This in a place where many still remembered that they had pioneered the noble and innovative experiment of democracy, where it was difficult for the citizens to feel a full measure of pride in the achievements of the past, to preen as heirs of Cleisthenes and Pericles when such palpable outside influence was omnipresent and their client status so apparent. So with Demetrius making little attempt to veil a supremacy so distasteful that it was later referred to as a time of oligarchic rule, opposition activists had little problem wooing support among all classes from potters and small farmers to landed gentry for whom the constitutional life of the community was more than just a sham.

To many citizens all this must have been redolent of Demetrius' hard-hand conduct towards the Boeotians between 294 and 291 where the imposition of Hieronymus had seemed as little conducive to Greek freedom as was the monopoly of their great offices by Antigonid placemen. There was a difference: the former was a family agent who would serve generations of Antigonids while in Athens he was sponsoring locals like Stratocles and Dromocleides, as tricky a politician as any who rose to prominence at this time whose reputation never recovered from his suggesting that Antigonid garrisons should be left permanently in both the Piraeus and the museum after the city fell in 295. Now how grim things had become was emphasized in 291 or 290 when, after Demetrius returned from Corfu, a hymn to his divinity was inserted in the liturgy at the Mysteries, celebrated when the white-robed, myrtle-decked devotees progressed along the 17 miles of the Sacred Way to Eleusis, which proposed that while the other gods were far away and uninvolved, Demetrius was on hand to be appealed to. The context was a need for his help against the Aetolians who controlled Delphi and who because of their alliance with Thebes were blocking the rededication of Athenian shields from the great victory over the Persians at Plataea in 479. The Theban people had of course turned quisling and Medized during the great patriotic war and felt the proposed dedication as the deepest personal slight. Yet despite this rationale, to so prostitute the city's most sacred ritual could not but sear the soul of pious, irreligious, rich and poor alike.

Much of the detail of Athenian Antigonid relations depends on the interpretation of inscriptions, usually fashioned several years after the events they refer to, that makes chronological determination usually dependent on often perplexing listings of Archonic years. The confusion of manipulated complexities is such that people have been able to argue that there were several sieges of the Piraeus and Athens in the 280s and

270s and that the port and its fort were recaptured by the Athenians before being retaken by Antigonus Gonatus. Much less adventurous modern scholarship has been reluctant to accept much of this, but what is not contested by most is the upheaval that occurred in 287. Revolution would not come out of the blue; outside factors would be fundamental, not just that tracking events when it looked like Demetrius' tenure on the Macedonian throne would soon be ended but that concrete results had accrued from the diplomatic approaches that Athenian opponents of the Antigonids had made to the great powers. Something definitely happened in a body politic long restless under outside control as the kings raised their coalition; there were exiles sniffing the air and dispatching feelers to friends still in town to advertise that their ruler's position was under threat with a menacing combination of enemies preparing against him.

Faction hatreds could be relaxed and bridges built as opposition to occupation was now all that mattered. Even those Demetrius had previously sponsored, their resolution charged by an alloy of patriotism and self-interest, conceived he was a man who had had his day. Not all recognized it but many realized that without his standing as king at Pella, any reservoir of support among the population of Attica and indeed much of the rest of Greece was pitifully small. There were some collaborators so totally committed that they had no wriggle room at all, but this was only a small faction; the people on the whole gagged for the return of that sovereignty rent from them in recent decades by a series of foreign monarchs, home-grown tyrants and oligarchs. It was power to the people bubbling away beneath before coming into its own, a real autonomy, but one where these adaptable placemen could still flourish, a programme carefully crafted and radical enough but hardly without precedent. So with resistance sufficiently fuelled, the drive for change was unstoppable, ensuring that when in July 288 Egyptian ships were spotted coasting along the Attic shore near Cape Sunium, many began to envisage how they might take advantage of circumstances. Talk became general about the feasibility of rebuffing their hegemon and making another bid for independence.

In the spring of 287 in the drive for liberation, with loyalties finely calibrated, key men sensitive to the political weather smoothly changed sides. Olympiodorus and Xanthippos might not have garnered the kind of reputation that made believable that they could sacrilegiously knock the phalluses off people's doorpost herma, but they certainly had an Alcibiadean propensity to switch parties and were now among the most important, turning into keen enthusiasts for autonomy, despite their being famous for holding Elateia for Demetrius against Cassander's men in 301. Now it was the former, a veteran of democratic debate and tempered in the exacting Athenian school of political hard knocks, who found himself at the centre of events, using all his powers of persuasion to enlist volunteers to besiege the Antigonid garrison in the Museum. This man had long been an Antigonid stalwart; it was he who had been the stooge who had been archon in succeeding years, but now he changed from Antigonid lackey to independence fighter and was in command when the Athenian combatants arrived under the walls of the fort on the Hill of the Muses. There they found the defenders sufficiently confident in their ability to intimidate these citizen soldiers for them to sally out, understandable enough if most, as Pausanias says, were 'old men and boys'. Yet in the street-fighting that followed, it soon became clear that the Athenians were far from being an incompetent rabble and that the garrison had weak links in their ranks. The Athenians, favourites of the goddess of wisdom, were notoriously wily and intelligent and would always turn to stratagem where brute force might not win the day. So during the carefree days before the crisis, it had been easy enough to make contact with the officers and men of the garrison in the bars and brothels of the Ceramicus, and in a captain of mercenaries called Strombichus they found a man open to the corrupting effect of easy money. Now this turncoat came through, joining the Athenians with his men, and pushed back the garrison until Olympiodorus with his commando of determined patriots stormed the ramparts. Under a fine blue summer sky, the intentions of those involved in the assault were grand and portentous: to free the city that boasted the battle honours of Marathon and Salamis and we even know the name of the first man over the wall, the hero Leocritus, who got the posthumous plaudits[6] with his shield dedicated to Zeus, the giver of liberty, while the thirteen Athenians who died in the assault were entombed along the high road, joining the long row of those who had fallen in the Athenian cause since the Persian wars.

The change in allegiance indicated by this military triumph was constitutionally emphasized as Diphilus,[7] the priest of the saviour gods who had been keeping the place warm for his sponsor, was toppled and expelled with the Athenians declared independent and free, electing their own archons and generals in the time-honoured democratic manner. This had been a fateful and perilous step, virtually a declaration of war against their old saviour god, and in the first flush of success many perhaps did not understand the challenge they had taken on, but they were soon to find out. Neither the senior nor the junior Antigonid was prepared to accept this reverse lying down; family honour absolutely obliged them to reject any acceptance of this ejection from Athens even if they had to from Pella. So while Antigonus Gonatus held their headquarters at Demetrias, his father gathered troops to bring the nest of rebels in Athens to heel. That there had been some time between his being dumped out of Macedon and the Athenian coup is shown by the fact that Demetrius was in the Peloponnese suppressing rebels when news reached him, but now he was ready and took the attack directly against the enemy. He moved across the isthmus to put the city under siege with the gawping residents experiencing a shudder of horror as they saw the approaching dust of the army, even before the lines of soldiers began preparing their siege works and assembling their engines.

Getting the food in before their arrival had been crucial, but they had needed help. A light Lagid squadron led by Zeno is noticed bringing a supply of corn to Athens on the 11th Hekatombaion (July) and more than this, summertime assistance came from a man named Callias, scion of a famous family with a father who held high office and who himself had been in voluntary exile since the time of the oligarchs and made a considerable career as a mercenary captain in Ptolemy I's service, who had arrived with a force of 1,000 elite soldiers and landed first at Andros. That the Lagids controlled here showed how deep their influence had become among the League of Islanders with more and more places submitting to their rule over recent years. From there Callias crossed over to the mainland and with help of his brother Phaedrus acted to protect those bringing in the harvest, an intervention that turned out to be hot work, shown by his receiving a minor wound in a skirmish with troops from the Piraeus garrison trying to interrupt the labour.

Bulging granaries meant that the Athenians could hope to wait Demetrius out as that king with his Asian agenda would not want to be delayed too long in front of the long walls. It is possible there was getting on for a year between his expulsion from the Macedonian throne and the tight siege being established in early summer 287 with entrenchments dug and sheds and engines deployed, sending a shudder of dread down Athenian spines. However long it had been, now the threat was palpable with Piraeus as a base still firmly in the besiegers' hands and the inhabitants no longer having the consolation of Ptolemy's fleet being in the offing. On top of that there seemed little prospect of succour from the other kings who were clearly preoccupied sorting out the new regime in Macedonia. The story is that the citizenry soon became scared enough that, despite the early successes of Olympiodorus in taking the Museum fort, they felt they were bound to finally succumb to the famed besieger of cities. It was in this context they made an attempt to deflect the wrath of their old hegemon by different means. The siege had interrupted the students, whether Athenian or foreign devotees, who attended lectures at Plato's Academy, the Peripatos of Aristotle, the Stoic school of Zeno or Epicurus' garden so the leaders of these highly prestigious institutions could be harnessed to the patriotic cause. The task was not anyway much of a stretch as these celebrities had often led the city's embassies in the past, so now Polemon, the head of Plato's Academy, was first requested to try to intercede with Demetrius, but he refused and the second choice fell on Crates the Cynic, another mentor of Zeno. The claim is that he persuaded the besieger there were other 'courses that were to his own advantage' rather than attacking the city. Much more likely was that Demetrius, not in any mood to be placated and hardly influenced by this cerebral interplay, was swayed by another factor: that an embassy the new Athenian government had sent to Pyrrhus bore fruit.

If Pyrrhus was unclear on the direction the fugitive had taken when Demetrius had given up on his fickle soldiery and departed the encampment near Beroea, what was abundantly apparent was that Macedonia was lost to him, though who would pick up the bauble was far less obvious. The Epirot had little inclination to indulge in a military face-off with Lysimachus; after all, recent events did not suggest that the Macedonians could be depended on in extremis, particularly as that old marshal was one of them in a way he could never be. The resources even of his kingdom of Greater Epirus would just not weigh in the balance against those of the ruler of Thrace and Anatolia. So with diplomacy his best resort, when Lysimachus arrived on the scene with his bloodied but still formidable army, halted after an orderly march and improvised his camp, envoys were dispatched to test the intentions of this ally. On this occasion there are no reports of forged letters or portentous sacrifices and it seems agreement was swiftly reached to divide the kingdom where a speedy removal of the incumbent had left a power vacuum. This post-Demetrius disposal in all likelihood mirrored the one that had been arrived at between the sons of Cassander back in 295 with a boundary along the River Axius, very likely leaving Amphipolis and Cassandreia on Lysimachus' side of the dividing line, though there is another tradition[8] that declares the River Nestus east of Philippi as the new border.

With his Thracian frontier sorted, the king of both Epirus and west Macedonia could regard himself as well rewarded for striking the decisive blow against Demetrius, yet he still showed that restful enjoyment of the applause of his new subjects was far from his style. Glamour and glory had always been what he lived for and now events rolling out around the hallowed walls of Athens drew him irresistibly. Here the dynamic was different from many other parts of central Greece with the opposition still seeing the exiled king as the greatest threat to their autonomy and considering Pyrrhus, even though now installed at Pella, as a sponsor who might offer crucial succour. Now he would respond to the Athenian request for assistance and soon would climb the Acropolis to make sacrifices to Athena with an admiring crowd on his heels before descending to address the citizenry in assembly. There showing himself a very different man from the one from whom he had just saved the city; not for him to dictate a new constitution and neither accepting trappings of authority nor outstaying his welcome, Pyrrhus only left his hosts with a piece of advice: that they should never open their gates again to any king 'nor admit them into the city',[9] oozing a disinterestedness that perhaps really warranted the busts that were set up in his honour.

It was undoubtedly this man that had counted, prepared to deal with the problem posed by an apparently resurgent Demetrius throwing his weight around. The threat of Pyrrhus' considerable forces marching down through the states of central Greece, coupled with the appearance of a Lagid fleet sent in response to an Athenian embassy to Alexandria, had been much more than any representations from the philosopher Crates that made the besieger consider withdrawing from his works round the city. However, this relaxation of the siege had been but a hiatus and only time would tell if a permanent settlement could be forged. Fortunately for the suffering residents, Athens was now a sideshow for a man deeply concerned to adhere to his Asian invasion timetable and looking for a way out in which he could save face. So he jumped when Ptolemy gave him the opportunity, sending Sostratos of Knidos, famous for sponsoring the lighthouse at Alexandria, tripping ashore with a proposal for compromise. The diplomatic manoeuvrings are obscure; there was no official Athenian representation at the talks, Demetrius could not countenance that, but the credible man from the Lagid court found a formula and Callias with his Ptolemaic credentials looked after Athenian interests and acted as a link to facilitate a peace brokered at Piraeus not later than July 287. So the archonship of Cimon saw the implementation of satisfactory arrangements and Athenian autonomy was assured that would stand for twenty years, though the Antigonid garrison at Piraeus remained, as did other fortified places around Attica.

We are not absolutely sure of the other terms of the treaty, but certainly a compact between Demetrius and Pyrrhus was concluded as well that presumably included recognition of the latter as king of Macedon while he accepted Antigonid control in key places in Thessaly and Greece. So Demetrius, still holding Corinth, Chalcis, Piraeus, Eleusis, Salamis and other Attica forts could be sufficiently content; he lost little by these arrangements as he prepared to undertake the last great gamble of his life. Yet if the Athenians observed his withdrawal with satisfaction, they were a roughed-up polity far from completely happy with the conditions they had been obliged to concede and not only looked to shore up their just-won autonomy but nurtured ambitions to reacquire not only the places their old hegemon had retained but others like Oropus that would in fact be lost to the Boeotian league for 115 years. Nor could it be just self-reliance, though by bringing back the likes of Demochares from exile they acquired home-grown talent and experience that would soon be required. They needed friends, but how to procure them?

Fecund minds had already been ratcheting into gear. Missions were equipped involving some of the city's most renowned celebrities. Envoys visited the rulers of Paeonia and the Crimea, and Spartokos, the ruler of the latter place, sent grain for which his kingdom was famous, but others seemed less generous, though after Demochares contacted Lysimachus he did unbend to the extent of 30 talents, useful to a people still feeling vulnerable and eager to spend money on refitting their defences. A return trip to Lysimachia even garnered another 100 talents, while Antipater, Lysimachus' son-in-law, came through with 20 more, so appreciative statues were erected to the king and honours awarded to his friends. The comic playwright Philippides was particularly lionized. He had made a name for himself for bitterly lampooning Stratocles, a track record of opposition that went back to 307 and had allowed him to win a corn donation from his friend Lysimachus for the regime that came after Ipsus, ending with being honoured in 284 as director of a splendid dramatic contest and later recognized by the people in assembly. Another embassy to Ptolemy was dispatched back to a grateful city with 50 talents and close association with the Lagids was well illustrated when admiral Philocles of Sidon not only visited, making offering to Athena, but around the mid-280s was also granted Athenian citizenship. Indeed, by winter 287 or spring 286 with the response from these wealthy backers they were sufficiently financially liquid to mobilize enough troops to recapture Eleusis.

The change of regime also allowed improved relations with nearer neighbours. Demetrius had been continually at odds with the Aetolians as the custodians of Delphi, but with him gone and the mountain men's old friend Olympiodorus high in influence, bridges could be rebuilt. After these successes ambition grew; now they wanted Piraeus back and hoped that the Antigonid officers there might be susceptible to gold in the same way that Strombichus had been at the Museum. This time, however, these soldiers for hire under their commandant Heracleides proved true to their salt and the Athenians found themselves hoist with their own petard. Two Athenian generals called Hipparchus and Mnesidemus approached Hierocles of Caria, one of the garrison's officers, when he was attending a religious festival, but this officer, while feigning interest, on returning to the Munychia informed his commander. The trap was baited and the Athenians were told by Hierocles to come in secret to a postern gate that he would open to them. The eager citizen heroes threw themselves into the fort but once through the entrance 420 attackers found themselves surrounded and exterminated by 2,000 men from the garrison, with the intriguer Mnesidemus having the smile wiped from his face when he suffered fatally among his men for the Athenians' ambition to regain control of the key port.

While Athens was enjoying mixed dividends from investing in home defence and local belligerence, Demetrius had shown again what an extraordinary character he was. This man who had campaigned from Egypt to Anatolia and from Thrace to Cyprus would demonstrate in the year 286 that none of his aspirations had been stifled by decades of ups and downs. He might be unstable, but he had charisma in abundance and if it had been decades since his great triumphs at Cyprian Salamis and Athens, even since then there had been plenty on the credit side as well as the debit. If his career had been unorthodox, the reputation he would gain would not fade away, even after the passage of centuries. Now key themes in his life came together in what would prove to be a climactic project. A yearning to win back his father's Asian empire was made only more poignant by his hatred for an old man who had, after completing the annexation of the Antigonid Anatolian heartland, also virtually concluded his takeover of the Greek cities on the Aegean coast that had been the jewels of the empire destroyed at Ipsus. For the evicted king of Macedon there was only one real road to greatness: to regain what had been lost and anything else would be a second-rate outcome. He had a choice between consolidating the realm left to him that had been held tight by the Fetters of Greece and his son Antigonus or going for broke in an Asian effort and Demetrius' decision was never in doubt nor was it one he was prepared to postpone.

He was drawn irresistibly across the Aegean like a moth to a flame and it had only been because he did not want to leave Gonatus with too many loose ends that he had delayed coming to terms with Pyrrhus before freeing up the resources he had left to allow a final reckoning with Lysimachus. No disasters in Macedonia could damp his enthusiasm, no panic among his retainers could restrain his staggering ambition and extraordinary optimism, although how much of his fleet of 500 ships was left to him is far from clear. Most of the vessels posted in Macedonia at the shipyards at the head of the Thermaic Gulf would have no longer been available, and if those at Corinth, Chaklis and elsewhere were still accessible, he would hardly have had the resources to finish, equip and crew much more than a bare minimum to transport the army he had gathered for what would turn out to be his last adventure. The expeditionary force consisted of 11,000 infantry and all his cavalry, hardly an overwhelming force for such a long-awaited enterprise; though Demetrius showed no sign of being afraid it was too little too late. Still, after the adventurers pushed out into the open sea and disappeared over the horizon onto the course mapped out it must have left his son with little beyond just the garrison soldiers required to hold onto those footholds that remained true to the Antigonid cause. At least he would have been well supplied with sound advice from the likes of Hieronymus who, now well into his 60s, surely would have remained behind with some relief as the man he had served so long headed out into the unknown.

Lysimachus would have been infuriated when the news of the arrangements reached him. The implication was clear: that his erstwhile ally Pyrrhus and friends in Attica had in their own interests discharged a dangerous man, whose patent intention was to fulfil his worst nightmare by descending on his Anatolian realm. However small the force with which Demetrius crossed the water, for his target the danger must have seemed profound. In fact this Asian war turned out to comprise a bizarre series of campaigns as the invaders island-hopping across the Aegean first retook a number of old Antigonid seaside strongholds, only pausing at Miletus for their commander to marry Ptolemias, Eurydice's daughter by Ptolemy to whom he had been betrothed since 299 when he had become friends with Egypt at the instigation of Seleucus. Then he marched north as far as Sardis before allowing himself to be driven east into the Taurus fastness by Lysimachus' son Agathocles, who had by then had time to gather his strength. Yet bold strategies were not enough, particularly as no army, however loyal, would find it comfortable to be stranded in the desolate mountains where Demetrius had led them. So, after tangling with Seleucus by trespassing on that ruler's Cilician and Syrian holdings, the adventurer ended with the rump of his depleted force surrendering to the lord of Asia, and after an extraordinary manhunt, a wild chase across southern Anatolia that ended with capture and being hauled off in chains by the officers of a ruler who was both an ex-ally and his current father-in-law.

The incarceration of Demetrius and the fragmentation of the Antigonid fleet marked the effective termination of an extraordinary career, but the question was what else would these developments portend? When news of what had happened in Syria percolated the Balkans, it was a happy monarch in Lysimachia who heard that his greatest enemy had passed from the political scene, the rival who had traduced his manhood by suggesting he was a eunuch and denigrated his liberality, that quality so crucial in keeping adherents content, had finally ceased to be a significant factor. Though having neither forgotten nor forgiven his insults, nor completely content that he was not dead, Lysimachus offered 2,000 talents to Seleucus to finish him off for good. Seleucus refused out of concern for his reputation or perhaps thinking that his prisoner might still be a useful pawn in future power-plays. Others, however, had much less cause for celebration than Lysimachus. Pyrrhus knew the reality was that no sooner was he established in Eastern Macedonia according to their arrangement than that ruthless man would be casting about for an opportunity to gobble up the rest. While he was still occupied with containing a rampant Demetrius, the Epirot had himself showed aggression in early summer of 286 when, using the excuse that any treaties had been invalidated by the invasion of Asia, he overran Thessaly. He had prepared the way with agents who undermined local confidence in Antigonid rule and soon found that Gonatus did not have the strength to do much more than hold the area around his stronghold of Demetrias and perhaps Magnesia.

After entering his name in a list of kings of Thessaly, it may well have been around this time or certainly not much later that not only did he incorporate part of southern Illyria into his realm[10] but that his son Ptolemy took back Corfu with an expedition numbering only sixty men. Yet despite these successes, the haunting reality was that there was no denying the man with whom he shared Macedonia would now have a free hand to direct his victorious armies in different directions, particularly as he was clearly refusing to be distracted by any conflict with Seleucus. Pyrrhus knew from his own experience with Neoptolemus in Epirus how little honour might be expected between the parties in this kind of co-kingship arrangement and with Lysimachus having no distractions along his Taurus Mountain front, the danger to those sharing his western borders was bound to be concomitantly greater. That Pyrrhus was cognizant of this menace and looking on with mounting alarm is demonstrated by his opening a diplomatic dialogue with Antigonus Gonatus. The relationship between these two had immediately turned bitter after the Epirot's gobbling up of Thessaly but nothing of that mattered for long; he was now no longer seen as an enemy to be faced outside Demetrias but a potential friend who, having inherited a feud from his father, might be as afraid of a raging Lysimachus as was Pyrrhus. It was a terrific coup for the Epirot to make a friend of this ruler he had so recently despoiled and one of the few people around who might significantly boost his numbers when it came to a meeting on the battlefield. A reference to a secret accord between the two is found in an extract from a play by Phoenicides called *The Flute Player* showing these two members of the younger generation of successors were very sensible of the threats emanating from the old king squatting so proximate on their doorstep.

In less than a year spies were reporting that Lysimachus' main army was regrouping back over the European shore of the Hellespont, hardly more than a few days' hard march from Pyrrhus' border. The intention to take over all the Macedonian kingdom had been there since Demetrius had been caged in 295, but it would have taken time to bring veteran regiments back from south-east Anatolia where they had been posted to protect against any return by that pirate king whose capacity to make trouble, despite almost any setback, had been shown so often before. Now, with him definitely no longer a factor, Lysimachus had an opportunity to turn against an ally who had done so much to pull the claws of that dangerous man. Determined to become master of the whole of his homeland, any inclination to share was clearly ditched when a rumour confirmed that Antipater, son of Cassander, had disappeared, probably killed. It had long been clear that he had no more real use for this puppet since he had formally proclaimed himself king of Macedon.[11] There had been human ties with his son-in-law here, but set against realpolitik they had not mattered. However, if the removal of this irritant had posed little of a problem, Pyrrhus was a different matter and no pushover, the Eagle king ruling as he did not just the choicest portion of Macedonia but Greater Epirus, including the parts of upper Macedonia taken over almost a decade before, plus the Thessalian country so recently acquired.

Early summer was the usual time to prepare to fight, so at this season in 285 the old man moved; with the tally of his years mounting, there would be no half measures. Lysimachus felt he could delay no longer and recent reports had been encouraging. He knew through contacts who had been fermenting dissent at Pella that Pyrrhus' support was not rock solid. Launching an unprovoked attack, he came over the border in force with all the strength he could mobilize. Veterans ferried over from Anatolia joined with the guards units from the capital in the marshalling fields outside Lysimachia where they had combined with thousands of Thracians, always eager for a fight. The old king, grimly confident, led the way west, the heaviest troops carrying an energy-sapping load of perhaps up to 70lb of arms as they trailed north of the Chalcidice peninsula and into the Axius valley where the invader found he had calculated correctly. Resistance was tepid and reports brought in by his scouts showed that Pyrrhus had abandoned the capital and withdrawn west where the mountains rose out of the plain and the terrain might even out the odds against him. So with the Epirot caught on the hop and aware that many of his Macedonian subjects were not about to sell their lives for him in battle, the old king came tobogganing into Pella on the scree of local support from those who had duly deserted the incumbent.

When the threat from the east materialized and with far from all the levy responding to his call to arms, it soon became apparent to Pyrrhus that he lacked the numbers to face the invader in the open. So, convinced he would be unable to check his progress, he ordered the abandonment of the capital and faded back to Edessa, hoping to hang on in that natural fortress. High in the hills above a towering waterfall framed against a backdrop of tree-covered cliffs, there at least he could pause and hope to hold his own while keeping a nervous eye out, even hoping that his enemy might have his hands full in incorporating lower Macedonia into his already extensive realm or be drawn away by action elsewhere. With a bit of luck he could even fall ill or die; not so unlikely for a man of his advanced age. However, any such dreams proved illusory as his problems became clear: that if he was at least temporarily safe in his eyrie, he was also bottled up and soon enough from his camp above a sparkling cataract falling over the precipice he saw a swarming army deploying below intent on his destruction. Well before Pyrrhus could receive much in the way of reinforcements from other parts of his dominion he found his rival in action, manoeuvring his troops with great skill. Lysimachus' main force was pushing down the road west from Pella, but the old king, who had the numbers, was not only approaching the defenders' camp by the direct route that was both dramatic and challenging, he was also able to send detachments to discover other ways around an occupied choke-point that he was reluctant to directly assail. These parties soon found other passes through the mountains and word reached Pyrrhus that his enemies were cutting off those men out collecting supplies and that his soldiers, with the squeeze put on, would soon be subject to serious want. More than this, a significant body of the enemy soon 'captured his supply columns', butchering the waggon-drivers and muleteers and threatening to cut his lines of communications. So in the camp it was hungry, unhappy and dispirited Macedonians whose officers received letters sent from Lysimachus or heard whispers that they were suffering in the cause of a man who was not only a foreigner but one whose people had once been Macedonian vassals. Efforts at subversion had worked, and Pyrrhus soon had to ask himself whether his Macedonians would fight for him at all and the answer that soon became clear was a resounding no.

Lysimachus' relations with the Epirot had never been as bad as that with Demetrius, but still the old man's unforgiving nature would have suggested that if he ever came into his power it might easily cost him his life. So despite the defensive strength of his starting position with numbers so decisively against him, finally he was left with little choice and even the Eagle king had to admit defeat. To ensure survival, he struck camp and moved west again to escape the enclosing enemy pincers. There was no formal engagement; he slipped away with just his Epirots and other allies leaving the field to an old man who had finally come into his own. The retreating army took a route back through the grass- and rock-covered hillsides of the upper cantons of Lyncestis and Orestis until they reached the border established after Cassander's son Alexander had alienated Macedon's most westerly provinces. Back where he had started when Demetrius had been the sitting monarch on the throne at Pella, showing that if Lysimachus lacked his rival's charisma, he was clearly ruthlessly efficient.

This is not the only version of how Lysimachus' last great imperial land grab played out. Others purport a struggle involving three of the big hitters of these years: that he fought out a campaign in Thessaly where Antigonus Gonatus had formed a strong and cohesive partnership with Pyrrhus and provided soldiers[12] to help out against a perceived threat to both of them. Also there is a differing account of the campaign fought in Macedonia between the incumbent and the invader: that initially sufficient Macedonians had stayed loyal, that ever belligerent Pyrrhus had offered battle in the open country around Pella and only withdrew to Edessa with the remnants of his army after he had been defeated. Whatever the precise details the upshot was incontrovertible, though hardly a foregone conclusion, that while the Epirot tide waned, that of Lysimachus waxed, as was made abundantly clear when his soldiers occupied all of upper Macedonia except for parts of Parauaea and Tymphaea. Not content with just claiming back much of the country that had been part of Greater Epirus since 295, in the following year the new king of all Macedonia showed he had no intention of leaving his rival to lick his wounds in peace. The year 284 saw Lysimachus' men passing in considerable numbers into Epirus itself. Pyrrhus was absent, distracted by ambitions to the north where he was making real headway gobbling up Illyrian territory, so the invaders not only had little trouble from the home army, allowing them to loot far and wide, but comprehensibly rubbed in their advantage when Thracian troops trashed the tombs of the Molossian kings. Yet the story that they 'destroyed the tombs and cast out the bones of the dead', deriving as it did from Hieronymus, has the definite stench of partiality, an example of this historian's prejudice, partly because of his bias in favour of Antigonus and Demetrius but also because he blamed Lysimachus for destroying his home town of Cardia when he founded Lysimachia. He intended to make sure that even if he won out in the struggle for Macedon, his impiety would run down the generations. Certainly the transcriber of these events[13] is himself not totally convinced, making the valid point that no Macedonian would have countenanced the destruction of the tombs of those who were ancestors of Alexander through his Epirot mother.

Pyrrhus had recognized what seemed the chance of a lifetime back in 288 when Demetrius' world fell apart, but now he found himself in the self-same predicament, but while his enemy's triumph may have given him bitter fruit for reflection, even amid the wreckage of his fortunes he remained formidable. He was far from being a lightweight and people knew it at the time. This was not just the golden glow of hindsight and his dashing reputation would soon be registering in a world to the west before he returned again to a very different Balkan cosmos over half a decade later. Not only did he retain a strong constituency among his own Molossians, but there always seemed to be some among both the elite and the rank and file in Macedon who thought his chariot worth hitching to. After all, rumours of his approach in the last decade had set the palace halls in Pella a-twitter, not always necessarily with alarm. So the administration at Lysimachia, worrying about what was happening in Pella, was never going to underestimate this mercurial king and even after their recent success was reluctant to risk the full-scale war that would result from any major invasion of Epirus. It was enough to enjoy the benefits of a massive raid while standing guard on their western boundary.

War elephant, Hermitage Museum.

The Tumulus Museum at Vergina.

Bust of Lysimachus, Naples
Archaeological Museum.

Bust of Demetrius Poliorcetes, Prado, Madrid.

Bust of the Odrysian king Seuthes III found
in his tomb and now at the historical museum
of Kazanlak.

Looking down the hill to the sea from where
the Munychia fort stood at Piraeus.

The harbour at Piraeus where trireme sheds have been found.

Speaking platform on Pnyx, Athens.

Looking at Acrocorinth from temple at Nemea.

Medieval fortifications atop Acrocorinth.

Bust of Pyrrhus, Naples Archaeological Museum.

Ancient fortifications at Ambracia built by Pyrrhus, modern-day Arta.

Modern statue of Pyrrhus at Arta.

The theatre at Dodona.

Ancient defences
at Messene in
the Peloponnese.

Looking down from the waterfall at Edessa.

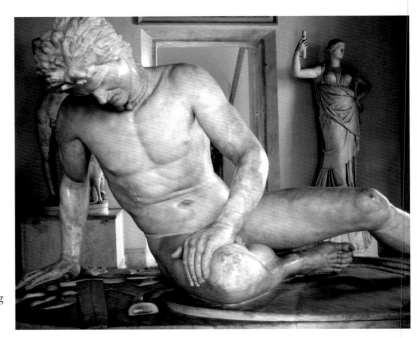

Sculpture of dying
Gaul, Capitoline
Museum, Rome.

Depiction of Hellenistic arms, Side Archaeological Museum.

The pass at Thermopylae.

Tetradrachm coin
with the face of
Antigonus Gonatus
horned like Pan.

Ancient
fortifications at
Nea Poteidaia
(Cassandreia).

Looking down on the
Eurotas River near
Sparta.

Chapter Six

A Passing Thunderbolt

Three successors had stood proud in the wake of Demetrius being caged up in the Syrian Chersonese and by the time of his actual death this circumstance seemed even more pronounced. While that other unmanageable man Pyrrhus had been boxed up back in Epirus, Ptolemy I was well ensconced in his Egyptian core and had expanded into Phoenicia and Coele-Syria while making sure of a Thalassocracy that covered almost all the Eastern Mediterranean and had long been muscling into the south Aegean. This farsighted dynast had also solved the succession problem by making his son by Berenice joint monarch as Ptolemy II. Seleucus also ruled a massive realm that distance had forced him to divide into two halves, declaring his son and heir Antiochus sub-king in the eastern satrapies. Still, despite the achievements of these two, a case can certainly be made that Lysimachus had done the best of all those who had fought over the empire Alexander had conquered. His territory now included Macedonia, Thessaly, Thrace and much of Anatolia, representing a large yet compact kingdom with an excellent tax base in the rich cities of the Aegean coasts of Asia, the Black Sea littoral and including the riches to be drawn from the extensive transit trade passing through the Hellespont and Propontis. He had great military resources too, not just from his Macedonians-in-arms but from the numerous warriors of Thrace, the Greek and non-Greek peoples of Anatolia, all available to be directly enrolled or hired as mercenaries. His navy might not have been quite up to that of the Lagids, particularly since the Phoenician cities and the squadrons they supported were now all under Ptolemy's control, yet he did have access to a maritime potential that might allow him in time to take on rivals such as Antigonus Gonatus or Seleucus.

This shrewd monarch also managed a trick that other rulers at Pella had found impossible: he stayed on excellent terms with the Aetolians, a people who named two towns after the king and his wife Arsinoe and indeed his reputation in the rest of central Greece was such that the Phocians felt so much confidence in his friendship that they drove an Antigonid garrison out of Elateia and his ties with the Athenians were strong since their dumping of Demetrius. However, this old king was not calling it a day just yet; what was left of a long life would be full of even more projects of expansion. Apart from ensuring against trouble in some problematic statelets in northern Anatolia and taking direct control of the important Black Sea port of Heraclea, he also had ambitions in Europe where forces of change were at work. Though high-toned hangers-on at court revelling in contacts with refined Athenians may not have been terribly interested in what was happening in semi-barbarous Paeonia, it was far from insignificant to their master, still driven by imperial imperatives. The country had long had associations with both Macedonia and Epirus, more powerful political entities situated along her southern border and Ariston, a leading cavalry commander in Alexander's conquering army was Paeonian royalty, while his son was the long-lived monarch Audoleon, himself a considerable figure in the north Balkan arena. He was not only Pyrrhus' father-in-law but had been recently noticed encouraging the Athenian attempt to reclaim Piraeus, though his dependence on Macedon had been highlighted back in 310 when he was required to go cap in hand to Cassander to bail him out when his territory was about to be overrun by the Illyrian Autariatae.[1] These people were dangerously on the move after suffering biblical plagues of frogs and mice until Cassander solved his neighbours' problem by settling all 20,000 of them near the mountain of Orbelus north of the Pangaion Hills.

In either 285 or 284 this Audoleon died, occasioning a succession crisis in which Lysimachus saw opportunity. The Paeonian king's son Ariston was at that moment in exile in Thrace, driven out by an opposition faction, and when he heard news of his father's death the ousted prince, gazing around for assistance, made a fatal miscalculation. He found Lysimachus willing and able to stump up the troops required to instate him but though he threw his decisive weight behind this contender, finally this prince's patron proved that where he could assist, he could also threaten. When Ariston returned in state to his father's kingdom Lysimachus accompanied him, apparently eager to supervise as the heir underwent the traditional coronation bath in the Arisbus River and to ensure the accession was celebrated by an appropriately sumptuous banquet. However, during these coronation revels Ariston was warned that his sponsor was contemplating treachery and had prepared armed guards to arrest him and, finding this kind of behaviour only too believable from a man with Lysimachus' ruthless reputation, he jumped on the first horse he could find and fled over the border north-west to exile in the territory of the Dardani.[2] Whether he really took control so soon after he had hoisted Ariston onto the throne is not clear. It may be it was the result of a contraction of time imposed by our informants with events really occurring after the prince, who was intended as a tractable puppet, started to appear inconveniently non-compliant. Yet it is also said[3] that the lure of a royal treasure trove was part of the old king's motivation when one of Audoleon's long-standing advisors revealed its situation hidden beneath the bed of the River Sargentius. What is certain is that by the time of the conclusion of Lysimachus' reign, Paeonia was part of European holdings that stretched from Macedonia, across Thrace to the Black Sea and Hellespont, south through Thessaly and included some north Aegean islands.

Yet this old king who had shown himself such a terrible neighbour to both Pyrrhus and Ariston was not destined to enjoy his pre-eminence for long. 'The harder they come the harder they fall' was something all too true in his case. Yet it would not be outside rivals or internal enemies that would be at the root of his difficulties, it would be two things that were almost impossible to guard against: the passage of time and his own personality. Not inappropriately, it was a product of a dysfunctional family who was the major actor in the events that were going to be central to the future of Macedonian Europe as another decade faded out. Around 319 a son had been born to Eurydice, daughter of Antipater and wife of Ptolemy I, the Lagid ruler of Egypt. This man, also christened Ptolemy, emerged in a short career as one of the era's most dangerous characters and the shocking crimes laid at his door ensured that times were never calm in the places he came to settle. His father had not long remained content with just one spouse and soon took a fancy to one of Eurydice's ladies-in-waiting called Berenice. She was the daughter of a Macedonian princess named Antigone and after her first husband had died, this high-born widow had joined the household of the queen of Egypt. Polygamy was not at all unusual for these Macedonian warlords, so when the king married her in 317, relations in the seraglio remained smooth enough until well into the new century. Then we know Eurydice and her daughter left Alexandria and had arrived in Miletus by 287 at the latest when Demetris, passing on his way to invade Asia, paused to marry the younger woman. During this period with King Ptolemy I flaunting his preference for Berenice's progeny, Ptolemy lost his position of pre-eminence at the court of his father who by 282 had made his eldest son by his second wife co-ruler. Already long cut out of the running, the firstborn was bound to have potential as a focus for political opposition so it is no surprise to find him turning up in exile at the court of Seleucus, but this was but a staging post. Finding little in the way of opportunity at the court of the king of Asia, who perhaps perceived something of the iniquity of the man and at most saw him as a useful counter in his diplomatic game with Alexandria and not somebody to invest much in the way of resources, he packed his bags and made his way to Lysimachia, hoping pickings might be better there.

No royal court was ever lacking in internal divisions, but now events conspired to push huge wedges between the contending parties at Lysimachus' headquarters. While ensconced with his new host Ptolemy discovered family affairs becoming increasingly toxic as the king had by this time also found a new spouse, having around 300 married Arsinoe, another daughter of Ptolemy I of Egypt and one of the extraordinary characters of the age. She had been about 15 and he was already near 60, but this infusion of young blood had not apparently upset the household for almost twenty years until the inevitable occurred when the younger wife's children approached the age of majority only to find that the heir to the throne, their mature, experienced, capable and popular half-brother, looked set to block any chances they might have of succeeding a declining father. However this might be dressed up, few were under any illusion that the issue of succession could be extremely complicated, with the court likely to prove too small to accommodate the ambitions of all concerned. Later it was alleged that political tremors had started to build not long after a destructive earthquake, a portent of disaster that struck Lysimachia in 287, but if all this was not sufficient to ensure turbulent times ahead, gossip gave it out that Arsinoe, tired of the old king, made sexual advances to this same heir Agathocles and it was his rejection of her that motivated her policy. However, the bursting of this salacious scandal to dramatically seal Agathocles' doom is not required to explain what is, after all, an even more hoary topos than the vindictive malice of a frustrated woman, that of a mother prepared to risk all to win the great prize for her child. Anyway, with motive enough Arsinoe managed to convince her husband that his eldest son and the prop of his throne was really an ingrate, a traitor, who tired of waiting for nature to take its course, was plotting to remove his father and seize the throne for himself. In these intrigues Arsinoe found a willing assistant in her own half-brother, the reckless and cynical Ptolemy, who was happy to execute the design against a man from whom, despite Agathocles being married to his own full sister, he expected little once he had succeeded to the throne of his father.

How the filicide was accomplished is not certain, but one lurid account has it that in 283 the paranoid old king, wracked by his destructive obsession, tried to poison 'the oldest and best of his sons',[4] but initially failed because on tasting the tainted offering, he spat it out. The reprieve was only temporary, as claiming he was plotting against him, Lysimachus had Agathocles flung into prison where Ptolemy, his fingerprints over the whole intrigue, 'slew him with his own hand, an act that won for himself the name of Ceraunus, the thunderbolt'. In the early days of the Diadochi Wars Antipater had distributed his daughters like confetti to the great men of the age and now one grandson, the offspring of Eurydice, wife of Ptolemy, had slaughtered another grandson by another daughter Nicaea who had been married to Lysimachus. There are certainly contradictory opinions on old Lysimachus: he is either a classic tyrant, hands dripping with the blood of his child, or a feeble ancient putty in the hands of his young wife, all coming from a range of primary sources from Hieronymus to Duris of Samos and various historians from Pontic Heraclea. Because of partiality here, we cannot be sure how much is credible, although we can certainly surmise that the bloody murder was followed by a purge of those who stood close to the assassinated man. Agathocles had been a real force in the realm with plenty of clients and supporters in important posts and it is likely there was an attempt to neutralize this group by a king now desperate to smooth the path for his new heirs. Circumstances that made it hardly a surprise that many felt at risk and this in a state where anyway, if many reports are believed, most in the Greek cities regarded Lysimachus as an unforgiving and oppressive tyrant. The terrible act soon turned out to be a catalyst for the beginning of a real political unravelling and the question must be why he risked everything by this precipitate and hazardous disposal? Surely his age must be the key: that at nearly 80 years of age, only immediate and drastic action would solve the succession problem to his satisfaction. It is clear that by 283 he no longer intended Agathocles as his heir; there would certainly be no dual kingship here as with the Seleucids and the Ptolemies despite his son being a popular, able general and administrator who had shown his worth over more than two decades. Perhaps this was part of the reason. In decline, Lysimachus was overcome with a lethal cocktail of jealousy and resentment against a man that he realized so many saw as the future and who represented a brighter and more popular prospect than any he could offer. This and that his eldest son in unfettered power would almost inevitably represent a threat to the young family he fathered by Arsinoe meant that Agathocles had to go and from that certitude, settled upon some time in 283, all else followed.

A cavalcade of discontent led by Lysandra, Agathocles' wife, was soon appearing over the Taurus Mountains asking for refuge at the court of Seleucus. Most significantly Alexander, another son of Lysimachus by an Odrysian spouse, took the same road, worried that he too might be marked down for an identical fate to his half-brother. This fragility in the ruling elite of such a proximate and wealthy neighbour could not help but entice the still ambitious ruler at Antioch. Here was an enterprise indeed, to finally reassemble the whole of Alexander's empire outside of Africa. We do not know whether Seleucus had already been meddling in his neighbours' business waiting for his opportunity, but when it came knocking he was not about to spurn it. As the exiles poured reassuring words in his ear about the weakness of Lysimachus' administration, the Seleucid military was mobilized, settler soldiers from Syria, elephants from their permanent stables at Apamea and a myriad of auxiliaries from the wide lands under the great king's control. Late 282 saw Seleucid armies swinging into action, moving west through Cilicia and into the heart of Anatolia with agents going ahead sowing dissention in a population already disturbed by the deep fissures showing among their rulers. Alexander, son of Lysimachus, headed one of the columns of soldiers in the hope that his credibility with those who had been attached to Agathocles would be greater than that of some outside invader. Certainly something made a difference as we know plenty of towns opened their gates, including Pergamon where Philetaerus, the later founder of the Attalid dynasty, defected to the Seleucid cause with a treasury of 9,000 talents and the keys to one of the most important strongholds in western Anatolia. Lysimachus soon awoke to the fact that this threat was not just alarmist exaggeration on the part of his most nervous councillors and with so much of his kingdom seeming on the point of slipping away, he steeled his nerves and, like another ruler two decades earlier, opted to confront an implacable opponent, to risk all on the lottery of battle.

The period of the first generation of successors had been fabulous and extraordinary with sources for some events being detailed and accurate, but unfortunately regarding the denouement that transpired in February 281 on the wide plains of Corupedion there are hardly any reliable details, only a plethora of improbable stories around this final bout in the struggles of the original Diadochi. Inland of modern Izmir and not far from Magnesia by Sipylos, where ninety years later Rome would burst bomb-like into the Asian world, the king of Thrace determined on his last throw of the dice. Presumably taking as few chances as he could, mobilizing all the soldiers available and calling on his allies and auxiliaries, was to no avail as heading west the invading Seleucid hosts were brilliantly coordinated and after joining battle their success ensured that Lysimachus' broken old body, despoiled of its finery, was found among so many others on the field of blood; their extravagant pretensions ended in dust. He had been sent tumbling from his horse when a soldier from Pontic Heraclea called Malacon struck him with a lucky throw of his spear while only a faithful dog guarded the body against the ravages of carrion birds. This is surely far more probable than the tradition that has him dying in a personal duel with Seleucus, a desperate brawl between old men that is far too elegant a conclusion to be credited. It was even touch and go as to whether the royal corpse of the penultimate Diadochi would end up mutilated by the vengeful wife of Agathocles before his less vindictive son Alexander forestalled the desecration and ensured his father got some sort of burial.[5]

If the last but one of Alexander's companions was dead, another man came through the bloody contest intact. Ptolemy Ceraunus was among the prisoners rounded up by Seleucus' victorious warriors as Lysimachus' army crumbled and the men laid down their arms in anticipation of switching to the Seleucid military roster or tried to save themselves by flight. In double-quick time, this chancer wheedled himself into his captor's good books. Seleucus was in a forgiving mood anyway; for him there was no better place to be the last of the first successors of Alexander standing with no real focus of opposition after the death of his rival to worry him. After all, his dead antagonist's adult offspring were already committed to his cause and Arsenio's brood were children, so in the happy atmosphere of a triumphal parade Ptolemy Ceraunus, who Seleucus had briefly known before, could make himself agreeable, suggesting to his new sponsor that he could be a useful chip in his ongoing poker game with the rival administration at Alexandria. So Ptolemy Ceraunus was there in the winter of 281–80. 'He was not despised like a prisoner, but given the honour and consideration due to the son of a king.... However, though he was honoured with so much attention, these favours failed to improve the disposition of an evil man.'6 Taking in the spectacle in a great sweep as long lines of armoured men accompanied by the sounds of animals, either meat on the hoof or carrying packs in the army's trains, sumpter traders and other camp followers prepared to embark for a short trip across the Hellespont. After hours and hours of ferrying there would have been elephants noticed in the cavalcade that Seleucus was leading over the narrow straits; after all, they advertised power like nothing else in the post-Alexander world of ostentatious monarchs. At the head came the old king himself, the last of a breed with his bull's horn and anchor insignia showing on the banners of those close companions, councillors and administrators surging after him, leading Asia into Europe, though none taking part or gawping from a roadside could have conceived that this glorious cavalcade would finally be the reagent for an apocalypse. This army he had concentrated was not anticipating opposition. There had been no reports of any Lysimachid stalwart busying up a defence to block the Hellespont or raise Thrace and Macedonia against what the invaders considered spear-won land, earned by the spectacular victory at Corupedium. Soon the road that led past the modern-day Dardanelles was crowded with warriors and their beasts kicking up great clouds of dust as they marched towards Lysimachus' old capital.

Now an utterly unscrupulous man took his opportunity. He might be short of a power base in a foreign land but he was not short on daring, and being an exiled son of the ruler of Egypt must have given him some cachet. Devious and dangerous, this man who was probably the murderer of Agathocles determined on another bloody coup in a world where almost anything seemed up for grabs. So he jumped at the chance when Seleucus decided to cross over to Europe. A ruler in a sedentary court would be surrounded by impenetrable security, but on the road there might be openings. Why Seleucus was so solicitous to this man whose unsavoury reputation he must have known is a mystery. He perhaps had considerable personal charm and this ensured he was beside the last first-generation Diadochi when he decided to indulge in some sightseeing as rest and relaxation. Near Lysimachia there was 'a splendid great altar' that locals called Argos because the claim was it had been built by Jason and his Argonauts as they sailed to Colchis to find the Golden Fleece, though there was another story that it was constructed by the Achaeans on the way to or coming back from assaulting Troy and named from the home town of the sons of Atreus.[7] Seleucus had had his warnings. Years before the great oracle at Didyma in the Asian Aegean had declared 'Do not hurry back to Europe; Asia will be much better for you', and another even more specific portent had told him to stay clear of Argos. There was nothing too cryptic here and whatever questions had been put to the fortune-tellers, the sense should have made the old conqueror call a halt at the Hellespont. However, if his advisors were alarmed over the implications, either Seleucus did not make the connection or did not share the alarm of these soothsayers, so this blithe monarch-turned-tourist hurried surrounded by friends and courtiers to see the local attractions and if in the ranks of his companions he recognized Ptolemy his presence raised no concerns. Some time during the day Seleucus' bodyguards were distracted or had been subverted and with the ruler of the world vulnerable, Ptolemy, playing for the highest stakes, acted. Having armed himself beforehand, he cut his over-trusting host down in cold blood. It had not been difficult to deal with a man enfeebled by many years, but the limit of the conspiracy did not terminate with the bloody corpse spread-eagled on the ground; the assassin wanted what his victim had had and in concluding that by beheading the administration of the greatest power in the world he would leave his followers bereaved and alarmed, he was right.

In late summer 281 the thunderbolt had struck and now he intended to reap the rewards. He had had a horse ready and, leaping aboard, galloped at full tilt towards Lysimachia. Once there, after finding a diadem to wear and surrounded by supporters and a 'splendid bodyguard', he met the army in assembly. They were like a deer in a car's headlights. There was no plan of what to do after such an occurrence; there was an heir but he was thousands of miles away and there was no deputy present in the army or among the courtiers caught cold on the road to Pella. Ambitious men in both the officers' quarters or the regimental tents might have indulged in heated talk, but nobody had a formula except the murderer. So the eyes of many who just wanted to be told what to do inevitably turned to him; the grim reality was that he seemed to be the only person who was offering any alternative to complete disorder. Accepted with no record of any reluctance, this again, like the fact that no one seems to have attempted to arrest him after the murder, suggests he had been hard at work subverting important officers before he took such decisive action. There had to be an audience for such talk, ambitious people again worried by the imperative of time passing and conscious that well into his 70s, Seleucus could not remain at the helm much longer. Soldiers, many of whom had come north with Seleucus and others who had joined from Lysimachus after his defeat, accepted the new king as a fait accompli. He had qualities that appealed, despite the universal verdict of him being treacherous and murderous; that he was decisive no one could deny and this may have been enough for many with really no other candidate near to hand.

In a few bare months so much had happened; the demise of Seleucus at the age of at least 73 after a reign of forty-two years had seen an epoch of ancient marshals contending for Alexander's diadem ending in an extraordinary sequence of events, from the thunderous heroics at the Battle of Corupedium to a seedy murder conducted during a daytime sightseeing excursion. An implosion of familial relationships had destroyed the Macedonian state contrived by Philip and sustained by Antipater and his son Cassander and now another poisoned polity had been thrown into chaos and foundered. In the Europe that had emerged out of the blood-soaked world of Alexander's successors, perhaps appropriately the man who climbed into the saddle in the aftermath was the gory man who had wielded the sword that ended the life of Seleucus I Nicator. If most of the dead ruler's Asian lands would fall smoothly into the hands of his son Antiochus west of the Hellespont there was a vacuum, but could Ptolemy Ceraunus fill it?

Clearly he had discovered enough of a constituency in the royal army camped on the Chersonese as they swiftly acclaimed him their king; particularly he had been able to count on troops from Lysimachus' army who had joined Seleucus after Corupedium, who saw his act as revenge for the death of their old chief, while he guaranteed complicity from some others of the chief men by the simple expedient of allowing them to plunder Seleucus' treasury. Not that all concerned were quite so egregiously venal: decency and propriety could be found as was discovered when Philetaerus of Pergamon handed over good money to procure Seleucus' corpse so as to render him the proper rites before sending his ashes to Antiochus in Seleucia by the sea, where a temple named the Nicatoreum was built to house them. What is clear is that this prince from Egypt must have had a silver tongue to both insinuate himself into a place where he could murder Seleucus and garner sufficient support to replace him at the army's head. No doubt many surrounding the just acclaimed king thought the chalice that Ptolemy had grabbed so energetically was pretty poisonous, as potential rivals and enemies abounded. A world of striving contenders was in situ, from Pyrrhus still a power in Greater Epirus, Arsenio and Lysimachus' sons holed up in Cassandreia and kin of Cassander still around as well.

While these vicissitudes of fortune were playing out at the hinge of Europe and Asia, most immediately someone else was sweeping open horizons with acquisitive eyes. Antigonus Gonatus had registered the news from the north with real interest. If he was a considerable downgrade from his forebear in terms of glamour and ambition, he had still proved capable enough in the years since his errant father had left him in charge of the family's interests. His kingdom by the sea on the map looked an unimpressive patchwork, but from the start he showed he was of a new generation, a new strain of ruler who valued stability over adventure, consistent fidelity over extravagant talent and his realm had enjoyed a considerable period of administrative continuity where loyalties had been fostered and interests reinforced. Now from many parts of Macedonian Europe where the very opposite of these qualities were prevalent, this must have looked increasingly impressive, so if the realm Ceraunus was claiming was a chaotic mess, a nest of competing interest where nothing approaching persistent stability had been on offer for years, many must have looked south and noted the contrast. Particularly in Epirus Pyrrhus, who while he had played an expanding hand for over a decade, now had his eyes fixed steadily west towards Italy and was not inclined to be delayed by any number of opportunities elsewhere. A key question for the strategists in Antigonus' camp was to what extent Ceraunus had been able to establish himself in Macedonia since his bloody intervention at Lysimachia. In the weeks since the demise of Seleucus there was much conjecture as to whether this interloper would have had time to find many powerful adherents. How many of the great men of Macedonia would have scurried to adhere to the new incumbent? Surely not such a large number. Many were bound to be disturbed by the reputation of this murderous prince whose life since leaving his father's court had seemed to consist of one outrage after another.

The resource Antigonus disposed of might not have looked so impressive when weighed against peers like Ptolemy II or Antiochus I, yet even so he controlled thousands of experienced mercenaries garrisoning many of the great fortresses in Greece and could field a marine of substantial size and quality. It was not quite the navy that Demetrius had led over to Asia in his last adventure, but it was considerably more than a mere rump. Antigonus' father is recorded building a huge fleet of 500 ships to attack his hated rival Lysimachus and shipwrights had surpassed themselves by constructing fifteens or sixteens, warships that even outshone the Sea King's earlier efforts at gigantism. Whether there had been exaggeration or not and plenty of the giant armada were probably transports required for the huge army of invasion he was mobilizing, a considerable navy had been created, much of which would have remained available for the son of its architect. Nor was it just mint new vessels; there were plenty of veteran warships that had been in his service for years. After all, when Demetrius had visited Seleucus in 299 his flagship is noted as having thirteen banks of oars. The evidence we have suggests that the warships of this period were serviceable for at least twenty years if not longer, so it is possible some of the ships that had fought in the triumph at Salamis in 306 might have still been available.

However, only a proportion of the armament Demetrius had taken across the Aegean had returned. The warships had been left first in the great harbour of Miletus when he had struck inland, waiting there for their commander's return. As the months went by officers and crews would have been bound to have considered their options, particularly when the place eventually opened its gates to Agathocles on his way to driving Demetrius inland into Seleucus' unwelcoming arms. The question was how would the great adventurer's matelots respond? They had been loyal for decades and bonds were not easily broken as most of the war fleet slipped its moorings and sailed south to Kaunos, leaving just a few to stay put and take service with the greatest power in Anatolia.

Still the great majority awaited the arrival of the man they had followed so long, and only when definite news arrived that he had been ensnared by Seleucus' hunters while trying to make his way back to them did tough choices finally have to be made. Many again stayed loyal to the dynasty, setting sail to return to Gonatus waiting anxiously in Demetrias to discover what he might recover from the wreck of his father's fortunes, but for others there was another offer on the table. Philocles, prince of Sidon, the commander of the Phoenician squadrons whose homeland produced some of the best fighting galleys, received an irresistible proposition from the court at Alexandria. So swiftly turning his coat, he secured the port of Kaunos in Egyptian interests and took the vessels raised from Tyre and the other Phoenician port cities over to Ptolemy. So Antigonus would have seen with disappointment that key components had not returned to him; those vastly experienced and expert squadrons that had made the Persian and later the marine of the Antigonid kings so formidable had jumped in a different direction. Such a step would advance the career of the man who led them even more than he could have hoped. The fruits of Philocles' betrayal included becoming the Lagid commander over the league of Aegean islands that was in the process of being appropriated from the crumbling Antigonid realm.

Numbers are unknown, but it is difficult to believe that many more than half of Demetrius' ships returned to his son, but still sufficient to give him confidence in dealing with most local maritime rivals. Antigonus was not the natural risk-taker his father had been, so we may assume this more modest ruler would have had very good reason to think that if he acted swiftly to intervene in Macedon, any opposition might be inconsiderable. He would have heard that Ptolemy Ceraunus was at Lysimachia trying to win over the key players in the army and at court, though to judge his success at such a distance would have been difficult; he almost certainly expected the murderer of Seleucus to have trouble in winning sufficient adherents to his side. After all, the soldiers in the murdered man's army would surely be reluctant to take orders from the butcher of their old commander, even if there was no obvious alternative to hand. Even if Ceraunus was blessed with charisma and people skills in abundance before these events, he had hardly been a major figure in the power firmament; indeed, not long before he had been languishing as a prisoner of war. Antigonus could have reasonably expected he would have trouble enough gaining the necessary influence in the army to make a sustained effort for the crown, never mind being able to immediately appropriate and deploy the military and naval resources of the Macedonian kingdom as warships in particular never came cheap. The fruits of his reflection would be war, but in assuming a naval superiority Antigonus, it turned out, would be wrong and in the time it took for him to organize his own fleet and embark his troops his opponent was not only able to persuade Lysimachus' old naval establishment over to his side, but he had been reinforced by a substantial fleet from Pontic Heraclea.

We know from a local historian[8] that Dionysius the Good, the ruler of this city on the south shore of the Pontic sea, prospered when a passing Alexander the Great dented Persian power in the region. Not that the conqueror's impact was all advantage, as once he had become the dominant power in the region some exiled democrats looked like they might persuade him to remove the tyrant until Dionysius enrolled the king's sister Cleopatra on his side. Later Perdiccas also looked for a while like he might sponsor the émigrés, but he had far too much else on his plate so 'Dionysius enjoyed prosperity in all his undertakings'.[9] A golden age was enshrined when he wed Amastris, who had not only been married to the great Craterus before an amicable separation but was a niece of Darius III and cousin of Stateira, one of Alexander's wives. This kind of connection and the dowries they brought placed the city on the world stage and its ruler ensured it stayed there by befriending Antigonus the One-Eyed and marrying one of his daughters to his nephew Ptolemaeus, even taking the diadem of royalty after a reign of thirty years before leaving Amastris as regent for his three children. Some time before the Battle of Ipsus, the Heraclean chancery changed diplomatic tack, offering support to the anti-Antigonid coalition and arranging for the regent to marry Lysimachus. Success in that combat ensured that the city was something less of a priority for the king of Thrace, and his new queen 'took control, she revived the place by her presence, and created the new city of Amastris'. Meanwhile, Dionysius' sons kept well in with their stepfather. For a time both stood high in royal favour, lavished with honours and confirmed in prominent military posts, with Clearchus, the eldest, even suffering capture alongside his stepfather after defeat by the Getae. This close relationship remained until this loyal vassal with his brother fell out with their mother. Rumour had it that they arranged for her to be shipwrecked and drowned 'by a terrible and evil device', prefiguring a similar but unsuccessful attempted matricide by the Emperor Nero by 350 years.

Unfortunately for this fraternal duo, the fate of his ex-wife had refocused Lysimachus' attention and now ensconced as king of Macedon there was no gainsaying his diktat. He apparently even visited the city and personally ordered the death of the brothers before taking direct control, establishing a man called Heracleides of Cyme who took charge on behalf of his queen Arsinoe in the years leading up to the implosion of the Lysimachid state. So Lysimachus had long been a dominant presence in this part of the world through marriage into the ruling family or direct control, and it is no surprise that there was some residual affection for the man and that in these circumstances Ptolemy Ceraunus, being perceived as his avenger after he bloodily disposed of Seleucus, found himself heir to considerable goodwill. Beyond that, the strategists in control at Pontic Heraclea, knowing that the greatest threat to their new-found independence was from Seleucus' heir Antiochus, recognized Ptolemy Ceraunus as a natural ally and counterweight to this threat, motives enough to make them content to fight in tandem with the putative king of Macedon.

This city had long been a crucial conduit for Black Sea trade on the north Anatolian coast and a significant naval power, so was easily able to dispatch a squadron to the Aegean to support Ceraunus. The fleet included as flagship an eighter 'of extraordinary size and beauty' that was named 'the lion-bearer' and the contention is that it was manned by a total of 1,600 oarsmen with two steersmen while 1,200 soldiers filled the decks. This is difficult to credit as it would mean there would be 100 rowing sections along the hull, more than three times as many as was usual for a trireme, and is contrary to the evidence that these larger vessels, if much broader, were not much longer than the smaller ships. Whatever the truth, it showed that they could deploy a real maritime giant as well as a significant number of sixers, fivers and transports that added their weight to the Macedonian navy. Indeed, they came in sufficient strength that Ceraunus, from the very brink of catastrophe, now found himself in command of a fleet of such potency that he was prepared to risk confronting the expeditionary force that he learned Antigonus Gonatus was leading against him.

Great sea battles were rare enough in the east Mediterranean in the Hellenistic period. The celebrated victory at Cypriot Salamis had set the tone for a generation and only with the fragmentation of the Antigonid marine, after Demetrius' defeat and capture in 285, did the Egyptians complete a sea-power comeback in the region. Now the potential effects of the coming contest could have been almost as climactic with either the prospect of Antigonid ambition coming to a shuddering halt or in the case of victory Demetrius' son being well-positioned to contest for his father's old throne of Macedon, where once ensconced he would be able to combine that country's naval potential with his own already considerable maritime resources. A victory at sea was the prerequisite against a man who was always a gambler and who, while considering the odds around the cooking fires of his men encamped with their beached warships, had no idea of doing anything but challenging his rival head-on. Antigonus' fleet, well-equipped from the arsenals at Corinth, Demetrias and Chalcis, had approached past the north shore of Euboea, funnelling through the bottleneck between the mainland and the island of Skiathos rising out of the sea, north along the coast of Magnesia, with Mount Olympus showing above the coastal plain on the left, his warships entered the Thermaic Gulf aiming to appear off the coast of Macedonia before the enemy could respond. Yet there would be no welcome as he appeared in these tranquil waters; the incumbent intent on defending his new-won realm was sailing to take up the challenge, so as the prow of Antigonus' flagship cleaved the waves, it was battle he was driving towards, not a hospitable homecoming.

When intelligence initially arrived that Antigonus was preparing to move, Ptolemy Ceraunus would have considered that the timing could hardly have been less convenient, but with the arrival of the ships from Pontic Heraclea everything had changed and now he considered himself handily placed to not just face the danger but just perhaps wreak havoc among the intruder's fleet. His captains, after debating stratagems between themselves in council as they waited, acted when scout cutters or the distant pinnacle of a fire beacon warned of the enemy's approach. Knowing now where they were heading, they launched their beached vessels into the sand and pebbly shallows to ready themselves for battle. Soon the enemy hove in view, stretching ahead their line of warships struggling to get in proper position to not foul their neighbours or get in each other's way. Veiled in spray, various contingents breasted the shoreline gliding to their stations; neither side would have been far from the land and both had a wing hugging the coast to ensure they could not be outflanked on that side. It was somewhere in the Thermaic Gulf that in the spring of 280 the two fleets clashed in a moment of truth: a panorama where warships, sleek galleys and high-sided fours and fives and more were sashaying into position, massing out in the open sea, and a great contest between some of the largest vessels of the age was in the offing.

It took a little time after the initial alarm and anxiety for the lines to properly deploy and make contact as the arching oars rose and dipped with water droplets caught sparkling in the sun and hammer blows prepared against the advancing opposition. Gaudy craft with decorated figureheads showed in awful advantage towards the vessels approaching them and, gazing across to the lines of these enemy craft, Antigonus Gonatus may, as he paced the deck of his flagship, have had some inkling of the trouble he was in. He had no great experience of naval combat and far from being the most inspirational war leader, he depended on his veteran naval officers and from the start it looked like they might have failed him. He was suckered into a deadly confrontation, a contest in the warm blue waters of the Aegean that were black with ships of his enemy, naval squadrons manned by Macedonian and Heraclean seamen who looked the equal or more of the crews manning his own craft, matching them when it came to manoeuvring at ramming speed and equally adept at grappling and boarding their high-sided opponents.

When soon enough the lines had engaged, the boldest captains would have been seen darting ahead of the line while their more jittery comrades held their places bobbing on the sparkling water; slim, ram-headed triremes escorting fully-decked cataphracts, ponderous ancient dreadnoughts, all came on as war songs and the cheers of the crews filled the air. With bronze-clad beaks pushing forward, there was no option but to fight. The classic tactics in such naval warfare were either periplus or diekplous, to run in between the enemy ships before turning to ram them in flank or rear, or to turn the flank of the line, going around to again attack the side and ends of the enemy vessels. The usual response to the periplus was to have a second line that could counter enemies thrusting between the ships of the front line, but this of course meant that the formation itself would be curtailed and so more susceptible to the diekplous. Combat became general with confusion and terror the order of the day as light but deadly craft sped across the open water bearing down on each other with hands clammy, nerves taut and stomachs lurching in the final moments of wild uproar or silent prayer before contact, when bronze rams sheared off enemy oars or shattered planking to let the seawater rush in as galleys locked together in a fragmenting of timbers.

Rowers' aching muscles flexed as they quickened their oar strokes in the stinking bowels of creaking leviathans, suffering in sweltering heat that reeked of the sweat exuded by hundreds of men, not to mention the stench of those whose bowels and bladders had been loosened by the terror of combat. On their cushioned benches cut off from the sights around, with the water lapping inches away it would have been a nervous time, listening for any noises that might tell them what was happening above them on the decks. Officers' orders would have given some indication and the men by the planking might just see something, while for others it was just the tunnel vision of sweating backs and wood-framed benches reaching in front along the line of the hulls they were propelling, all to the music of drums thumping and war chants voiced by the more ferocious matching those of the marines on deck who were gripping their shields, javelins, bows and swords in preparation for crunching contact. After brutal bond was made, the crews and marines stampeded down the deck, stumbling over the hand rails to reach the enemy, hacking at the limbs of the men opposing them or finding themselves pitched back overboard.

Losses were considerable on both sides with desperate fighting the order of the day as captains and squadron commanders tried to keep control, but it would have been almost impossible in the heat of battle where glamorous deeds of heroism were particularly celebrated among the fighters manning the great Heraclean flagship 'the lion-bearer', a high-sided eighter with its hundreds of marines shooting arrows, throwing javelins from her decks and aiming catapults at any enemy that came in range. We do not know how long the Antigonids maintained themselves, with officers and men shouting encouragement across the roiling waters, but in the face of the numbers their rivals threw against them, vessels with timbers creaking were gradually driven back by macerating force until formations began to dissolve with the vulnerable rammed and the rest no longer able to hold. Captains in one part of the line did not have a view of the whole milling prospect, so it was not possible to reinforce where the ranks were fractured and no directing hand was able to stem the inevitable outcome. The only consolation for Antigonus, seeing his fleet crumble into chaos around him, was that it was not a complete disaster as after hours of bloodletting even his enemy's aggression gradually petered out with both sides bone-weary and the water, illuminated by burning wrecks, was filled with bobbing corpses and debris, while a few wounded clung on to any spars they could find, desperate for help from victorious crews intent on gathering prizes from a dreadful contest.

The reason for Ptolemy Ceraunus' success is not made clear, though he may have caught the Antigonids unprepared. Comprehensively ensnared, they would have still had their masts and rigging raised when they found the great line of enemy vessels filling the horizon, while Ptolemy's craft had been able to ship these impediments, leaving spars and sails beached under guard, ensuring their warships were considerably more manoeuvrable than their alarmed and frantic prey. There was a downside as the presence of masts and sails would have given the Antigonids the advantage when, after recognizing defeat, they made a dash for safety. Antigonus had lost the fight and lost it comprehensively, but despite his vexation at the failure of his plans, he cosseted and encouraged the survivors as they regrouped out of danger of pursuit; it would not have been politic to vent any resentment against followers who were his only shield against a dangerous and rampant enemy. There are no precise numbers for the lost or disabled in this fleet that made its escape bid through the billows of a darkening gulf, but if battered and scarred it remained a fighting force and we know that a considerable number evaded the chasing pack. Once there were no more sightings of pursuing vessels, the battle-scarred remnants limped away to the shipyards at Demetrias, Chalcis and Piraeus where gangs of expert craftsmen put in the hours to repair and overhaul them, sufficient indeed for Antigonus to be able to deploy a substantial naval presence in only a few years' time.

Antigonus' intervention had turned out a fatal miscalculation, though perhaps even in hindsight hardly surprising considering how chaotic was the power balance at the time. Having been taught a lesson concerning overreach, the defeated party now withdrew to Boeotia[10] to lick their wounds and try to keep a lid on the boiling discontent in Greece that would be bound to arise after such a rebuff to their putative hegemon, while Ptolemy Ceraunus considered how best to exploit his success. In truth he had defeated what had been a real existential threat and could celebrate against a backdrop of flickering night-time fires where his soldiers and sailors were spitting animal carcasses on impromptu grills or building funeral pyres for their comrades alongside their beached ships. Yet the fuming effects of victory party wine did not affect what had been his intention from the start. His had been a defensive strategy and nothing had changed; what was required was to move might and main to secure control of Macedonia itself. There were, after all, plenty of others around with claims who might cramp his style: a nephew of Cassander who would have his fifteen minutes of fame soon enough, and the rump of Lysimachus' family including a son of Agathocles and even a name from way back, one Arrhidaeus who may have been the offspring of Alexander the Great's brother and his queen Eurydice who reigned briefly until disposed of by Olympias in 317.

Where these potential rivals were based or the magnitude of their support is not reported and there is no suggestion that they were able to put up any resistance when Ptolemy marched into Pella to inherit an administration that had so recently functioned at the behest of Lysimachus. He might claim the role of that king's avenger when he entered the capital but there remained a major problem: this was Arsinoe, his half-sister ensconced in Cassandreia with her sons, looking to many people as the only contenders with a rightful claim. Hearing of her presence, Ceraunus knew he needed to act quickly before his recently-won support began to erode away in her direction. This queen, experiencing the bitter fruit of her own sowing, had apparently escaped from the debacle of her husband's last war disguised as a beggar and reached her city of Ephesus, designated for her upkeep years before. Feeling the pressure of Seleucus' officers as they took control in spear-won Anatolia, she had taken ship to Macedonia, finding refuge in Cassandreia, a place that stood at the top of the most western of the three legs of the peninsula of Chalcidice.

Cassander's foundation had long been home of a cult to Lysimachus and once established there, the widowed queen looked to many like the real representative of the rightful line. Ceraunus could not help but know that many of high and low rank, despite having accepted him as their ruler, would still feel the draw of her young family, innocents freighting a legitimacy that made that won by the man whose only claim to their loyalty was that he had butchered Seleucus look poor and paltry. So from the beginning he was left with the conundrum of his half-sister.

There is no doubt about the reputation this man had acquired and the next episode only confirms earlier impressions: 'Having thus freed himself from the fear of foreign enemies, he turned his impious and unprincipled mind to the perpetration of wickedness.'[11] To try to assail Cassandreia would inevitably pollute the start of his reign; attacking other Macedonian royalty just would not look good in what was anyway a very difficult location to overrun, but could intrigue be made to work? To make the attempt, trusted envoys were dispatched down to the coast to open a line of communication with his half-sister. We can disregard Justin's contention that the marriage offer came with a claim to be in love with her; the nuptial arrangements on offer were political, as everybody involved would have been well aware. From the start Arsinoe's concerns were for the safety of her children and if such an agreement was to even be considered, she would be looking for sacerdotal guarantees. She eventually sent a partisan named Dion to obtain binding oaths from her wooer and he was amenable, so at the Temple to Zeus he

> took hold of the altar, and, touching the images and couches of the gods, vowed, with unheard-of and most solemn imprecations, that he sought a marriage with his sister in true sincerity, and that he would give her the title of Queen, nor would, to her dishonour, have any other wife, or any other children than her sons.[12]

Ptolemy Ceraunus had never had trouble in offering easy assurances, but what is extraordinary is that this intelligent and remarkable woman, who had a fascinating and impressive career in front of her, believed this man she knew well and whose perfidious past was so recent and so palpable. Yet this half-sibling who seldom showed herself naïve or foolish in her life listened eagerly to these assurances so transparently insincere. During furious discussions at the queen's council not all were taken in;

her eldest son, another Ptolemy, knew his uncle too well and exclaimed that 'there was treachery at the bottom'. In fact he was so trepidatious that he fled to Illyria to the court of a king who later backed him with soldiers in an attack on Ceraunus that, though unsuccessful, still led to even more destructive fighting in the Macedonian homeland. This eldest son departed, leaving his mother sufficiently convinced that she travelled to Pella and wed her dangerous fiancé in front of a court and army where many would have taken comfort from the junction of two parties that they had previously felt themselves torn between. With calculated duplicity, Ceraunus appeared the perfect groom, putting the diadem on Arsenio's brow and proclaiming her queen of Macedonia in front of the assembled army, stressing that he was raising her again to the status she had when wed to Lysimachus.

The inevitable was not long in coming after she allowed her new husband's officers to take control of Cassandreia while 'she appointed a festival in the city against his arrival, ordering the houses, temples, and all other places, to be magnificently decorated, altars and victims to be everywhere kept in readiness'.[13] Entering a town decked in festival bunting, the bridegroom was no longer concerned about hiding his intentions and sent troops into the citadel and once in complete control the handsome 16- and 13-year-old princes, who had met him with their mother outside the city gates and who he had sworn to protect and raise to the throne, were unceremoniously dispatched. All was conducted over the desperate protestations of his new wife who, finally realizing what she had done, tried to deflect with her own body the blows aimed at her offspring. Of no avail, the half-crazed mother 'with her garments torn and her hair dishevelled' was pitched into a ferry and taken to exile on the offshore island of Samothrace with only two servants to console the bereaved woman. She was soon on her way to Alexandria to become a sister queen of Ptolemy II and where she would re-encounter her eldest son who became for a period co-regent of the Egyptian kingdom after his mother's death before continuing in Lagid service as governor of Telmessos in Lycia.[14] There is something odd in this story, suggesting that we are missing a dimension. Why would this man, though certainly capable of such butchery, risk alienating so many of his new subjects with Lysimachian sympathies by so causelessly, blatantly and precipitately murdering that dead king's ex-wife and children? There may have been a trigger. At some stage Arsenio's eldest son Ptolemy who had escaped to the court of a neighbouring monarch returned backed by Illyrian swords and if Ceraunus interpreted this threat as a component of his new wife's plotting, such a potentially destabilizing disposal of his relatives becomes more understandable.

The kingdom Ptolemy Ceraunus had stolen may have looked like a comforting whole, stretching from the cantons of upper Macedonia to the eastern marches around Philippi and Amphipolis and coastal Thrace that would have been secured on the march from Lysimachia. Also from still-held Paeonia down to the Thermaic Gulf with the Greek towns settled on the coast that ran to the Vale of Tempe and the twin and rival foundations of Thessaloniki and Cassandreia were now well held. The latter place became home for Eurydice. This man may have been a vicious murderer but he looked after his mother, allocating the local revenues for her sustenance. So apart from a few pretenders of little account and perhaps Antigonus trying to reassert his presence in Thessaly, the new king was looking pretty safe as he came to terms with both Pyrrhus and Seleucus' heir Antiochus not long after coming to the throne. The question was how solid were the foundations of this most recent incumbent? Would his tenure at the Palace of Pella turn out more lasting than the last two? Both Pyrrhus and Lysimachus had been great figures, but neither had endured more than a few years. Would this new edifice be found fragile and where might the test come from that would determine it?

There is little doubt about the general view of this man who found himself facing the first major barbarian incursion for generations hardly eighteen months since he had come to the throne. 'Hurried on by the madness that distracted him for his unnatural crimes, went out to meet them with a few undisciplined troops',[15] here was no suggestion of a martyr suffering to defend his people when he came to a sticky end. It was just deserts for a man with a rare talent for mischief whose hands were red with blood of family members with inconvenient connections as well as monarchs who had been unlucky enough to find themselves hosting this dangerous exile driven out by a father who perhaps had some inkling of his egregious character. This universally reviled character had hardly begun to settle on his throne when in 279 storm clouds were suggested by an embassy arriving from the Dardanian kingdom situated on Macedon's north-western border on the cusp of Illyrian influence in the west and Thracian in the east. Monunius I was the royal head of a people who may have had some connection with those close relatives of the Trojans mentioned by Homer and who gave their name to the Dardanelles. Savage fighters, his people were famous for only bathing three times in their lives – at birth, on their wedding day and after death – though a condescending Greek geographer[16] suggests that if dirty, they were at least musical. A king called Bardylis reigning during most of the first half of the fourth century made them a power that even dominated Macedonia through quisling stooges in part of the 390s and 380s and terrorized the Molossians as well. As recently as 359 they had defeated and killed a king of Macedon and one of Philip's first marital forays was to wed a Dardani princess, to establish an entente that allowed him the time to turn the tables on a people who were still able to worry Alexander's Macedon in tandem with some other Illyrians in 334.

Monunius was a considerable figure himself, the first of his line to strike chinking bright, silver coins, he dominated part of an Adriatic shore necklaced by Greek colonies and was sufficiently credible that Pyrrhus was happy to form an alliance with him. Relations with Macedon had seldom been happy even in recent times, but the menace from northern invaders had served to concentrate his mind. Understanding the big picture and realizing that a united front was the best hope, the Dardanian monarch sent emissaries offering to assist Ptolemy Ceraunus in defending his borders with 10,000 or even 20,000 of his best men, but this offer of solidarity against the emerging threat was thrown back in his teeth with insults. The Macedonian ruler, a lot more relaxed than he should have been, spurned the offer, adding in insulting language that

> the Macedonians were in a sad condition if, after having subdued the whole east without assistance, they now required aid from the Dardanians to defend their country; and that he had for soldiers the sons of those who had served under Alexander the Great, and had been victorious throughout the world.[17]

If this reflected the arrogance of a people who had so recently been masters of the world, it also highlighted their recklessness. In such a circumstance, Monunius might well, on hearing this response, have said that 'The famous kingdom of Macedonia would soon fall a sacrifice to the rashness of a raw youth',[18] a comment that if actually made showed considerable prescience.

This failure to accept proffered help in itself was bad enough, but having no prospect of making a common front the Dardanians, with little option, joined the Gauls, showing their new friends the easiest invasion routes leading between Illyria and Paeonia that followed the Pena River west of modern-day Skopje and down past Kichevo north of Lake Ohrid and into Macedonia by the Monastir Gap. Then it would follow a corridor of grass running down from the pass to where in Roman times the Via Egnatia would run, near modern-day Florina, east into the heart of Lower Macedonia. It was probably early spring 279 when, without waiting for many of his men who were still working their farms and against advice, the volatile ruler left Pella and marched into upper Macedonia to face an invasion army that now included thousands of Dardanians. All Ptolemy Ceraunus' career may have borne witness to an aptitude for infamous intrigues, but he was inexperienced in military matters. There is no evidence that he had ever led troops in battle before. That he had been captured fighting for Lysimachus in no way implies that he was in any position of command; he could just as easily have been at his monarch's side as an aide or even been scooped up when Seleucus took over his opponent's court. So it was a military tyro who found himself facing an existential menace but one who saw himself as representing the invincible royal line of Philip and Alexander, though the reality was that hardly secure on his throne, surely cursed by the murderous impiety of his recent past, he took up the perilous commission of hurling back the invaders while disdaining advisors who stressed the importance of assembling as much of the national levy as was possible. These characters, the elite of a marcher kingdom, could draw on generations of experience of combating wild men from the north, but the man who made the decisions was not listening and marched with many of his crucial phalangites still absent.

Nor was this his last chance to avoid disaster as the warlord at the head of the invading horde, on nearing the defenders' camp, sent agents to open negotiations. Putting their cards on the table, they made it clear that they were open to an arrangement; even at this late stage they would leave the Macedonians in peace for a price. However, this man who had rebuffed the emissaries of a neighbour with offers of succour was hardly going to find appeasement coming easily and anyway convinced himself that this embassy carrying a proposal to leave him alone if he paid up betrayed the intruders' weakness. So for him any agreement could only be on his terms and the answer flung back in their faces was belligerent: he would only grant them peace if their commanders surrendered themselves as hostages and their followers gave up their weapons. These untamed men were unimpressed and, laughing at this foolishness, prepared to pounce on an opponent apparently determined to tweak the lion's tail. The predictable occurred and only days after these diplomatic passages, the invaders brought on decisive battle. The defending army in this moment of truth proved not only unskilled but undisciplined too, and 'the Macedonians were defeated and cut to pieces' with their king conscious at last of the effects of his temerity, finding his soldiers routed, slain or captured and himself attacked and wounded several times before finally being taken. He died hard, pulled bloody and suffering from the back of his injured elephant that had unseated him while he had been directing the battle, but with his captors hardly in a forgiving frame of mind there was going to be no mercy for this man who had insulted them. Pressed to his knees, a swordsman struck off his head and hoisted it high on a spear point to encourage their comrades and dismay any of the Macedonians who still showed fight. In the end the dead king had plenty of company in his misfortune as very few of his followers escaped the rout: 'the rest were either taken or slain.' The intruders had brought ruin to the new man who had just established himself on the throne after disposing of most of his local rivals. These challengers he had shown himself capable of dealing with, but not when a new and different menace had appeared on the horizon.

Nobody had any doubt that the man got his comeuppance, 'killed in a manner befitting his own cruelty'. It had been an extraordinary vision of the king dragged wounded off his fallen elephant, but is it really credible? There is no tradition of Hellenistic rulers commanding their armies from elephant-back; they usually fought with the cavalry or if this arm was absent or less relevant, with the infantry. No other examples exist, and if it was not some copying mistake, it is perhaps just an irresistible desire for the dramatic by some chronicler cognizant of King Porus confronting Alexander at the Hydaspes River from the back of such a beast. These events that had doomed Ceraunus to ignominy had now made it clear that the Macedonians were facing one of the greatest threats they had ever confronted. Not since the death in battle of Perdiccas III at the hands of Bardylis in 360 had they experienced such disaster, and if the tremors from this catastrophe would soon reverberate around the whole Balkan world, even those immediately experiencing them could not have imagined how far-reaching and damaging the upheavals that would follow were going to be. The impact would reach far south in Greece and even across the Hellespont into the heart of Asia Minor, ensuring that the happenings of the few years after 279 would be etched in dread on the Hellenic psyche.

Chapter Seven

A Gallic Fury

Who were these new intruders? People of the periphery who had downed a monarch who sat on the throne of Philip and Alexander and led the army with which those monarchs had conquered the world? The other question was how had they done what they had? When Alexander had not long to live in Babylon he received an embassy,[1] one of many, from a people who he had briefly encountered soon after coming to the throne and who, when in 335 he was rounding off a Thracian campaign by floating his men across the Danube on skins and canoes, piqued his interest because they claimed the only thing they feared was that the sky might fall on them. Any people in the ancient world could hardly claim a real pedigree unless there was a mystery and these Celts were no exception. The Celtic tongue probably originated as a language developed to facilitate trade along the Atlantic shores of Spain and France forming fully sometime in the second millennium BC (though there are claims for roots going back to the third millennium), before moving east and north, apparently the exact opposite of the expansion of the material culture going the other way.

The typical artifacts of the Celtic iron age, often found in warrior graves and covering the period between the ninth and the fifth centuries, were first uncovered in Austria at a salt-rich Hallstatt. This civilization centred on Austria, Bohemia and Bavaria stretching towards the Rhine, had built on the previous Urnfield culture and was probably influenced by horse-riding steppe peoples who had been migrating west into the plains of Hungary. Extraordinarily rich princely cart burials in southern Germany show how it spread and its connectivity is indicated by the unearthing of many Greek and Etruscan accoutrements for their wine-drinking parties. The lakeside settlement of La Tène in Switzerland highlights a second stage of stylistic development with chariot graves in the Moselle and Meuse river valleys showing the same expansion process for styles that were common to so much of a Celtic world that was to be subsumed by a Roman Empire, massively expanding between the third and first centuries. The practice of throwing La Tène pattern swords, shields and other artifacts into lakes has ensured wonderful finds from central Europe and southern France to the British Isles, despite the fact that the inhabitants of Britain or Ireland were never described as Celts in ancient times by the literate cultures of the south. Controversy continues about how and when the people or their styles travelled, since orthodoxy over various pulses of invasion reaching as far as Britain and Ireland have been largely replaced by more nuanced understanding of dispersal through trade, intermarriage and raiding rather than visions of whole people on the move.

This was a feasting and raiding culture with high-status bards singing the praises of warrior chiefs that had spread far and wide since at least the fourth century when some of these people began to dominate much of the Carpathians and the Danube basin while others were consolidating their position in northern Italy. Many tens of thousands had settled in Italy, Illyria and ancient Pannonia, places peppered with La Tène remains, while their hegemony covered much of west and south-central Europe with a presence felt as far away as the north-west Pontic region of modern Moldavia and the Ukraine and mineral-rich southern Poland as well. However debated the origins and spread of the Celts may be, the literate societies of the Mediterranean were pretty clear about who they meant when they referred to these Gauls or Galatians, people they had been in contact with on and off for centuries. Greeks from the Phocaean colony of Massalia in southern France had been first in their familiarity with peoples who were happy to swap slaves for wine and the intensity of other contacts is most dramatically illustrated at the Heuneburg hillfort in southern Germany, 15-odd miles from both Ulm and the Swiss border where there are unique mud-brick walls with protruding towers that surely must have been the handiwork of travelling Greek engineers familiar with the latest methods of fortification. Less adventurous compatriots of these men had become well acquainted with the Gauls as warriors for hire, fighting in the endemic wars in Magna Graecia between Greeks, Carthaginians, Sicels and Italians with Dionysius I of Syracuse establishing Ancona partly as a good contact point for mercenary recruitment. They had even been seen in combat alongside the Spartans when Dionysius had sent auxiliaries in 370 to fight in her Theban wars.[2]

Archaeological finds suggest military developments in the fourth and third centuries, with increased use of armour, heavier shields and longer swords that would have suited fighting from horseback, ensuring an enhanced warrior reputation and that a band of this frightening people had sacked the significant city of Rome in the early fourth century was well-known as far afield as Greece. The Gauls who inhabited the countries north of their own Balkan world would have been long known through trade, even if few were cognizant of political realities north of the Danube. Certainly raiding and population movements south of the great river were detected by the end of the fourth century, and there may even have been a considerable state organized around the conjunction of the Danube and Sava. These in fact were probably the people who are noticed roughing up a north Illyrian tribe called the Autariatae who lived in the centre of the Balkans around the Morava valley. There is a story[3] that the contest was long and indecisive with the intruders having to stoop to leaving poisoned food behind in their camp for the enemy to find and eat to gain advantage. From 310 the reports of Gallic activity are more convincing in detail and we get names of leaders like Molistomos who overran sufficient Tribelli country, Dardania and Paeonia for Cassander to take notice, thwarting the raiders in the Haemus Mountains. This probe had shown that the Macedonian frontier advertised by Alexander in 335 was still vigorously held, but fifty years down the line things had changed.

When word of the collapse of the stable Macedonian-Thracian state ruled by Lysimachus passed beyond the forests of Thrace and mountains and marshes of Illyria, it found listeners eager to try for the treasures of the civilized south. Even before in 298 the borders had been tested by a warlord called Cambaules, but he only reached Thrace before turning back through fear of the numbers of defending Greeks. Yet this was sufficient to give these northern boys a taste and many of 'Cambaules' veterans' were eager for another crack at a suddenly much more porous border. So another large force was mustered, its numbers enhanced by local warriors of non-Gallic extraction and womenfolk. It is also possible that these movements were encouraged by the arrival of Gauls from Italy like the Senones, who had recently been overwhelmed by the Romans and had escaped east through modern-day Slovenia.[4] The idea of peoples on the move in vast numbers has long gone out of fashion when describing the migrations of Celts or Germans from 400 through the Roman era and into the Dark Ages. That small elites or even cultural influences following long-used trade routes as explanations are now more accepted as agents of change, but certainly on this occasion raiders moved south through the Balkans in numbers, whether they were ethnic Celts or an admixture combining with the local Illyrians and Pannonians among whom they had spent the last few generations. Although it might be difficult to tell, torcs offering supernatural protection were common decorations in many cultures and locals joining up might well have copied the moustaches and lime-spiked hair of the successful marauders whose banners they were following while learning enough of the Gallic tongue to get by. Beyond this there are definite reports of 10,000 Dardanians enlisting as well as venal Greeks from near the Malian Gulf and Thessaly, while the story of the blood-drinking Scordisci is particularly indicative; known from the time of Philip V, they are claimed as a hybrid of Celts who retreated from Delphi commingled with Illyrians and Thracians to settle in present-day Serbia at the mouth of the Sava.

Whatever the exact ethnic formula, it is reasonable to assume that they came in very considerable numbers, with thousands upon thousands of raiders draped in plaid cloaks with long oval shields and carrying long vicious swords pouring out of the remote north. They erupted south in 281 and 280, encouraged after tidings reached them that the previously impervious kingdom of Lysimachus had been broken. He had been the dyke who in his recent takeover of Paeonia had reminded anybody thinking of making trouble that he was still very much in charge on this border of the Hellenic world. With the dam ruptured at the Battle of Corupedium, inactivity at the border posts suggested decadence and softness, so wild tribes looking for land and loot coalesced to take advantage, with 85,000 warriors purported to be on the move by 280 at the latest. Coming from the direction of Illyria and Pannonia, long-used riparian trade routes down into the Balkans and Greece that had acquainted them with the delights of the southern littoral now became invasion roads. The Maritza valley route from the Danube down through Thrace would have seen the great body pass before splitting into three waves that would leave hardly any part of the Balkan peninsula untouched. A leader named Cerethrius took 20,000 in the direction of the Tribelli and past them into Thrace; some of these probably sacked Seuthopolis, while another horde under Brennus and Acichorius terrorized Paeonia as Bolgius led more on a different trajectory. It was the last of these, taking advantage of an astonishing exhibition of mismanagement, who piled ruin on the head of the king who had just established himself at Pella.

A different group embarked on a peregrination that started in 279 or 278 that would take them to another continent where the imprint of their name remains to this day. This company may[5] have broken away from Brennus' horde under a couple of adventurous heads named Leonnorius and Lutarius who saw profit calling from the east. Some 20,000 of them, 10,000 being combatants, marched through Thrace demanding money with menaces as they went, arriving at Byzantium where, if they had not already intended to cross to Asia, the talk of the rich country over the Bosporus made up their minds. Having wrung all they could from the surrounding people and finding no transport to cross over the channel, they moved to the Chersonese where they are even reported capturing the old capital Lysimachia 'by treachery'. The local governor called Antipater in control along the Hellespont agreed to help them cross, but delays caused the fractious raiders to split again, with Leonnorius, the leader of the larger group, heading back to Byzantium where he found Nicomedes, king of Bithynia, willing to ferry his men across on condition they fought in a war with his brother. The rest got over once Antipater finally came through with a few ships, allowing both bands to reassemble for profitable service in Anatolia. However, this conflict that reunited Bithynia was only a staging post for a terrible people who, raging through Phrygia, would not settle until they reached the Halys River, from where they held large swathes of country in their thrall. Yet not everyone was so condemnatory, as there is a claim that they helped democracies in Anatolia: when the local kings tried to suppress them, the Galatians acted 'by repelling the city's oppressors'.[6] Despite this apparent attempt to make local friends, they were largely celebrated for decades of raiding and mercenary service before Attalus I of Pergamon tamed the descendants of those who had crossed to Asia and confined them to the region known to this day as Galatia.

We may know the names of the leaders that sent shivers down the spines of Macedonians, Thracians and Greeks alike but still search in vain for real personalities. Brennus is the closest that it is possible to get and we are not even sure whether his name is really a title, as surely it is too much of a coincidence that the two most notorious Gallic marauders, one who captured Rome in the very early 300s and one who invaded Greece, would have the same personal name. What this latter Brennus did in Paeonia is unknown, the only clue being one attestation that he 'made an irruption into Greece',[7] though in the next years he emerges as the crucial figure indignant that many loot-laden Gauls were now looking to return home with so much of the wealth of the Hellenic world left unplundered. Brennus, with war always in his head, opened a real campaign of persuasion, circulating among his independent people at public meetings and in private conversations arguing that in not continuing on to Greece, they had missed a real payday, passing up the votive offerings of gold and silver deposited at the Greek sanctuaries over the centuries. To ensure his audience's cupidity was not diluted by worrying rumours he threatened to execute any Delphian captives who repeated what they had told him, that many of the statues at the sanctuary were of brass with a thin gold covering. He would have been uncomfortably aware that the more knowledgeable of his chiefs might have known of the depletion of the Delphic treasures during the Sacred Wars and wanted nothing to dull the rapacious gleam in the eyes of the men listening as he extolled the potential payday waiting in the sacred precincts at the navel of the world, the cherry on top of the cake of loot they could expect to acquire in the rest of Greece. Intent on showing that this rich fruit was to be had with almost effortless plucking,[8] he gathered as many of his compatriots as he could for an illuminating exhibition. A band of Greek prisoners was then paraded before them. Half-starved from months of captivity with shaved heads and threadbare clothes, these feeble scarecrows shuffled between the rows of his own followers. 'Stout handsome men, equipped with Gallic armour', so the comparison was unambiguous, emphasizing what a pushover the enemy defending the booty would be.

Once he had won over the men, eager like meat-famished dogs for wealth earned along a sword's edge, Acichorius was confirmed as his second-in-command in this smash-and-grab enterprise. The fearsome numbers claimed in the undertaking are frankly unbelievable; not only that these two led between 150,000 and 152,000 infantry and 15,000 to 20,400 horse, but that each cavalryman was supported by two servants who could join the fight to take their master's place or provide him with a remount when either were wounded or fatigued. The contention that this procedure somehow mirrored the Persian immortals is odd[9] but perhaps comprehensible as these new invaders would soon be treading the path followed by Xerxes two centuries earlier. What is far from certain concerning these Gallic intrusions after 280 is whether they were peoples on the move comprising not just armed men but also caravans of waggons laden with household goods followed by women and children. Or were they war bands of young warriors looking for easy pickings from plunder or as mercenaries for hire? The answer must be that they could be either; those that settled in Thrace and Anatolia certainly did bring at least some of their families along, just as their predecessors had done when they arrived in the Danube basin or ventured into Italy from north of the Alps well over a century before. Others we know were purely warrior bands whose members had little disposition to settle themselves where they had overrun, only looking to take away what they could. This other Brennus, making an attempt on the treasure houses of the Hellenic world, would surely have led this kind of fighting gang rather than any kind of people on the move. The numbers given, however, are a grotesque exaggeration. Even a tenth of the figures given would be a stretch, and if forced to venture an estimate it would be at most some few tens of thousands of armed men and if they had waggons in their train it was not to carry possessions and families but to take away the loot they were confident they would soon acquire in the urban centres and religious sanctuaries of Greece.

A path needed to be cleared for this larcenous horde and the first chore of a campaign that started late in the fighting season was to deal with the fragile arrangements put in place since the descent of Bolgius, to try to protect the core of the Macedonian kingdom around Pella and the Axius River country leading down to the Thermaic Gulf. Brennus, running along the tracks taken in the years before, burst in once again to find the only man who stood against him was the general Sosthenes who had managed to raise what was left of Macedonia's fighting men in an attempt to impede his progress. However, this patched-up army of home defence was defeated and again every soldier who survived with their civilian compatriots fled for the safety of the walled cities. Brennus, though his followers had suffered casualties, was in control and now ravaged the countryside, taking what little had been left from previous trashings. Yet his ambitions were grander and, far from satisfied with what remained of the riches of Macedonia, he pushed on. Having cleaned out the farms and barns along the way, the invaders pressed across the southern borders leaving chaos behind them with the fields untilled and fly-blown corpses of plough teams rotting in the sun. They exited down through the Vale of Tempe, their train of men and waggons so long that by the time the last units passed it would have been evening with the silhouette of Mount Olympus showing dark behind them. They then pressed on with restless violence down into Greece and debouched into the proud old world that retained a glorious reputation, despite a decline in real influence since the rise of Macedon under Philip II. Larissa was passed and the plains of Thessaly covered with bands of rapacious marauders picking up everything that was portable in the rich estates of the horse-riding cattle barons who dominated the region, then down through country where in the past great battles had been fought and would be in the future: at the Crocus Field near Phylace where Philip II bested a Phocian-Athenian alliance; at Crannon between Greeks and Macedonians; at Cynoscephalae where Macedonians and Romans would clash; and Pharsalus where Caesar was destined to confront Pompey the Great in a terrible civil war.

The brutality of the invaders ensured word of their coming was soon circulating south on the wings of rumour, substantiated by hordes of refugees fleeing the Gallic terror. With the advent of these Gauls the future for Greece never looked darker, so despite their usual preoccupation with their own squabbles, local faction leaders now forswore the temptation to work for the ruin of old rivals, class warriors sheathed their rhetoric, ancient grievances between rival cities were shelved and while the invaders poured south, delegates from round central Greece, sober men with solitary inclinations and aware of the jeopardy facing their people, were in communication about the strategy and numbers they would need to confront the approaching menace. Unlike with the invasion of the Persians, they did not have many months to prepare themselves. There could be no question this time of asking for aid from the diaspora. There was no chance of an heir of Gelon, who had been approached in 480, coming to their assistance from Syracuse or from some other place in Magna Graecia. There was just no time to make such kin contacts, never mind for them to mobilize and ride to the rescue. Apart from this, there was little evidence of any lessening of the local bickering that would have made national unity any more probable than 200 years earlier as even this critical invasion scare would not unite everybody on the mainland. Some places were too touchy and provincial to conceive of united action and local anxieties still dominated even the city governments that struggled to coordinate a defence. There was hardly any involvement from the warrior peoples of the Peloponnese; just a few Achaeans came later to help their neighbours over the Gulf of Corinth. Though at least on this occasion the country was not going to be rife with Medizers; even if for some it had made sense to make quisling arrangements with the Empire of Persia to avoid the grim consequences of defeat and conquest, such a procedure was hardly really possible with the Gauls. Xerxes and his followers may have been barbarians but they had been civilized ones; these latest invaders were wolves from who little could be expected except rending and destruction wherever they passed. There may have been some who might have had hopes of paying them off (an arrangement that had, after all, been offered to Ceraunus), and the future would show some individuals would even join up for the grand tour of larceny, but for the moment these weaker links kept their mouths shut.

News of the incursions in the countries to their north had been circulating for long enough to not allow the slightest doubt of the seriousness of the danger and those most threatened knew they had to choose between surrender and fighting. Despite the risks of retribution, they had acted and answering the appeal to preserve the homeland, task forces were dispatched by the citizens of Aetolia, Boeotia, Athens, Phocis and others from central Greece. Alert to how menacing the situation was and in a unusual moment of co-operation, they determined to try to halt the avalanche of terrible northerners who they now knew were on their way. Their wise heads had good knowledge of both their geography and their history and the inevitability of being outnumbered demanded that they find a bulwark, so Thermopylae was decided upon as the natural site to try to stem the tide. Though the traditions[10] that provide details of what occurred were bound to indulge in comparison with the earlier existential threat posed by the Persians, the names and numbers given suggest real veracity concerning the confederacy that decided to try to repeat the previous stand at the Hot Gates where history steamed and fizzed like the waters of the springs themselves. Among peoples across central Greece assemblies had met, and with self-defence decided upon they were eager now as arrangements were made for the call-up.

When the men brought down weapons from lofts or took them from their walls and assembled, the names in the air were redolent of ages past when the bronze-clad warriors of old Greece led by heroes shining with intelligence and courage had not flinched to face the greatest empire in the world in a war of epic dimensions. To face this latest test 10,000 hoplites and 500 horse from Boeotia were present under their generals Cephisodotus, Thearidas, Diogenes and Lysander, while the fretful Phocians, who would most immediately bear the brunt of any enemy who penetrated the pass, brought 500 cavalry and 3,000 infantry under Critobulus and Antiochus. Locris, hardly less threatened, sent 700 infantry led by Meidias, while from Megara came 400 hoplites following Hipponicus, the Aetolians, self-appointed protectors of Delphi, led by three generals Polyarchus, Polyphron and Lacrates were mob-handed including 7,000 hoplites, 790 skirmishers and some horsemen. From Athens came Callippus, the son of Moerocles, exemplifying ancient valour dispatched at the head of all the triremes the city could launch, churning up the waters of the Euboean channel with their oars and eager to protect the coastal flank of Thermopylae just as their forebears had at Artemisium during Xerxes' invasion. Their land forces amounted to 1,000 foot and 500 horse to help defend the pass, enough of a contribution to apparently ensure their leader was given the high command, despite there being royal contingents present dispatched by monarchs who could not shrug aside responsibilities for defending people whose interests they always claimed as close to their hearts. Some 500 mercenaries under Aristodemus the Macedonian were forwarded by Antigonus Gonatus and another 500 officered by a man from Orontes in Syria called Telesarchus were dispatched by Antiochus; not that many, but as full-time warriors able to leaven the inexperience of the citizen soldiers.

This designation of Athenian leadership may well be apocryphal, a contrivance to play up Athenian involvement in an effort to mirror a Herodotean tradition, just like old times with an Athenian slant to put beside the epitaph 'Go tell them in Sparta, O passer by, that here, in obedience to their orders we lie'.[11] Indeed, this Callippus is only otherwise mentioned again during the Chremonidean War and may not have been as important as claimed as no inscriptions confirm his involvement, while the Athenian naval contribution equally could be exaggerated.[12] Whoever was in charge by the time this holding force had been led into place, information had already located the invaders at Magnesia and Phthiotis and forward scouts scanning the skyline would have seen great clouds of dust appearing along the horizon in the direction of Thessaly, indicating the time of waiting was over. Learning of this and disdaining just to wait upon events, the Greeks decided on a forward defence along the Spercheus River where it ran down from the Dolopos Mountains to the Malian Gulf. An allied council approved the hazard and all the cavalry and 1,000 light armed men were pushed forward a few miles, determined to make the river crossing as costly as possible for the intruders. Swiftly traversing familiar paths, on reaching the river they looked up from the banks to see the enemy columns not far away, but still they had time to break down the bridges and encamp along the southern bank. Their hope was that the foe would be predictable in their ignorance of tactical expertise and in making a wild rush would expose themselves to being overcome in detail while in the process of crossing the river. However, Brennus was a capable military leader and learning what was waiting for his army he sent 10,000 of his best swimmers and tallest men down river towards the sea near where its waters joined the gulf. There the defenders had taken no precautions, thinking the lakes and marshes would be impassable, but the active men in this detachment either waded or swam across with some using their shields as rafts. Things had looked promising to begin with but now their enemy's enterprise was too much for the Greeks. When they realized they would soon have to face men who had already crossed over the river and were coming at them unobstructed, there was no longer any suggestion of maintaining a forward line. They pulled back in good order, returning safely to the main defences at Thermopylae having discovered the baleful reality that their opponents were cunning as well as terrifying.

The invaders pressed their advantage with enthusiasm, utilizing the locals, eager enough to see the intruders on their way, to rebuild the bridges so the whole army could cross over this last major obstacle between them and the army blocking the way. They continued marching south, trashing the countryside as they went, until they passed by Heraclea in Trachis and if they failed to take the city itself, well defended by a garrison of steady Aetolians who had recently welcomed the place into their league, they were able to pause to rest by the Asopus River. Giving up on the well-walled town, they swarmed forward, on and on, aiming to crash through at Thermopylae and reach the riches of central Greece. The Gauls clearly had their sympathizers as deserters kept Brennus well-informed about the enemy he was about to encounter and, feeling confident in his numbers, he thrust forward towards the pass. However much their totals were exaggerated by our sources, there would still have been sufficient for the earth to shake as they drove forward before showing a great haze of smoke from pluming fires as they settled into their forward camp.

The Greeks manning the walls they had managed to repair in the brief time they had been there would have had cause for panic at the intimidating sight, but were able to keep such fears in check as they ordered their lines with previous regional hatreds sufficiently suppressed to ensure cohesion. They were well-officered by men tutored in the martial arts from absorbing tactical manuals and listening to peripatetic military instructors and weapons experts, attentive pupils who knew well how to use to best effect the troops that were present. Light infantry were deployed so their javelins, slings and arrows could have the most impact against attackers, many of whom were unarmoured, while the hoplites were deployed in phalanx formation, keeping an eerie silence that unnerved an enemy used to attacking while screaming war cries at the top of their voices. In this time of fear at least they were comfortable in their formations and if the normal pattern was adhered to, seven files stood behind the front-rank men, those rearward prepared to replace wilting and bloodied comrades used up by holding the line under a broiling sun. With comrades tucked in snugly to protect their flanks, it was a wall robust enough to break up the enemy attacks: 'When they came to close quarters, the infantry did not rush out of their line far enough to disturb their proper formation.'[13] Steady and determined with shimmering light waves flickering from the brisling mass of spearheads, these men were still relieved they would not have to face the enemy cavalry who were always some of the most effective soldiers. There was no room for wheeling horsemen to manoeuvre between the looming cliffs and the sea and much of the ground comprised smooth rocks covered by running water that would have made it difficult for horses to keep their feet.

This time there was no embassy with a proposal that the Greeks could pay them off as had been offered to the Macedonians; the invaders wanted everything these people had, not just some tithe to leave them alone. Anyway, since they had emerged out of their Pannonian and Illyrian habitats and through the Balkan passes they had experienced only thumping victory and nothing now suggested history would not repeat itself. Even if they were surprised at the combined front facing them, given their knowledge of the usual interminable feuding and snarling backstabbing habits of the Greeks, it gave them little pause.

So as the sun showed, Brennus hurled his warriors forward. The shock force approached, showing on the narrow plain in front of the defenders: a ground filled with a ferocious enemy sufficient to chill the blood, reaching to within a few hundred yards of the defensive line before increasing their speed as they got closer, then it was into a jog as the first knots of northern warriors reached the wall and tried to smash it down. Yet it was no easy task in the face of obdurate men whose forbidding visages could be perceived behind their shields, stabbing again and again at any sword-swinging attacker who approached them. Grimly resolved to stand firm in this historic corridor against a lethal threat, the example of 300 iron-hard Spartans and their hero king Leonidas were in the forefront of many minds as the enemy poured forward, filling the gap between the tree-pocked cliffs of Mount Callidromus and the marshy salt water rolling up the beach. They maintained discipline against increasing pressure, crowding in behind their stout shields and spearing where they could see an opening to reach the head or torso of the enemy fighters raising their weapons in preparation for a slashing blow. Men fell on both sides, crushed to death by enemies and comrades alike, but more of the attackers. They were less well-protected and less adept at keeping formation in such a head-on fray. Natural duellists, most were intent on isolating an opponent and hacking him down, but the encounter was not like this; in the closeness of the setting it was impossible to find the space needed. All it could ever be was a frontal assault against well-drilled armoured hoplites whose very raison d'être was this kind of fighting and who from early on realized they had the measure of their foe.

As the outlandishly apparelled horde surged forward, the sun picked out the glittering chain mail armour of the Gallic leaders through the morning haze while below a cloud of dust, high horns, shaped into animal heads, blasted out their singular cacophony. Yet with only their narrow shields for protection many attackers blanched under a hail of blows from spears and missiles while the rest were troubled by the solidity of the unbroken line of defenders facing them toe to toe. Yet bravery was a given, so they came on in fearsome assaults, ranks bunching together as the stones and javelins picked them off, and ferocity was apparent as they ground implacably forward: 'Slashed with axe or sword they kept their desperation while they still breathed; pierced by arrow or javelin, they did not abate of their passion so long as life remained.'[14] Their wounded, drawing out the spears that skewered them, fought on, even using the same weapons that had hurt them to throw or stab at the enemy. Like the Medes, Persians and Sakai centuries before, with no way round the flanks they exhausted their bodies and expended their blood against a barrier that would not give way and this was not the worst; steady at their station offshore the Athenians' warships cruised along the muddy waters of the coast 'and raked them' with deadly accurate arrows, javelins and slingshot.

Among those who fell under Gallic swords in this thunderous assault was an Athenian who showed particular courage in holding the battle line. He was a youngster called Cydias who was so marked out as a hero that his family dedicated his shield to Zeus with the following inscription: 'Here hang I, yearning for the still youthful bloom of Cydias, The shield of a glorious man, an offering to Zeus. I was the very first through which at this battle he thrust his left arm, When the battle raged furiously against the Gaul',[15] which apparently could still be seen in the time of Sulla's siege of Athens in 86–87. In these minutes fraught with incident and jeopardy, he had died a true hero and the courage of the young soldier and his peers would be recollected as long as stories were told or accounts read in their home districts. If Athens already had Marathon as the gold standard of courage and civic sacrifice, for other places this now would be that encounter where all who had fought there would be held up as exemplars. Altogether it was not immediately clear who was having the better of the fight, but the defenders, their ash spears stabbing like the flicking tongues of thousands of snakes, fought with such valour and skill that 'The Celts were in unspeakable distress, and in the confined space they inflicted few losses but suffered twice or four times as many.'[16] The weight of numbers was not telling, even in the moments of absolute collision, and many of those fallen wounded among their comrades or just exhausted from pointless battering against the Greek shield wall must have felt they had been fed a line when Brennus spiced his recruiting efforts with displays of feeble and dishevelled Greek prisoners, an appreciation that if for the moment did not impact would in time rebound on its author.

Men began to seep away from the rear of the attacking column, while in the front blood-spattered and wearied men flinched when ordered back into the fray. Finally hopes of victory dimmed until they had had enough and their chiefs had no option but to give the signal for recall from the battle line, first to catch a breath and then to find some succour in their camp. Some even lost their lives in the crush as they attempted to escape the terrible combat they found themselves in, while their enemies continued their deadly labour. 'Many others fell into the swamp and disappeared under the mud. Their loss in the retreat was no less than the loss that occurred while the battle raged.'[17] The first test had been passed, and resting under the canopy of a night-time sky illuminated by an autumn moon, the defenders, after removing panoplies and dressing wounds, could congratulate themselves on having held the pass. The hefty white bodies of the attackers lying in piles were soon despoiled of anything of value, while the forty Greek dead were buried and their wounded tended with the defenders only confirmed in their contempt for the invaders when they left their corpses for the carrion, not even sending a herald to ask for permission to remove them for proper ritual. Not being familiar with the Gauls' particular version of sacred magic, they already assumed these barbarians were far from properly pious from their failure to practice divination before the fight and this final failure of civilized practice confirmed prejudices ingrained by centuries of cultural programming.

Could they hope to continue to hold the line against this impious scourge? For a time after the bloody repulse Brennus was baffled, staring over the field of blood at the unbroken ranks of his enemies, firm behind their defences and clearly prepared to stay as long as necessary. One day passed without attack and then another shredding nerves among the defenders, who knowing their enemies were not going away wondered what was afoot. The deadlock had lasted seven days when after a council of war Brennus considered the option of another frontal assault. Deciding against this, he resolved to try strategy against his unwavering foe, choosing to emulate the Persian king who had come this way before, though his flanking force was directed to take a different route to the one the egregious traitor Ephialtes had shown to Xerxes, one that led towards Mount Oeta before turning off along a narrow track around the walls of Heraclea in Trachis, perched above the rock-cut Asopus River.

Typically for this army of banditti, this was not all about strategy; the Gauls had also heard of riches deposited in a sanctuary to Athena in the locality. Yet as if following a hallowed script, when the chosen Gauls pushed along the trail they discovered a force led by Telesarchos, the officer sent by Antiochus, barring their way so, just like Hydarnes leading his Persian immortals, this later flanking expedition found itself blocked by armed men. However, unlike those guardians from an earlier age who withdrew to a nearby knoll and let the attackers pass by, those these Gauls encountered stood firm across their track, despite in the ferocious contest that ensued, their commander was soon dropped in his own gore. Hours of fighting could not clear a path through the guardians' ranks, so with their flanking move aborted, the survivors returned to Brennus' camp.

If history had not repeated itself in his favour, the Gallic chief was determined that the campaign should not be overwhelmed by any sense of drift, particularly with such a multitude to feed and a primitive commissariat ensuring belts would soon have to be tightened and he resolved to find another stratagem up his sleeve. True, the confederacy of Greeks had proved confident, brave and rock-solid so far, but these were people who had not long since been at each others' throats and a ruse suggested itself, an opportunity to rend their alliance into pieces. As his men rested and tended their wounds, it was decided to test this show of solidarity. Brennus and his officers knew enough of their enemies to play on their weakness: that however much they considered themselves Greeks, it was always their individual city or people that in the final analysis came first. So they would foster division by dispatching a force in the direction of Aetolia, expecting this to persuade their soldiers defending the narrows to depart in an effort to preserve their threatened homes. The detachment was claimed as numbering 40,000 foot and 800 horse under a couple of chiefs called Orestorius and Combutis who left the camp in an interminable column of men, retracing their steps past the looming cliffs by the sea to reach the crossings over the Spercheus River before branching left and rounding a shoulder of mountains in the direction of Callium. Once there they began to burn and butcher, leaving the country they travelled through under a pall of black billowing smoke greasy with burned human and animal flesh. Understanding the concept of psychological warfare, they encouraged the flesh-crawling reports of their drinking blood and eating babies that fuelled a rising tide of terror, while their outrages against the local women were spoken of as the trigger for numerous suicides. Horror at their deeds sped word of their passing and eye-witness accounts from those finding refuge in flight gave dramatic evidence of barbarian brutality that would inevitably be the fate of all Aetolia if the invaders were allowed to penetrate further. With fear for families and loved ones pervading the ranks, the Aetolians holding in the pass reacted exactly as the perpetrators intended. 'At once they raced back from Thermopylae', and when these seasoned warriors travelling past Elateia in Phocis and through Doris reached home, they found that all the reserves of young and old men had been called out to defend the motherland: 'Their very women gladly served with them, being even more enraged against the Gauls than were the men.'[18]

Raiding in the direction of Aetolia and advertising their presence by awful cruelty, the Gauls ensured that the Aetolians, faced with a prospect from their worst nightmares, called their best men back home, but having achieved their purpose and then reversed their march they found they had stirred up a hornets' nest. Achaean hoplites who shipped over from Patrae had linked up with the locals and, gathering in sufficient numbers to take on the intruders, they deployed, determined on revenge. Catching them on the march while the armoured spearmen occupied the invaders in a frontal fight, the Aetolians supported by their women flailed the enemy with incessant missile fire from the flanks before melting back into the woods or rocks. So despite roughly handling the hoplites in their front, when the Gauls continued to withdraw it was only to find themselves pursued by an eager and dangerous enemy. Aware of the need to keep out of the range of the enemy swords, the Aetolians skirmished from a distance and it is asserted that no more than half the invaders were able to get back to the main force at Thermopylae, the rest falling 'along every road' to the projectiles of the inhabitants. Yet the battered and bloody task force, trailing its comet's tail of missile-pierced corpses already crawling with carrion flies, had done what was asked of them. What is not reported is what the others thought when the Aetolians declared their intention to leave. Many of these Greeks had long histories of rivalry, sometimes including instances of shocking outrages against each other, so it is difficult to believe that accusations of treachery were not bandied about, particularly after they had recently heard that locals from Thessaly and elsewhere had actually joined the invaders' ranks. Yet we not only do not hear of any such thing; there is no mention of any inter-allied tension in the fighting to come. None had an interest in destabilizing the confederation; all were too aware of the ever-present danger that the alliance might fragment and then dissolve, sinking any chance of success, to be critical of any one member's decision-making.

Once it was confirmed that the defenders' numbers were significantly reduced, Brennus determined on another attack, but still not feeling that his opponents had been sufficiently diminished for a direct assault it was decided to attempt yet another flanking move. The Gallic high command had been apprised of another path, less steep than the one leading above Heraclea in Trachis, that instead proceeded over Mount Oeta and skirted Aeniania before joining the track that the Persians had used in the fatal year of 480. The locals around the Gallic camp were prepared to do anything to be rid of their unwelcome guests who were stripping out every barn and orchard they owned, so self-interest trumped any patriotism as they offered guides to lead them up and over the mountains. Brennus took the lead now in what he intended as the decisive blow after leaving his lieutenant Acichorius in charge of the main army with instructions to attempt another onslaught when the flanking force had got behind the Thermopylae defences. Taking a detachment that again is claimed to comprise some 40,000 men, they attempted the highland path, a journey that took them first a few miles west, tens of thousands of feet pounding along the shore in a cloud of dust beside the sparkling sea, before the hike around the pass was truly begun with the sweating men climbing higher and higher until a thick and threatening mist came rolling down, masking the sunshine. This was troubling to men who had never travelled these difficult wooded paths before, but they huddled together and for hours kept on and on. Difficult as the shadow-darkened terrain was, as they breasted oak- and pine-covered ridges where leaves and twigs crunched underfoot, it became clear the lack of visibility gave them an advantage, as stumbling through the mist-shrouded trees, the Gauls found themselves confronted by a Phocian formation posted in their way on a stretch of open greensward. These men were surprised and rolled over almost before they knew it. The sound of surprised sentries shouting warnings broke the silence as the rest of the defenders, though appalled by the danger, struggled to grab their shields and spears with little choice but to brace themselves for a gallant last stand. It turned into a frightful combat with just-formed Phocian spearmen confronting big-boned, be-torqued swordsmen emerging from the gloom. Outnumbered and far from fully aware of their attackers' whereabouts or intentions, they were forced back and out of the path of the onrushing column, though the delay at least allowed time for runners to carry bleak news of the imminent blood-red danger sweeping towards the main confederate forces in the pass.

The Greeks in Thermopylae did not panic, but nothing could hide what was self-evident: they could still see the extensive enemy camp in front from which at any time a tidal wave of Gauls might howl into the assault and now it was only hours before another teeming detachment would arrive in their rear. The implication for the stalwarts there was clear: it was only ever by fighting on one front that they had any hope of surviving, so in near-desperate alarm they realized the defence of the pass was no longer tenable and all they could do was to make provisions to ensure they were not surrounded and annihilated. It was an almost exact mirror of the earlier Persian assault, except this time rather than most of the defenders withdrawing down the pass leaving the doomed Spartans, Thespians, exiled Thebans and helots to make their heroic last stand, instead they all packed up their arms and baggage as the adept mariners of the Athenian fleet, as if in answer to their prayers, came to the rescue. As the war cries and flashing spear tips of the flanking Gauls came into sight, the Greek warriors massing along the beach were hauled aboard in a fighting withdrawal through the marshy shallows to escape an enemy determined to drive them into the sea and seize and burn any ships they could capture. With boat decks crowded with rescued soldiers, the warships backwatered out of the Malian Gulf and manoeuvred down the Euboean channel, conveying each national detachment back to their homes intent on spearheading the resistance of communities haunted by the question, would they be next to face an increasingly imminent Gallic menace?

The Hot Gates were clear and Brennus did not hesitate; without waiting for the forces under Acichorius to catch up, having descended to the shore he ordered his officers to press on along an invasion road to Delphi. The target they were in motion to reach after plundering the rest of the riches of Locris and Phocis was a sacred precinct, home of Apollo for most of the year and where glimpses of the future might be mistily perceived. It nestled in the pine-clad heights of Mount Parnassus that were themselves sacred to the god Pan and the Muses, where Orpheus learned his licks from Apollo and young Odysseus came to grief in a boar hunt, leaving him with a recognizably scarred thigh.[19] The town was situated in a steep and defensible place, 'not walls, but precipices, not defences formed by the hand, but by nature, protect the temple and the city'.[20] Near the centre was a great natural amphitheatre where echoes from shouts and blaring trumpets, constantly repeated and increasing in volume, were interpreted by ignorant visitors as an awful illustration of the powers of Apollo, while winding up the hill the sacred fissure itself is found 'for a cold exhalation, driven upwards by some force, as it were by a wind, produces in the minds of the priestesses a certain madness, and compels them, filled with the influence of the god, to give answers to such as consult them.'[21] Since time immemorial, people had come to ask guidance of the oracle from the hugely rich Croesus of Lydia to proud king Tarquin of Rome and the tyrants of Syracuse; all beat a path to Delphi and the cities and states of mainland Greece, the islands and coastal Asia Minor regularly sent envoys to receive either mischievous riddles or at best highly ambiguous advice during key moments of communal crisis. Nor was it just rich fees for the service of the priestess (Pythia), but temple dedications of precious metals that were deposited from the loot of warfare from half the world. The devout and the expectant came either across the plains of Boeotia and Phocis to reach this greatest of cult centres or disembarked from the Gulf of Corinth at the port of Cirrha to make the short journey up to the sanctuary.

Delphi had suffered disasters in the past: as early as the mid-sixth century, fire had consumed Apollo's temple, and even before that there had begun a centuries-long sequence of destructive Sacred Wars. It was horror from the start when the Amphictyonic League ('league of neighbours', organized originally to manage the affairs of the sanctuary of Apollo at Delphi) states attacked Cirrha, the port of Delphi, blaming them for harassing pilgrims but really wanting their land, and cursed annihilation followed an assault against a population weakened by hellebore added to the city wells. More than 100 years later, a Pericles-inspired Athens backed the Phocians destructively contesting with a Spartan-sponsored coalition of locals to control the sacred places. It was the third war in over ten years in the 350s and 340s that saw the most terrible desecration when the Phocians, stirred up by a fine demanded by the Amphictyonic

League, dared to risk anathema by seizing many of Apollo's treasures to fund mercenary armies. Some 10,000 looted talents translated into an army of 10,000 mercenaries, paid premium rates to overcome any scruples about 'dirty money', that allowed them to punch considerably above their weight in central Greece in opposition to a Thebes intent on humiliating a hated neighbour. Years of conflict ended finally with the eruption of Macedonian power, first south of the Vale of Tempe and later below Thermopylae, that merged into a conflict with an Athenian-Theban alliance that ended at the Battle of Chaeronea. Dramatic stories littered these years, with a Phocian leader throwing himself to his death off a mountain rather than be captured after being injured in battle, leaving his second-in-command Onomarchos to salvage the army by liquidating his opponents and sequestering their property.

Phocians stripping the temple treasuries to fund their military had been bad enough, but at least they had been Greeks who honoured the home of Apollo; they respected the Pythia, even if they tried to manipulate her, and had an interest in preserving a place they knew had such importance for the whole Hellenic world. Now the terrible host approaching on the pilgrim road was intent not on leaving riches behind but on taking everything away. Crossing Phocis had been easy until the Gallic army reached the walls of the Parnassus range that came as a real shock. Jagged limestone ridges that reached heights of 8,000ft showed ahead and the roads they were crowding down seemed to threaten the possibility of ambush at every turn, a region that looked more like the habitation of wild beasts than sophisticated men dripping with the precious possessions they were after. Not that they had not seen plenty of mountains before in Illyria, Thrace and Macedonia, but this was not the soft country they had been promised. For nearly 10 miles they snaked along with Brennus and his officers at their head, a Gallic command that was careful as they travelled the unfamiliar and threatening valleys, sending out scouts who would have warned them that despite seeing so few inhabitants on the immediate approach, a considerable force was waiting in defence of Delphi.

Along with now knowing they would have to fight for the treasures of the gods came the realization of how difficult this might be. The narrow road pushing below a mountain ridge made their immediate approach to their target deeply problematic; even the small number of hoplites on hand for defence could easily fill the passage that the Gauls needed to push through and there seemed no way round as coming up from the valley below entailed climbing something like a cliff that could hardly be assailed even if it was only lightly held. As the designs on the hoplite shields and bristling spears came in sight, Brennus was in two minds, calculating whether to attack immediately or allow his exhausted men to rest overnight before sending them in to the attack. Spokesmen from the Aenianians, Greeks living west of the Malian Gulf and Thessalians, who had joined the Gauls in a murky compact when they traversed their country and who knew the foes they were challenging, were eager to attack straight away so as not to give the defenders a breathing space to receive further reinforcements, organize themselves and block the approaches with stone walls. It was indiscipline in the ranks that eventually decided the matter as many of Brennus' warriors dispersed over the country, finding wine and food in the houses and barns that the locals had left behind at the behest of the oracle, suggestive of a stratagem against people notorious for liking a drink and one that achieved exactly what was intended.

So it was perhaps with surprise that many of the defenders realized they had been granted a temporary reprieve, allowing the inhabitants of the country who had fled to Delphi to arm themselves to aid in guarding the home of Apollo, to integrate with the allied soldiers who had arrived almost at the last minute. These locals had not been abandoned to their fate; Phocians from all over had appeared eager to make amends for the sack of Delphi by Philomelos in 356 that started the Third Sacred War, as had 400 hoplites from Amphissa a few miles to the north-west. To back them up were some Aetolians who soon found themselves reinforced by 1,200 more of their compatriots under another Philomelos. What of the rest of these formidable people? They had not been dilatory, but had redirected their steps through Doris to harass Acichorius as he moved with the main army through the Hot Gates into Phocis and now they continued to pin him down, delaying decisively any attempt to follow his leader's orders and press swiftly on past Thermopylae with all his remaining men and the baggage containing the invaders' already accumulated loot. If many Aetolians would not be present to defend Delphi itself, they at least made sure that Acichorius' horde would find no easy pickings in central Greece or reach Brennus in time to offer the crucial reinforcements he looked for.

So it was just what was left of his own detachment that had travelled the mountain track behind Thermopylae that Brennus could bring to the battle. Not even all of these were in the best of moods, believing the upcoming contest was not what they had been led to expect. Greece had been advertised as a sunny land of easy pickings, but now they found themselves between threatening, craggy promontories, ramparts of jagged and fissured rocks where the wind whipped through gusts of snow and frost lay white on the terrain that might conceal lurking enemies. Yet these disappointed men knew they had to fight; they may have been hoping to get rich quick, but now thoughts were concentrated almost as much on survival as they wound up the track towards the complex of buildings, religious and secular, that made up the sacerdotal centre of Delphi. The position must have seemed like Thermopylae all over again, but now there was no possibility of an outflanking movement; all that could be attempted was a battering assault against men at the edge of mortality who called on all they knew to try to increase their chances against an enemy they saw massing in apparently irresistible might. The large round shield carried by each defender covered not just himself but his comrade on his left, meaning perfect confidence in the next man was required in an atmosphere where savage yells etched the air and reminded the Greeks of the worst stories they had heard of Gallic fury as the whole weight of Brennus' horde swept forward like a terrible beast of prey eager to feast on the farmers and artisans manning the hoplite line to their front.

Even if the numbers in Brennus' raiding party were exaggerated, the defenders were still facing monstrous odds with troops from different places, among whom spite had been the theme of ages, trying to coordinate in the face of annihilation. Still, it helped that in the lull before the storm, as the hoplites hefted the shields and levelled their spears and the light troops prepared their missiles, word went round that divine figures, gods, ghosts and phantoms, guardians of the sacred places, had been seen inspiring the struggle against the impious intruders who were determined on stealing what belonged to the gods. 'Two priests, as well as the priestesses themselves, with their hair loose, and with their decorations and fillets, rushed, trembling and frantic, into the front ranks of the combatants',[22] yelling encouragement that they had seen Apollo himself leap down into his temple, seconded by Artemis and Athena appearing in armour and carrying bows to the sound of clashing arms. That there is a tradition of heavenly intervention is inevitable in such a hallowed place as Delphi where the gods would always be near and it is easy to imagine the rumours of sanctified assistance causing a surge of confidence among people already animated in defence of their homes and families. The assistance of the gods was always a mystery, but it was not to be sniffed at, particularly here at the portal to the celestial world.

Some of the attackers were still under the influence of a night spent drinking wine, so went forward uphill towards the enemy with enthusiasm and little 'fear of danger', while others were hungry, yet more hung-over and some not a little resentful that they were having to fight for their lives when they should have been piling up their waggons with loot. Yet all had been raised tough and had the confidence of born warriors, while to enhance their motivation, 'Brennus, to rouse the courage of his men, pointed to the vast quantity of spoil before them, declaring that the statues, and four-horse chariots, of which a great number were visible at a distance, were made of solid gold'[23] as they approached the 4,000-odd defenders in a formidable defensive position blocking their way. Jostling lines wavered and bent as biting winds whistled down between the crags, blowing out the plaid cloaks of one side and bristling the horsehair helmet plumes of the other. The front ranks crashed together with spears splintering and the attackers trying to break the enemy with great slashing sword strokes or lance thrusts and the Greeks defying all behind their wall of shields. Holding firm, the defenders found themselves not just aided by divine apparitions but by nature itself. It was said that part of the mountain fell on a section of the Gallic line, which sounds improbable, though a modern sign near the approach to the archaeological site does warn of falling rocks, suggesting that seismic intervention was not impossible. All this was while an increasing storm of wind and hail lashed the attackers, leaving their wounded in great discomfort. Hardly able to hear the orders of their officers, there were stories of warriors struck by lightning and that they too saw the apparition of heroic Greek divinities fighting beside their enemies.

Not that the casualties were only on one side: Greeks fell too and a Phocian warrior named Aleximachos was noticed falling to a fatal wound as the hero of the defence, so that a statue of him was later dedicated in the sanctuary to Apollo, but it was worth the sacrifice as it was their gods they were defending against northern demons; a crusade against warriors of the dark. After desperate combat, the sides fell apart with the attackers fading back to collapse fatigued in their temporary camp formed among the dark masses of the mountains, while the Greeks, pressing forward, moved in close to prevent the invaders from foraging for the provender they now so desperately needed. Scattering to settle down to try to sleep with little order kept and with minimal defences built, the Gauls spent a dreadful night in such terror and panic that some, thinking a huge Greek host was attacking them, started slashing at each other. It turned out it was not just imagination because as the sky began to lighten the following day, it became clear that the enemy was in no mood to leave them alone. Picking themselves up from the hard frosty ground, limbs cramped and minds hardly rested, the Gauls knew they must arm themselves for another bout of fighting. Those mandated as piquets were already raising the alarm as slingshot and javelins screamed out of the dawn into the sleeping ranks as Brennus and his officers fabricated a fighting line.

The Greeks came on, deep files of men behind their solid round shields, with only their eyes showing between rim and helmet, while Brennus led from the front with a bodyguard of tall, brave warriors slashing wildly with their long swords to hold back the spearmen driving their weapons at their torsos. He and the other chiefs would have been much better protected in fine mail shirts and decorated helmets, but they suffered too as the defenders utilized home advantage. Local men who knew every track and passable ledge led their peltasts and other light infantry beneath the broken crags, edging their way along rock shelves to get above their enemies and once in place they loosed volleys of missiles against the unguarded flanks and heads of an enemy who could not get back at them. The impact was immediate and the Greeks, revitalized, exploited this real advantage, which rather more than any airy apparitions counted as the armoured hoplites stood against the Gallic fury. Soon they were able to take the initiative with the Phocians in the lead. Sternly ordered forward, they launched an attack against the wavering enemy line that was bunching up as many tried to turn their shields to protect against the slings, javelins and arrows that were lashing them both from the wings and above where the Greek skirmishers had found positions of prominence in country they knew so well.

The Gauls were struck on their unprotected bodies or where there were weaknesses in their armour and those wounded, even if carried back out of the fight, could find no comfort in a world of frost and snow. Pushed to and then past breaking-point, the sweat-soaked and blood-flecked northerners were soon in open retreat and the Greeks saw an opportunity to rend at the heart of the sacrilegious intruders who had intended to loot their holy places. Paeans were raised and spread along the lines as a tide of hoplites swept forward past the bodies of the wounded men put out of their misery by comrades who could no longer carry them away. They followed an enemy who were hoping to find a stronger position where they could make a stand and recoup their strength, but discovered they were not allowed any such breathing space as they retreated, picking their way through unfamiliar terrain. Things may not have gone to plan but at least the Gauls could hope to get out with their lives, despite knowing their foes were shadowing the route they were bound to take, waiting to strike. There was little chance to get up speed, burdened as they were with casualties and needing to protect themselves at every step. If not exactly inching, still it was slow progress, picking their way over an unfamiliar route with groups fragmenting in an atmosphere close to panic, with so many having lost confidence in leaders who seemed to have no answer to the enemy tactics. Clan leaders and tribal chiefs might push the men in their war bands to hold their ranks and drive back the puny southerners who were daring to attack them, but few took notice. For the Greeks it was now hit and run, ceaselessly harrying a tormented enemy with stones and javelins, tactics in which the Aetolians particularly excelled.

'Scorched thresholds testify to Brennus' sacrilege, attacking the Pythian kingdom of Apollo, the unshorn god: and then Parnassus shook its laurel-crowned summit, and scattered fearful snow over the army of Gaul.'[24] It had been terrible, a sure sign of the anger of the gods with reports of 6,000 Gauls falling in battle and the loss of a further 4,000 in the wintry storms and panic that followed; an overstatement, but one suggestive of how roughly the intruders had been handled. Nor was this anything like the end, and even if we question that another 10,000 starved to death on the road, the interlopers without doubt suffered constant harassment during their retreat. The survivors, dead-eyed and exhausted, found and joined up with Acichorius who had been delayed on his journey by the attentions of the Aetolians wanting payback for the losses their people had suffered when the Gauls trashed their country. The whole army, thirsty and hungry, now pressed on to make camp near the town of Heraclea in Trachis, a nightmare march not helped because of the attentions of the Athenians who had found out from their agents what had happened at Delphi and with no cautious voices heeded and all possible men mobilized, they hurried through Boeotia, picking up local soldiers on the way to unite with the pursuers coming from the sanctuary: 'Thus the combined armies followed the barbarians, lying in wait and killing those who happened to be the last.'[25] The Athenians had taken the road north to join others committed to revenge, ensuring the invaders left their blood to mingle with the earth they had hoped to conquer.

The image of the heroic Gaul or Galatian was made concrete after Attalus of Pergamon commemorated his victory over one of the bands despoiling Anatolia in the 230s by the dedication of groups of sculptures. One in Pergamon itself and another on the Acropolis at Athens that is reported[26] standing next to a statue of Olympiodorus. Roman copies can still be seen of these noble, uncorrupted savages who in defeat could become particularly appealing to people who loved their own sophistication but knew they had lost something in the transition from the simple days of their ancestors. One of the most impressive is the Ludovisi Gaul housed in the Museo Nazionale di Roma, Palazzo Altemps depicting a warrior stabbing himself while supporting his dying woman. Whether Brennus expressed such a forceful combination of naturalism and theatricality in his own passing is unknown, but having been wounded in the fighting at Delphi the tradition is well-established that he died on the road by taking his own life. Dragged down in ruin by puny Greeks, the outcome was not uncharacteristic among Gallic leaders when they had aroused their countrymen's anger by military failure. Fiasco had to find a target of blame to satisfy his testy followers and with his officers intent on finding excuses for themselves, it is unsurprising that he had to shoulder the responsibility. With it came self-destruction, though the method is uncertain, ranging from drinking himself to death with unwatered wine to ending it all with a knife when in unendurable pain from a wound. In whichever way, so perished the second famous Brennus, the only one of the Gallic chiefs of this period whose name lived long in the memory.

That Brennus had been wounded is no surprise as he was very far from alone with 10,000 injured warriors carried or hobbling back from the Greek campaign. These survivors and their intact comrades accomplished the hazardous journey north, despite after crossing back over the Spercheus River the stragglers were pounced on by local Thessalians and Malians eager for retribution. The details of their woes on this trail of tears entail nothing but terrible hardships; that they had already consumed most of their food and wine meant that famine dogged their steps and their suffering was enhanced by rain, frost and fatigue in the open where they were unable to find shelter or peace to sleep and were consumed by fear of the enemy falling on their rear. All this was compounded by guerrilla attacks from the people whose country they crossed, where laggards were finished off and no rest was to be had before they left Greece behind. Many more would have succumbed during the retreat, though 'that not a Gaul returned home in safety'[27] is clearly hyperbole; their assailants would have become sated with slaughter well before such a complete extirpation could have been accomplished.

Much of all this was far-fetched yarns repeated to comfort traumatized victims as it was clear that a large proportion of the invaders saved themselves, many dispersing all the way back to Illyrian and Pannonian homes, despite receiving hard knocks on the road when they passed through Dardania. There were a people reportedly living in Illyria who were plagued by the vengeance of Apollo for taking part in the attack on Delphi; they came home to a land where the rivers and streams were filled with numberless frogs producing vapours that led to a devastating plague. Others seem to have travelled even further, sufficient for a legend to arise that booty from Delphi made its way to Tolosa, modern-day Toulouse in France.[28] Some 15,000 talents of silver and gold were hoarded there before being filched by a particularly grasping Roman proconsul called Quintus Servilius Caepio who, cursed by his actions, suffered by his army being annihilated by the Cimbri at the Battle of Arausio, a holocaust that fittingly saw this deeply unpleasant man stripped of his citizenship and driven into exile. Other bands of survivors joined compatriots who had continued trashing Thrace and parts of Macedonia before running up against Antigonus Gonatus or under Comontorius enjoying a lucrative protection racket at the expense of Byzantium before setting up the short-lived kingdom of Tylis in Thrace, probably in the Haemus Mountains in what is now Eastern Bulgaria.

The Greeks were still in shock in the wake of the violent fury of the Gauls' attack when realization dawned at last that the threat was over, they had cleared the invaders out of their homeland and that age's heroes could return to their homes without fear. It had seemed a dazzling triumph, yet there are question marks; how otherwise to explain stories like the Tolosa treasure, clearly suggesting that Delphi was sacked, even if the polluted looters were driven off afterwards? Was their departure before or after they had got their hands on Apollo's riches? What some Hellenistic powers would become uncomfortably aware of was that the people who year by year had gained in power and reputation by the retelling of this campaign were the Aetolians. Admiration for their stirring resolve was general, despite the fact that they had left their post at Thermopylae to return and defend their homeland and however unorthodox their guerrilla tactics had been. Since steeling themselves to fight a nation of thaumaturges (magicians), they had found a way of winning and they would benefit from the repeated rendition of a heroic tale of peerless glory to be put alongside Salamis and Plataea. If the flyblown Gallic corpses lying along the road north were mute and pitiable, the Aetolians were not; they trumpeted achievements that put them into a line of greatness stretching back from Thebes and Sparta through to Athens. Those places had had their day and now it was surely theirs. The dominance of the Aetolian League at Delphi was physically advertised by a victory stele incorporating examples of captured Gallic armour and spiritually by their admittance to an Amphictyonic League that they substantially dominated for some decades after. Their recent acquisition of Heraclea in Trachis emphasizes a capacity to control the stretch of country right across the middle of central Greece where the gulfs of Actium and Malia pull in tight like a belt around the country's waist. Were these the hardy cockroaches who had survived a barbarian Armageddon to become the advance guard of a glorious future for Greece in a post-Galatian age?

Chapter Eight

An Improbable Hero

What would a world after the deluge look like, particularly now that Demetrius, after a record of evanescent achievement, of ups and downs without parallel, would never come back again? The sybarite warlord whose inflated and eccentric policy had been the shaping factor in so much of what had happened in Macedonian Europe after the turn of the century had since 285 been held captive in the shadows by Seleucus. For three years the great besieger of cities had rotted under house arrest in the Syrian Chersonese where the Orontes River bent towards Antioch. It is easy to imagine that, bored and humiliated, his resistance to plentiful food and drink provided by his captors was pretty limited and 'in the fifty-fifth year of his life' this brooding presence passed from the land of the living, despite him being almost twenty years younger than both his hated enemy Lysimachus and his captor Seleucus. One of the most extraordinary of the successors had died; a man who, if like his exemplar Alexander, had loved to immerse himself in Dionysian mysteries still was really more in thrall to Tyche, the goddess of chance, already increasing in importance in the Hellenistic pantheon. Partying on the Acropolis where as a saviour god he could dally with Athena in her own temple; when not attacking cities with siege towers the height of mountains had been his style, as had been leading fleets with maritime goliaths that would have overawed Poseidon himself and preferring to throw himself into an impossible invasion of Asia rather than accepting a quiet life as a monarch over the Fetters of Greece. A heroic reputation won by blazing across a world made huge by the great Alexander had been everything for Demetrius and just as it had been for that conquering king, both these men would undoubtedly have preferred a Homeric death in battle, bringing immortal fame, but it had not been in their stars and both had been brought down with a liver pickled in alcohol rather than by a foeman's sword. Gossip certainly gave it out that Seleucus had encouraged the dissipation that led to his demise, to be rid of this rogue king without suffering the odium that would have come from outright murder, but this is not completely credible. It was after all this same ruler who refused a shower of gold from Lysimachus to kill his captive soon after Demetrius had surrendered to him and more than this he had to be of some value as a pawn in the diplomatic game he intended to play in the years ahead. He even offered some hope to the caged king by suggesting that he would reconsider his sentence once Demetrius' daughter came to Syria from the east with her husband Antiochus.

There is emphatically no suggestion in his disposal of the dead man's remains of any sort of personal enmity. Seleucus notified Antigonus Gonatus that he would be sending his father's ashes to him in a golden urn so he might meet the transport vessel and do due honour to one of the greatest figures of the age. That such a giant would pass away without some spectacle was not a possibility, and his final send-off was attended by some of the grandest pageantry reported during the whole period. With his entire fleet, the grieving offspring sailed to meet the Seleucid ship 'off the islands' along the Aegean coast of Anatolia and took the great golden urn that contained his father's remains onto 'the largest of his admiral's ships'. From then it was a funereal cavalcade around the realm that Antigonus had inherited: 'Of the cities where the fleet touched in its passage, some brought garlands to adorn the urn, others sent men in funeral attire to assist in escorting it home and burying it.'[1] The importance of Corinth to the Antigonids is well demonstrated when the funereal armada approached the port with the vase with the dead king's ashes exhibited in glorious pageant, wrapped around in cloth of royal purple with a diadem mounted on the top. Youths from the best families stood as escort around the magnificent catafalque as the most distinguished living flute-player called Xenophantus performed a melody to keep the rowers in perfect time as their oars splashed through the water, 'like funereal beatings of the breast, answered to the cadences of the flute-tones.'[2] Once the ceremony at Corinth was completed and 'garlands and other honours had been bestowed upon the remains', the caravan was directed to Demetrias where the final interment of the remarkable adventurer was to be concluded.

The son of the extraordinary father just entombed had already shown himself a very different man and ruler from his sire. A third-generation successor, Antigonus Gonatus, perhaps so-called for having been raised at Gonni in Thessaly, had been hanging on for years, bailing out the leaky ship of state inherited from his parent since Seleucus had clamped fetters on him after a preposterous battle on the plains of Syria.[3] Apart from orchestrating the grand pageant required for Demetrius' funeral, another significant occurrence in recent years had seen him for once overstep himself and allow inopportune ambition to drive, leading to a significant naval defeat at the hands of Ptolemy Ceraunus. Beyond this, his role had largely been about holding on while his veteran mercenary corps secured the Fetters of Greece on top of the other places in Attica, the Argolid and eastern Achaea where his friends and agents were in power. This coastal statelet was a fragile entity without a sizable terrestrial kingdom, and the tax base was insignificant outside the enclaves like Chalcis, Corinth and Piraeus where they could levy tolls on the merchant princes of Greece and the Aegean grown rich on a considerable transit trade. Though this was only at the expense of an increasing unpopularity among those who were bound to resent the continuing cost of funding his forces, especially after the years of shakedown they had experienced as Demetrius wrung every drachma he could to outfit his invasion of Asia.

Yet when from the windows of his palace at Demetrias Antigonus scanned the political firmament at the commencement of the third decade of the third century, there were considerable pluses to be noticed. Firstly that dangerous monarch Pyrrhus was no longer a notable menace, having succumbed to the rival temptations of a wider world, as after concluding an entente with Ceraunus and taken his daughter in marriage, that mercurial man, buoyed by a promise to provide him with Macedonian soldiers, was putting the final touches to his putative adventure and waving goodbye on the way to Italy. Beyond this, Demetrius' heir also had good men on his side. There was the likes of his half-brother Craterus, Phila's son by Alexander's redoubtable general who long governed in Corinth, on both sides of the isthmus including places held in Attica and down towards the Argolid and perhaps with overall control of Euboea, but never seeming tempted to make a play for independence. Another was Heracleides, the long-time commandant at Piraeus who showed impressive loyalty on at least one occasion. Equally he was on good terms with a considerable if criminal constituency of maritime freebooters who Demetrius had befriended in the past and who retained an affection for his family. To be sure, there were others among the grand old cities of Hellas where after the demise of his father he had found his standing eroded; the loss of Elateia in Phocis had highlighted what was more than just a local problem, it showed that the hard-won position of the Antigonids in Boeotia had become less secure, ensuring land communications between Corinth and Demetrias were much more troublesome, concerns amplified by an awareness that the hand of Lysimachus could be detected in these developments. The year 284 had seen Antigonus feeling his most insecure, cosying up to Pyrrhus despite that king having just thrown him out of Thessaly, only to end on the losing side when Lysimachus drove the Epirot out of Macedon, raided Epirus and re-established Acarnania in the west as a local bulwark against Pyrrhus' Aetolian allies. With new friends showing themselves hardly able to sustain themselves in a changing world, nothing could hide the fact that Lysimachus represented a real sword of Damocles hanging over his head, though time would show that this naked blade would never fall, something that became more and more apparent as that monarch's activity abroad was paralyzed by conflicts within his own family.

So at Antigonid headquarters after intelligence reports had been scrutinized they certainly could breathe a little more easily as the ruin of Lysimachus at the hands of Seleucus suggested a considerable notch on the credit side of the balance sheet. Yet it was far from a time to rub their hands in glee as the aborted attempt to compete for the crown of Macedon meant considerable risk for a magnate with resources as skimpy as Antigonus and when it went wrong he would pay the price. It was not just the sour taste left in his mouth from his miscalculation; there were also enemies all around determined to kick a man when he was down and it looked for a while that after his defeat at sea he would be beaten out of much of Greece. Enemies mobilized to take advantage when news leached in that only a battered remnant of Antigonus' task force had returned from his Macedonian escapade. Especially long-standing enemies in Sparta, headed by their king Areus, were looking to resuscitate a Peloponnesian league that might effectively oppose Antigonid influence in the peninsula. The membership ended including much of the Argolid, Arcadia, Elis and towns in western Achaea like Patrai, Dyme, Tritaia and Pharai, while Argos and Megalopolis, places that normally had no time for following in a Lacedaemon wake, threw out their Antigonid garrisons and pledged themselves to severe neutrality.

Nor were these eruptions confined to the peninsula. Boeotia and Megara⁴ may have reacted with Athens possibly involved as well, although the chronology is a mystery for which there is no completely satisfactory explanation. These few years had seen a continuing war of posts in which Antigonus still retained hopes of holding his own, as even if he failed to keep control in Boeotia, with the fetters at Corinth, Euboea and Piraeus well held his watery communications were secure and his enemies effectively separated from each other. However, in Areus he had an enemy who understood strategy well enough too, who in 280 attempted to make an impression in central Greece by marching to Patrai and shipping his army over the Gulf of Corinth to attack the Aetolians who otherwise might have come to Antigonus' aid in Boeotia. The cunning of the planning was not matched by a concomitant outcome as when they landed on the seaside below Delphi and occupied the Cirrhaean plain, laying the country in ashes, this only served to stir up the locals. The Aetolians, assembling 500 warriors, launched nimble attacks on the separate raiding parties until the invaders, confused by the smoke of the fires, badly ordered and loaded down by booty, not realizing what a small party they were facing were cut up and routed, losing an improbable-sounding 9,000 men. This setback meant the Spartans found few takers to restart the campaign after this poor showing, particularly when many communities had long appreciated the hollowness of any Laconian assurances about any autonomy agenda .No one either on the Peloponnese or outside was eager to swap an Antigonid hegemony for a Spartan one, encouragement that for Antigonus was made sweeter when circulating Spartan ambassadors advertised a resurgence that scared sufficient Achaean towns, many of which had recently expelled their Antigonid garrisons, into creating their own league as a counterweight. Finally, policy had been directed by the uneasy glances they had long cast at the bully in their own backyard from whose Peloponnesian ambition so many still bore scars.

While the Antigonid administration worried over the arrival of heterogeneous news from Greece, everything was flung in the air by the intervention of wild men from the north. The intrusion of Gallic war bands into the Balkans effected an awful trauma among the Hellenic polities from Thessaly to Aetolia, while places as far off as Athens and Boeotia worried whether it might be their turn next on the barbarians' hit list. Antigonus himself had been involved peripherally, sending a few hundred men to help at the defence of Thermopylae, but mainly he just hoped his holdings would not come directly into the crosshairs of a novel and ferocious enemy, but as the dust settled he realized that the new circumstances might offer as much opportunity as threat. He was bound to seem a natural for many apprehensive people to turn to after the last king of Macedonia had ended donating his skull as a drinking vessel to the foreign invaders. The cities of the Thracian Chersonese, the Troad and Aeolis, made nervous by the Gauls tramping over Thrace or crossing to Asia, would certainly have cause to look to Demetrias for a patron and if Antigonus Gonatus was no big beast in the mould of Antipater, Cassander or Lysimachus – after all, in 280 a few minor powers of Greece had run him ragged – in Europe the big beast seemed largely a thing of the past. At least he was still a ruler with cards to play, he controlled great fortresses with a solid mercenary corps to garrison them, a considerable field army and a marine significantly refurbished since the defeat in 280 and the financial reserves with which to fund them.

Opportunities in Macedon itself and at the hinge of Europe and Asia were inevitably where Antigonus' acquisitive inclinations were piqued, partly because openings in other areas were few and far between. In many ways the great winner in the last years of the 280s had been the Ptolemies, secure behind desert and a sea cruised by their first-class marine. To allow no doubt on his dynasty's standing in the world, Ptolemy II in 280 had instituted a great festival in honour of his father at Alexandria that he intended should equal the Olympics and in the enlarged League of Islanders the Lagids had plucked from an Antigonid grasp, they even began the practice of honouring Ptolemy II as a god just as they had his father. Where many polities suffered the blight of contesting factions, Egypt had seen a smooth transition from one very long-lived monarch to another; something that in pre-modern Europe was almost always a win-win situation unless the inheritor was both offensive and useless to a phenomenal degree. Ptolemy II Philadelphus was certainly not that. Responsible for turning Alexandria into the intellectual engine of the Hellenistic world by his sponsoring of the Great Library and with ventures like the royal menagerie and the extraordinary lighthouse on the Pharos being more to his liking than grand military adventures, his near forty-year reign allowed a stability and security that was almost unique in this era.

So any opportunity of expanding his influence into southern waters in the face of Lagid maritime might was almost closed off or at least very chancy, thus almost inevitably when Antigonus again looked to spread his wings it was towards the chaotic north that he directed his gaze. Gratifyingly, his spies would have made him aware that it was taking Antiochus a long time to secure control of those Anatolian positions his father won on the field of Corupedion, though once arrived on the scene from his secure bases in Syria and Mesopotamia it was likely to mean conflict with this powerful neighbour. Competition for influence around the Hellespont was going to provide a flashpoint for war, but when this outbreak of hostility occurred is difficult to know, although it could not have begun until some time after Ptolemy Ceraunus had established himself in Macedonia. It had been the demise of Seleucus at his hands that had been at the root of the power vacuum that formed around the Thracian Chersonese, where it was a mess in a region where local administration had been ruptured twice within a year. There must have been some communities where officials and garrison units with Lysimachid inclinations were still in place, while others would have recently welcomed Seleucid governments that were left hanging in the wind while the new Macedonian king had his hands full at Pella. Certainly Ptolemy Ceraunus held little sway there, while Antiochus, still in inner Asia, was just digesting the news of his father's bloody end.

This prince from the East had years of experience ruling the old Mesopotamian and Persian upper satrapies, but now he had been hoisted onto the throne of a realm expanding to include Phoenicia, Syria, Anatolia and more. Seleucid Asia was a famously multicultural place and where different elites had been flattered and seduced into compliance since Alexander had arrived, happy to pay considerate attention to the practices and gods of so many people. The first two Seleucids not in the least averse to syncretism proved adept in navigating this world, recognizing the need to find friends in strategic lands and partners in rich and brilliant localities where an investment of courtesy and esteem would pay dividends. However, just its extent of over 2,000 miles east-west and 1,500 miles north-south as the crow flies meant that centrifugal forces were bound to come into play, threatening dissolution, and indeed it had been this imperative that had meant Seleucus had set Antiochus up as his proxy in the East in the first place. Just in north-west Anatolia the new king would find more than one enemy eager to contest his hegemony; the Bithynians, bolstered by new-found Gallic allies, had no intention of giving up recently-won autonomy, while Pontic Heraclea had already fought off armies sent by Seleucus and had shown in recent combat against Antigonus Gonatus that her naval resources were formidable. It was the resistant autonomy of these two that saw the gestation of a northern league that would later include Byzantium, Pontus, Chalcedon and Teos, all of whom had worried about the threat initially from an all-conquering Seleucus coming to dominate Anatolia and Europe on top of his other Asian holdings. Zipoetes of Bithynia had been a moving force in the beginning and his role was taken up with enthusiasm by his successor Nicomedes, despite civil war with his brother initially undermining his position after his father's death early in the 270s. These local dynasts controlling one of the most important routes between Asia and Europe had long shown an independent inclination in their relations with Macedonian monarchs, fraught intercourse had on occasions deteriorated into bloodshed and there is evidence that Bas, an earlier ruler, had defeated a Macedonian general called Callas in the 320s, while more recently the Bithynians had driven off a commander that Lysimachus had sent to suppress them.

Pontic Heraclea, if less consistent in its anti-Macedonian stance,[5] had thrown off their shackles when Lysimachus' death became common knowledge, subverting their garrison and slighting their acropolis defences. Seleucus sent his agent to attempt to bring the rulers in Heraclea, Phrygia and upper Pontus into line, but found them resistant in independent combination with Byzantium and Chalcedon. After this it had been Antiochus' turn to try, dispatching his general Patrocles over the Taurus with a detachment which then delegated a man from Aspendos called Hermogenes to crush them and their allies. However, he was persuaded or his palms were greased and, leaving the country, he decided to concentrate on Bithynia where the unlucky man was ambushed, killed and his army destroyed, despite his fighting bravely in the defeated ranks. This sting only stirred up Antiochus, causing him to collect his resources to deal with Nicomedes, who himself looked desperately for help from the direction of an expanding Heraclea that had been purchasing territory at Cierus and Tius and from the Thynians that may have been theirs before, though failing in the cherished dream of recovering the town of Amastris.

If he could not suppress these independence fighters in the years 280 and 279, Antiochus made, with the aid of local stalwarts like Philetaerus of Pergamon, considerable strides in reclaiming those places Seleucus had won in battle from Lysimachus. Lycia, Caria and Lydia would largely have been brought back into the fold, although Miletus and other places on the south Anatolian coast were snapped up by Lagid forces,[6] and after this the energetic son of Seleucus was never going to easily countenance the loss of his father's spear-won rights to the lands where Troy had once stood. Troas, a region of ancient prestige and riches, was not going to be lost to Antigonid influence without a fight and spring 279 would have sprung with anticipation of both opportunity and danger at Antigonus' court. The soldiers of Antigonus and Antiochus had stood shoulder to shoulder at the pass of Thermopylae in the autumn in the face of the barbarian threat posed by Brennus' horde, but this truce had been an aberration ensured by the chaos that followed Ptolemy Ceraunus' demise. Tensions had always been pretty high between these two later-generation successors who each had a legal claim to the throne of Macedon through their fathers that could have been a *casus belli* as early as 279. Antiochus had previously not pressed his claims and instead made an accommodation with Ptolemy Ceraunus, but now he was dead all bets were off and after what had been hardly even a season of goodwill, by spring of 278 the war was on again, although the events of this year remain sufficiently obscure.

It is possible that by this time Antiochus had allied himself not just with both Sparta and other Greek enemies of the Antigonids but also with Apollodorus, the tyrant of Cassandreia as well. The problem for these confederates was that Antigonus remained the strongest naval power in the north Aegean and his squadrons ensured it was almost impossible for any members of the combination to coordinate military activity; a naval predominance that was buttressed by close connections with those inveterate enemies of Antiochus, Byzantium and Heraclea, whose significant navies were now on his side rather than confronting Antigonid warships in alliance with Ptolemy Ceraunus. The active involvement of these powerful friends and the welcome it promised must have been part of the explanation for Antigonus' confidence as he prepared both to cross over to Asia to fight Antiochus and boldly cruise the waters round the Chersonese. There is a mention of a major conflict[7] between Antigonus and Antiochus in 278 with 'Large forces ranged on either side, and the war lasted for a long time' and confirmation that other members of the confederacy faced off against Antiochus at sea. Heraclea sent thirteen triremes to aid Nicomedes of Bithynia which allowed that monarch to confront the Seleucid navy on an equal footing, ensuring that neither side was prepared to risk an open engagement and that a balance of naval power was realized. Why Antigonus had not sent his squadrons that clearly might have been decisive is unclear unless there is something in the suggestion that he was distracted by another abortive descent on Macedonia.[8]

If we are nowhere given details of the campaigns fought in 278, we are on firmer ground by spring of 277 when Antigonus is recorded trying to make his presence felt both in Thrace and the Chersonese. He was counting on the fact that the patriot general Sosthenes and any other significant Macedonian power-players were mired in their own troubles and could have had retained little influence in those regions, while he also hoped to coordinate trouble for Antiochus with his allies. At some stage during the campaigning season movements of a considerable number of well-known troublemakers stirred the pot. The pattern of Gallic perambulation had been confusing from the start, the draw of asportation taking them all over, but by now many were dead, dispersed, gone back north to Illyria or Pannonia, involved in either their own Asian adventure or spread around Macedonia plundering. Yet some were still dangerously assembled and in 278 these were travelling along the Thracian coast, plundering as they went and cutting a swath of destruction that amplified the terror just the news of their coming engendered. Some of them were the remnants of the band, most of whose members had crossed to Asia, while others were left over from Brennus' horde, whose leader was long gone, and after their thrash at Delphi had taken the road back north and east. This party, now led by a warlord named Cerethrius, had spent 278 overrunning the Getai and the Tribelli, peoples that Lysimachus in his pomp had failed to completely subdue, and then wintering in their territory. Now this most recent Gallic menace numbering 15,000 foot and 3,000 horse were discovered barrelling into the Thracian Chersonese where a real drama played out.

Despite once brilliant kingdoms having been almost reduced to wastelands and weeds risen in the footsteps of these roving Gallic bands, Cerethrius' followers still felt that Europe had plenty to offer and after storming settlements along the coast and passing the vicinity of Lysimachia could have been preparing to commence another invasion of Macedonia[9] when they learned from their scouts that Antigonus was not far off with a considerable army and fleet. Cruising the coast, he was looking for influence among the communities of the Thracian Chersonese rather than on a hunt for Gauls, but he was bound to respond when he found vulnerable people in the area searching round for protectors after the marauders were reported heading in their direction. Antigonus would have seen nothing but advantage in putting such people under his protection, and with his ships loaded up with all the men he could spare from his fortresses' garrisons, he had headed for the Hellespont. By the time he hove in sight in summer 277 the area was already occupied by the raiders, but the impression is that the presence of this army was something of a surprise, that he had failed in detailed reconnaissance and, having no well thought out plan, was essentially making policy on the hoof when events unfolded near Lysimachus' old headquarters. Antigonus ordered a landing in the Gulf of Melas where Hieronymus' old home Cardia, standing at the neck of the Thracian Chersonese, had long prospered from the grain trade until 309 when Lysimachus razed it so the inhabitants could people his new capital.

The outlaw combination, noticing the disembarkation, were a little unsure of what to make of this particular Macedonian commander they had not confronted before, so refrained from blindly stampeding straight into a fight, instead sending envoys and offering a peaceful way out if Antigonus would pay for it, but who could also judge his numbers and quality if the new arrivals seemed disinclined to respond to the proposal. The answer was polite and if no promise of tribute was made, they were invited to a luxurious banquet with foodstuff laid out on gold and silver salvers to impress the gawking visitors with Antigonus' wealth. This only had the effect of inflaming their cupidity and it is impossible not to believe that this was his intention, except that he apparently also showed off his elephants, suggesting much more of intimidation than entrapment. Antigonus' intentions in all these intrigues are not so easy to make out, but the extravagant exhibition of both his wealth and his power make it likely that he was eager to come to an understanding with the Gauls. After all, it had not been long since the Bithynian king had hired just such a horde as axillaries and these ferocious warriors might be useful allies either in confronting Antiochus or making a move on the Macedonian throne. It was only when it became clear that they had no intention of agreeing to such an arrangement and were almost certain to attack him that he made the fateful decision and laid his plans. Whatever the motivation, when the Gallic leaders heard their emissaries' account they determined on attack, supremely confident, having apart from Brennus' misadventures in Greece experienced a long string of successes since the day three years earlier when Bolgius had cut to pieces the army of Macedonia and butchered its king. The direction of their reasoning was clear: that Antigonus would prove easy pickings as 'his camp was filled with gold and silver, but secured neither by rampart nor trench, and that the Macedonians, as if they had sufficient protection in their wealth, neglected all military duties, apparently thinking that, as they had plenty of gold, they had no use for steel.'[10]

The general opinion was that these rich and amenable Macedonians who had invited their representatives to dinner were clearly up for being sequestered, so with spirits high and temptation immediate the Gauls prepared their assault for the following night, hoping that their prey, under the impression that there might be a peaceful outcome to this confrontation, would leave their defences incomplete and any sentries would be lax in keeping watch. In fact, Antigonus 'foreseeing the storm that threatened him', had detected the perfect occasion to ensnare his enemies and a textbook plan to achieve it. He had emptied his encampment of not only his men and camp followers but most of the baggage and placed all in an adjacent wood, though leaving in plain sight his ships drawn up on the beach behind the bivouac. This tricky customer did not even leave sentries on guard, so things went very far from according to plan and it was almost a farce when those scouting in advance of the Gallic columns crept forward, under the cover of dark, towards the enemy's perimeter. There they found no guards to rush and no foemen snoring and defenceless in their tents; all was eerily quiet without even a piquet left to raise the alarm. Milling around the gate and looking up at the deserted walls, the attackers, taken aback, reacted with fear, 'suspecting that there was not a flight, but some stratagem on the part of the enemy, were for some time afraid to enter the gates.'[11] The apprehensive freebooters imagined that a trap had been laid and it took some time before they collected their nerve and even then they only sent a few men to skirt warily around the deserted streets of the unnerving edifice. Once these spies confirmed the place was empty the rest entered, determined to carry anything valuable and movable away with them. Then those with plunder looking for more and those without even more eager, they pressed on out of the other side of the camp in the direction of the sea, rolling noisily up the beach. Having, after a very circumspect approach, worked up the nerve to occupy the camp and reached the other side, they now saw a line of what looked like defenceless ships sitting vulnerable just a few score yards away.

Voices may have again been raised suggesting caution, but the majority were greedy for loot and pushed on. If the night-shadowed vessels had been left as bait or had remained by accident without the crews having time to launch them the effect was exactly the same; the attackers fell on them like starving men on a feast, expecting to find those treasures on board that they had not discovered in the deserted tent lines. All were fairly disorganized now with officers unable to retain control in the darkness and everybody impatient to find spoils to carry away. A disorderly line of men with spiky lime-washed hair gleaming in the moonlight fanned out from the camp gates onto the shore and, stumbling through the sand, approached the ships hauled up all along the curve of the beach. With little order and plaid trousers or bare legs wet to the knees, groups picked out vessels to board and climbed up onto the decks with their shields slung on their backs and only a few with weapons in hand, but now for the first time they encountered resistance. They did not expect it; everything this far had been easy, so their guard was down when they discovered the warships were not deserted but full of armed sailors and corseleted marines, eager to make a fight of it. Javelins were hurled and slingshot launched down onto the milling assailants, while other defenders pushed shields forward or stabbed down with long pikes, driving at the enemy trying to climb the sides like the giant Ajax keeping the foe at bay as they attacked the Archean penteconters drawn up on the sands outside the city of Troy.

The attackers, pressing on with savage war cries on their lips, had located formidable opponents, and the defence in this later fight, not many miles away from where that legendary affray took place, was even more effective as many of the beached vessels were high-sided fours, fives or even bigger, carrying considerable complements of fighting men with bolt-throwing engines on their decks. The fighting was ferocious, decks became slippery with gore as the assailants who had climbed so far were butchered or defenders overcome, though without doubt the Gauls were far from coming out on top, but this was not the worst of it. Antigonus, looking on from his position in the woods, felt the time had come to unleash his main force. Suitably emboldened by the success of his ploy and after his priests had made the appropriate blood sacrifices, the prince and his commanders signalled the advance, urging their men on to revenge the awful damage these intruders had done to so many of their homes. So the soldiers kept in hiding, mercenaries and elephants and the rest, given the huge advantage of surprise, appeared in a mass of armoured men and animals. Critical reinforcements that in formed and serried ranks issued from their arboreal shelter surged forward like an army of phantoms as they passed through shadowed trees. The disorganized Gauls attacking the boats now found themselves closed in the jaws of a trap between those opponents on the high-sided vessels they had already been combating and the armoured Greek mercenaries with stout Aspis shields and stabbing spears in a solid phalanx rolling into their rear. Their comrades still in the camp or whose attention was all on the plunder they expected to scoop or who were occupied in dragging away what they had already acquired were in no position to or had no interest in helping them.

The men on the beach were thrown into a tossing ferment of confusion by this enterprising blow. The northerners, except for their nobles, fought without armour, sometimes even naked, so facing brazen foes, many with corselets and helmets beside their heavy shields, they were often struck down without being able to hurt their assailants in return. Besides the heavy foot, quick-thinking officers also unleashed the peltasts who nimbly circled behind the enemy mob, finding easy targets as they threw their javelins in deadly enfilade into unshielded backs before surging in with swords bared. Only the cavalry was redundant in this night-time affray, with horses left hobbled or corralled while their riders fought on foot if at all. Everything was orchestrated to the terrifying din of horns and elephants trumpeting terror in the night-time conflict with fearsome fighters emerging from the woods singing their paean and threatening to cut off any possibility of retreat to Cerethrius' camp where they might hope to find refuge. These Gauls were brave men, many giddy with violence, and they fought on with audacity, wielding spears and swords, until the sight of more closed enemy ranks appearing through the dark caused some of the faint-hearted to fall into panic. Though steeled from youth in combat, finding themselves under a rattling fusillade of javelins and hissing arrows with the enemy line smashing into them turned out too much. Fear wrenched their guts as they surveyed a nightmare prospect; in front bloody men speared them from the ships' decks, while others behind moved in for the kill. Sword arms wearying, they were being tested as never before and the outcome did not long hang in the balance. Leaders and braver hearts tried to rally them, but it was no use and many would have not just been afraid and desperate but they would have been bitter, blaming their leaders' carelessness that looked like it had thrown away an initial advantage.

It would be hard to imagine a more eerie picture than a full-scale battle raging in the dark, illuminated only by the few torches that both sides carried to light their way, but how long this kaleidoscope of draining combat lasted we do not know. When the Gauls realized they were in danger of being surrounded they inevitably looked for options, for a way out, but however desperate they were to escape they needed to be able to see a route before they began to run and without it many continued to defend themselves out of desperation when in a more conventional affray they would have already taken to their heels. Their chiefs were there too, men who had led them to victory and treasure so often before, around who they might unite until it became clear all was lost. If the night-time confusion had initially benefited the Antigonid forces, now they also would have been unsure who was friend or foe and unable to make out their comrades in a tangled mass of humanity or see how they were faring in other parts of the field. Runners carrying orders to try to coordinate their efforts would have found it all but impossible in the deepening obscurity to find the officers to whom they had been sent. Formations crumbled on both sides, and grim and glorious duelling pairs would have clashed and fallen apart in this wild melee, a tentative ebb and flow that made it unlikely that a decisive outcome could be swiftly achieved. Yet finally it ended, with the Gauls, their resolve long faltering, discovered methods to extract themselves, stumbling through the darkness along paths leading out of the fighting line and Antigonus' officers calling a halt for fear of their own men losing their way in pursuit and coming to grief. However, the end did not come before a terrific slaughter had been accomplished in the ranks of the northerners' army, and as the dawn broke over the field, a picture showed mounds of Gallic dead and wounded calling for aid and mercy from the victors. How many of their numbers fell is not recorded and the same was true of the far fewer casualties among Antigonus' sailors and soldiers, but it was sufficient that not only had this particular band ceased to be a threat but afterwards any other barbarian neighbours would think twice before following the Gallic example in threatening Antigonus' domains.

The first rays of the morning sun showed an elated Antigonus treading the blood-soaked fields and regarding with satisfaction the parade of wounded and captured Gauls his men were escorting away. His favoured deity Pan had done the business and everybody knew who was the clear victor against the people who had been terrorizing the civilized world for years. How to explain how this had happened in this bizarre battle that from the beginning had never been a formal affair? We do not hear that Antigonus himself was at the forefront of the melee, but then that was not his style. Many others might have tried to emulate Alexander in spearheading victorious battlefield assaults, but Antigonus was happier in the company of his philosophers. This man who valued intelligence certainly had good knowledge of his enemy when he hatched his plan, ensuring a tempting bait was offered: first an undefended camp and after that vulnerable ships to suck them in until he was ready to pounce. So doubtless, after preparing the snare, he left the hands-on stuff to his officers, mercenary generals who had done such a good job of holding tight in Greece over the past decades. Whatever the cause of victory his men did not care; they were jubilantly slapping each other's backs to celebrate having faced in open battle these frightful men who had been ravaging the land for so long and cut them to pieces; world conquerors who previously had swaggered almost wherever they chose had been humbled. Such events might precede a marvellous future when news of the triumph over an existential enemy permeated the heartland of not just Macedonia but that country's neighbours who had been suffering for years as well. Surely there would be a welcome in both towns and countryside for the leader who had shown himself as the best hope as protector in a world turned upside-down; the one man who might divert the awful fury of the northern invaders and bring the civilized world out into the light of peace and prosperity after a half-decade of despair.

Much would hang on the verdict of this encounter, but if word of success soon reached the worried citizens of Lysimachia, it would take considerably longer to spread through Macedonia and Greece. In the days it took for news of his sensational success to circulate, Antigonus found it confirmed that his reputation had been massively boosted in a battered world. The impact of his achievement was being registered in all the wide Hellenic sphere; Greek cities offered thanks, with the feat recorded in a temple to 'Athene the giver of victory' at Athens.[12] Yet it would not just be the Antigonid prince's standing in Greece that had been hugely burnished; achievements on the sands of the Thracian Chersonese would have ramifications in his national homeland as well. Ambitions that had recently seemed impossibly grandiose might now be more than feasible, and Macedon might finally be there for the taking. Since the death of Ptolemy Ceraunus, this country had been sunk in something close to anarchy. After that king's well-earned fatality, a ruling elite had tried to reconfigure themselves to deal with the emergency around his brother Meleager who had been hoisted onto the throne, but his reign had lasted for a bare two months before he was exposed as incompetent, being 'unfit to rule' and deposed, after which the army bestowed the crown on Antipater Etesias, the son of Cassander's brother Philip. However, this man showed none of the character or talent of either his uncle or his namesake and lasted hardly forty-five days, and because his fleeting reign coincided with the dog days when the etesian winds blew, he went down in history named for this phenomenon.

After this tumultuous interlude a general called Sosthenes, probably one of Lysimachus' officers, who because of evident capacity rather than any dynastic connection was made heir to the Macedonian government. He effectively re-ordered the army, recruiting young and old, and even bested one of the bands of roving Gallic desperados who were careless when they tried to re-enter the country. .He 'drove them off, and saved Macedonia from devastation.' Clearly an effective ruler, his resurrection of Macedonia's reputation in Greece is suggested when the Aetolians named a city Sosthenes in his honour, and extraordinary too, that when this selfless servant of the state, despite his lack of royal blood, was offered the diadem he refused the honour. 'For these great services, he, though of humble extraction, was chosen before many nobles that aspired to the throne of Macedonia. But though he was saluted as king by the army, he made the soldiers take an oath to him, not as king, but as general.'[13] He retained the reins of power in his hands, holding at least parts of the country together for almost two years, probably in the name of a number of legitimate but powerless monarchs. Yet even this competent man could not escape the wrath of the Gauls as the army he struggled to keep in the field was not sufficient to keep control of all Macedonia or Paeonia and finally in June 277 suffered fatal defeat in the field, with routed troops only able to find protection in walled cities closing their gates against the enemy hanging on their heels.

So in this world rich in hope and potential, a reputationally engorged Antigonus found himself with real prospects. Sosthenes, who had held a fragile sort of power in Macedonia, was dead and the population, traumatized and suspicious, was cringing behind city walls or out trying to repair the farms and estates under constant fear of attack, either by bands of blond northern men who had been filling their waking nightmares for years, or just bandits encouraged by a lawless environment. In an exhausted country seething with contesting factions and petrified by intimidating interlopers, both within and without its borders, the greatest prize was suddenly within Antigonus' grasp and the son of the man who had been so ignominiously chased out of Pella almost a decade before now returned, trailing clouds of military glory. We know that not long after the victory at Lysimachia, Antigonus' old mentor Menedemus of Eretria[14] was lauding his receipt of the royal diadem worn by Philip, Alexander and his own father; enough to crease the face of this latest Antigonid king of Macedonia with a broad smile. Even if we are not sure whether he arrived in armed panoply at the head of his victorious army, leaving his new subjects with no option but to welcome him with open arms, or perhaps that a significant faction gagging for a saviour of any kind invited him to take the throne.

The question that locals were bound to have asked was whether this Antigonus Gonatus would do any better than the parade of kings and commanders who had come and gone in the past five years, but if the answer was unknowable, hope always remained and it would be hope amply repaid despite an immediate future that remained full of menace. Seldom was the suggestion that 'uneasy lies the head that wears the crown' more apt than in the case of this most recent ruler of Macedon. No part of the kingdom had been left unaffected by the traumas of recent years and the people who the great Alexander had considered only interesting because they worried the sky might fall on their heads had damaged his homeland in a way that king would have considered incredible. Death, destruction of buildings and theft of livestock had stifled the economy and even after the hordes had passed, the disruption of order had encouraged the flourishing of local brigands and a perennial threat remained of roving bands of unemployed mercenaries released by Hellenistic employers. The attrition had been considerable: bloody deductions from the always finite number of phalangites who had fallen under Gallic swords first when Ptolemy Ceraunus was crushed and later when Sosthenes suffered defeat and those farmers and their families who failed to reach the protection of city walls had been killed or deported, deducting swathes from those who might have provided refurbishments for the home army.

Macedonia had bled out in these years; the upper cantons particularly had repeatedly suffered at the hands of the intruders, so any government infrastructure remained fragile in a region that had always been poorer and less populated than lower Macedonia. Even in that heartland things were hardly any better: on top of the loss of life, the people's morale was shot; from turbulent aristocrats to patient peasants, everybody wondered what had happened to the favour of the gods that had allowed them only decades earlier to conquer the Persian Empire but now brought them to a pass where they had to beg for mercy from despised barbarians. The most significant towns had to rely on their own efforts and particularly their stone ramparts to stave off Gallic assaults and now few felt much fidelity towards administrations at Pella that had so singularly failed to protect them. Nor was it just Philip and Alexander's kingdom: much of the territory around had suffered too; a world of ruin in the Balkans that ensured it would be at least a generation before things could begin to recover properly.

At least in these circumstances Antigonus had a personality that offered reassurance to communal leaders whose worlds had been rocked to the foundations in past years, not just in places that had only just survived the Gallic fury behind their stone defences but rural populations too, who could find in this man who was a grandchild of the great Antipater hope of stability and safety. This country that Philip II had transformed into an imperial engine wanted rest and consistent government more than anything, and a familiar figure from over two decades, now suddenly radiant with the new-found glamour of a Gaul-destroyer, must have looked like the best bet to provide it. He was no unknown quantity: many would have remembered him from Demetrius' reign as that ruler's dependable viceroy in Greece, a serious figure that Macedonian grandees might have met and dealt with during a reign that had, despite the incumbent's manifold failings, lasted far longer than any since the death of Cassander. The new monarch immediately had to confront more than one focus of opposition, with the likes of Antipater, king of the dog days, still around, all presumably with some adherents and possibly another pretender called Arrhidaeus or Alexander loitering in the wings. These claimants had done little to fill the power vacuum that Antigonus now intended to occupy, and with their legitimacy questionable and their resources meagre, few must have expected that they would mount even local opposition to the hero who had crushed the terrible Gauls at Lysimachia. Certainly they had been singularly ineffective in stopping what had been left of the governing elite welcoming the new king, or shown any will or capacity to trouble his victorious army when it travelled the road to Pella.

Once established, Antigonus Gonatus, like Ptolemy Ceraunus before him, moved to eradicate those domestic rivals within his reach. Antipater required a final solution, and these two definitely came to blows because we are told[15] that some of Antigonus' mercenaries after the encounter were so insistent on getting paid their coin, which would have amounted to between 30 and 100 talents depending on whether women and children were counted in the calculation, that hostages of high rank had to be given over until the money could be raised. The captives looked for a moment to be in considerable danger as the mercenaries, camping apart from the main army, threatened vengeance until, proving devious, Antigonus took some of their own leaders prisoner and forced them to accept the lower sum in full payment of arrears. These men who valued themselves so highly for getting rid of their commander's rival for the throne were the remnants of Cerethrius' Gauls hired to flesh out an army that Antigonus expected to need to fight his way to power. Hiring the very men he had just defeated was a doubly advantageous arrangement: these troops whose name still instilled terror and were notoriously effective on first contact could plug the gap as an exhausted Macedonia was in no position to provide him with troops, while it also gave employment to potential marauders still roiling in the country north of his kingdom's borders.

If Antigonus was early in employing these warriors to boost his military roster, he would be far from alone. One of the most noticeable features of the new world once the awful tide of destruction had reached its high mark was that as the waters receded, Gallic mercenaries became the new military of choice for the contenders trying to pick up the pieces. It would be a policy soon followed by almost all the other Hellenistic monarchs. 'The nation of the Gauls, however, was at that time so prolific, that they filled all Asia as with one swarm. The kings of the east then carried on no wars without a mercenary army of Gauls.'[16] Numerous, cheap and effective, from this time few armies that we hear of do not include such a component and as often as not it was the decisive one. These wild men would fight hard and for any protagonist with money in his pocket and to employ them was a win-win situation. Like Antigonus, such commanders would both acquire numerous bespoke soldiers to fight their battles and instil terror in the hearts of their enemies, but at the same time ensure these people were not employed in laying waste their own familiar country and killing their kinfolk. They became ubiquitous, just as they had in the previous century, providing cut-price warriors to fuel the wars in Magna Graecia in south Italy and Sicily. There were plenty to go around, fighting on the cheap, and soon enough any major encounter in the Balkans would see groups of them in significant action. Indeed, there could be few better tributes to their fighting qualities than how completely they had come to dominate the mercenary market in the few years since they had appeared on the scene.

If these fighters for hire ensured that the last remnants of the house of old Antipater were driven off never to be heard of again, by 276 most other pretenders also seem to have been disposed of. Yet if these threats had been contained without too great an effort and little record, the same could not be claimed in respect of the ruler of Cassandreia, sited where the old city of Potidaea had stood at the head of the Pallene peninsula, the most western of the three legs of the Chalcidice. From the demise of Lysimachus, this place had shown a tendency to go its own sweet way and Arsinoe had made her base there before foolishly believing the marital sweet talk of her half-brother. Some time after Ptolemy

Ceraunus' death and the chaos that it ushered in, a local dynast took over there. A significant figure for some years, Apollodorus had been considered a great patriot for sponsoring the removal of a character called Lachares who had become unpopular for both his despotic conduct and his friendship with Antiochus and crucially he was already well-liked for having headed popular opposition to an officer called Theodotus, who is known for commanding in Lysimachus' garrison at Sardis and when arriving at Cassandreia had tried the classic tyrant's ploy of suggesting his life was under threat and in consequence needed a bodyguard.

This Apollodorus, apart from these patriotic credentials, also had a considerable reputation for base cunning and brutality. Once when accused of setting himself up as a tyrant, he 'appeared in black, with his wife and daughters dressed in the same manner' to persuade his judges of his unthreatening humility, while soon after wheedling out of this prosecution he really did take control of the city, after which one of his first acts was to punish the very judges who had exonerated him. There is another story that to secure his takeover of power he organized a cannibal banquet, 'invited a young lad, one of his friends, to a sacrifice, slew him as an offering to the gods, gave the conspirators his vitals to eat, and when he had mixed the blood with wine, bade them drink it.'[17] Apart from these impious shenanigans, once he had taken over he marched into the citadel, previously occupied by Ceraunus' mother Eurydice and her mercenary guard who gave it up when he proffered self-proclaimed credentials as one of the leaders of the city's democratic party. Then he bolstered his chances of defending his assets by more practical measures, employing Gallic mercenaries as both his personal guard and core of a municipal defence force with citizen soldiers and other hired warriors prepared to man the stout walls that protected the city. These lavishly rewarded northern mercenaries were the key to not just the city defence but to internal control as well, allowing him first to mulch the rich but later 'to exact money from the citizens at large, and by inflicting the penalty of torture upon many men and more than a few women he forced everyone to hand over gold and silver.'[18] It is even said that he was advised by a man called Calliphon the Sicel who had cut his teeth on the courts of a Sicilian despot, who counselled him to arm gangs of slaves and workmen, all the tropes of a Greek city tyrant from Cypselus of Corinth to Pisistratus in Athens.

Whatever the shocking crimes he is claimed to have perpetrated and whatever the vileness of his reputation, it did not stop this man proving very effective in holding off Antigonus for almost a year. No small-time thinker, he approached anybody who might resent the new incumbent at Pella; there is evidence he may have looked for allies as far away as Sparta, where they always worried about Antigonid influence and even approached Antiochus who may at this time still have been contemplating a bid for the Macedonian throne. Determined to deal with this present enemy, the Antigonid military marched down to the Pallene peninsula, famous in legend as the site where the Gigantes, born of the blood of castrated Uranus, were vanquished by the Olympian gods before being dispatched to underground captivity to act as engines of volcanic and seismic activity. Much of the promontory was rich arable land, or pasture occupied by colonists mainly drawn from Eretria on Euboea, though Antigonus' target had been a Corinthian foundation before Cassander re-established it in 316. It was far from easy of approach, with a canal built years earlier fronting its northern defences that still looks impressive to this day. Plenty had come to grief there in the past. A Persian detachment from Xerxes' army was well on the way to taking the town in 479 when they were washed away by a tidal wave, and in the 430s the Athenians had to spend years besieging the place just to bring this recalcitrant member of their Delian League to heel.

Once established, those very Gauls who Antigonus had made his reputation by vanquishing could have been seen occupying the siege works around the town both to its north and south. Bare-chested, moustachioed warriors filled out the ranks of the besieging army, the rest comprising Antigonus' veteran Greek mercenaries and as many Macedonians as were prepared and able to fight for their new monarch after years of battering defeats. Just as important was the Antigonid marine, well capable of cutting off supplies to the defenders, despite them having outlets on two sides of the Pallene peninsula, particularly now that the regular numbers of Antigonid vessels had been supplemented by whatever portion of the Macedonian fleet was still in working order after years of chaos. The whole enterprise lasted ten months, the kind of undertaking that Antigonus had not been involved in since the last major siege of Athens, though the only details of its successful conclusion are peddled in an improbable story from a book of stratagems.[19] This concerned a Phocian buccaneer named

Ameinias who involved himself when Antigonus raised the siege after a ten-month blockade. Getting on Apollodorus' good side by helping to revictual the defenders, he then offered to broker a reconciliation between the two warring parties so that in this new atmosphere of compromise the defenders dropped their guard, allowing the pirate chief to reveal his true purpose. He was based at an advanced post called Bolus and from there, with the assault force deputed to an Aetolian pirate called Melatas, he provided his men with ladders cut to the height of the city defences, and then sent them over the walls. Success was immediate and once the town had fallen it was handed over to Antigonus and the beneficiary of these sea dogs' enterprise now had the satisfaction of having the troublesome Apollodorus eliminated while Ameinias remained on his payroll until at least 272 when he is again mentioned as a senior officer at Corinth involved in the Peloponnesian campaign against Pyrrhus.

With this stronghold reduced and Apollodorus disposed of, Antigonus showed he could woo as well as assault, with other cities in the region soon following in offering their adherence. Thessalonike, the most important foundation at the head of the Thermaic Gulf, is hardly mentioned despite its neighbour being a centre of opposition for at least two of the monarchs that came after Cassander and it is probably a deeply-felt contention between the two that explained this quiescence. As important as domestic security was the imperative need for Antigonus to clarify his position on the world stage. Achievements in his immediate world had been mixed: from his base at Demetrias it had been easy enough to recover Thessaly and include it into his new realm, but as for Paeonia this country, just ravaged by the Gauls, he was unable for the moment to recover. Cut loose, the locals reorganized themselves as an autonomous league for self-defence. Other items on the debit side are also recorded further south when Spartans decided to take advantage. Troezen was a venerable place well east of Argos near the Saronic Gulf named for sibling affection by a son of Pelops and grandfather of Theseus when two communities combined in legendary times.[20] In human memory it had been important as being where the Athenian civilian evacuees were sent for their protection before the day of decision at Salamis in 480, and was the mother city Sybaris where the exiles on the instep of the Italian boot had perfected the art of good living. This well-defended town was an important component of the fiefdom Craterus held for his half-brother around the Isthmus of Corinth, but around this time it was wrenched from his grasp by Laconians in expansionist mood. These first tried psychological warfare when they had messages declaring 'I have come to preserve the freedom of Troezen' bound round the shafts of javelins hurled over the walls and returned some citizens they had captured without ransom to plead their cause with the locals. This activity stirred some factional discord, but Craterus' garrison commander showed he was well up to combating these machinations, though in the end when it came to swords and spears the Spartan warriors, still formidable even in these degenerate days, 'scaled the walls' and took the place.[21]

There were also three Achaean towns that in 275 went the same way as Troezen, lost to the Antigonid cause. Aegium, situated below the foothills of the Panachaiko Mountains, included the territory of Helike, which has pretentions to being Plato's Atlantis.[22] Bura inland between Patrae and Corinth and recently rebuilt after a devastating earthquake and Eryneia, again inland from Aegium, were all lost, though we don't know how.[23] The Corinthian enclave was shrinking and would continue to do so after the fighting against Pyrrhus at the end of the 270s when other Achaean places may also have been lost to Craterus. Antigonus was now down to not much more than the three great Fetters, his Attic forts on top of Megara that he attacked and conquered around this time when the defenders used flaming pigs against his elephants and where a mutiny among the Gallic garrison years later indicates it was continuously in his hands.[24] In central Greece Aetolia, after her own heroic stand against the Gallic menace, was looming increasingly important from the Ambracian Gulf to Thermopylae, utilizing her dominance of the Amphictyonic League to exert influence on her neighbours. This hoary and highly reputable organizing had been crucial in Philip's significant military interruption into the Hellenic world during the Sacred Wars and Antigonus, though still theoretically commanding votes at the league council through cities he controlled in Thessaly, realized that taking up the option of attending would only thoroughly expose his own lack of clout in this arena.

To compensate for this loss of influence in the Peloponnese and central Greece, there are claims of a thawing of Macedonian relations with the Athenians. With their previous sponsors much less effective, Lysimachus long gone and Ptolemy II with more pacific inclinations than his father, it made sense for a people who had been fighting the Antigonids on and off since 287 to move to improve relations, particularly as their failure to take the Piraeus and the continued presence of Antigonid garrisons at Salamis, Eleusis, Sunium and Rhamnous ensured that corn imports would have had difficulty in getting through. There is evidence that an actively Macedonian-inclined administration took charge with a decree honouring the king for his defence of the Greeks by his victory near Lysimachia and another from 275 celebrating Phaidros of Sphettos, an old Antigonid stalwart who had been ousted from his generalship and replaced by Olympiodorus in 287 and even sacrifices made making mention of 'Antigonus the king'. Yet all this is very thin and if it is probable, dealings between Pella and Athens became noticeably less tense than they had been and after 287 there is certainly no suggestion of any kind of vassalage. Indeed, the delegation sent to Pyrrhus when he arrived in the Peloponnese in 272 may indicate that there were hawks in the Attic capital who hoped the Epirot king might provide troops to assist them in having another go at digging the Antigonid garrison out of the Piraeus.

Apart from these developments in Greece, the Seleucid ruler's attitude was bound to be key for Antigonus' immediate future. Fortunately there were reasons for optimism in this quarter because Antiochus was being troubled by a reconstituted northern league of Bithynia, Heraclea and Pontus while wandering Galatians remained a problem, so he was unlikely to have much stomach for a fight against the latest iteration of the Macedonian monarchy. When ambassadors tested the water, it turned out that he was happy to find a boundary along the Nestus River that again became a significant borderline with its waters running through difficult mountain country and wild canyons to reach a marshy delta near the border post of Abdera. That place controlled a pass through the mountains north of modern Xanthi and the routes along the Thracian coast and was wealthy from trade with the interior of Thrace. And that legend claimed as a Phoenician foundation that had benefited from a passing Xerxes' munificence when the great king was on his way to Greece. Such a demarcation line very much suited Antigonus who had more than enough on his plate in imbedding his dynasty at Pella, so could allow his interests in the Chersonese to wane, while in exchange Antiochus was content to give up claims in Macedonia that he had no immediate prospect of pressing. So an entente was enshrined and to put the seal on the second coming of the Antigonids to the Macedonian throne, Philo, a royal princess born of Stratonice, the bridegroom's full sister, and Seleucus I, married Antigonus in winter 276/75. This season of grand nuptial revelries included special honours given to the god Pan for filling Antigonus' enemies with his signature brand of terror during the epochal battle against the Gallic foe. However, the questions remained was it really time to discard residual dreads, were awful Gauls and predatory neighbours things of the past, and had peace truly come to bleeding Macedonia after her agonal years?

Chapter Nine

The Last of an Eagle

Pyrrhus may have just escaped an inferno of battles against Romans and Carthaginians but crestfallen was never a condition suggested by the man from Epirus and certainly not sometime in 274, the probable date for his return from Italy. This was despite the battered state of the army of 8,000 foot and 500 horse that survived the wreck of his western dreams and had mustered on the Adriatic shore, dispirited but determined to get paid. On his return he found his son Ptolemy, by Antigone, the princess he had married in Alexandria, had at least been fortunate when deputed to look after the homeland while his father took ship across the Ionian Sea. In the recent perilous years the Gauls had largely passed him by, considering his country not high on their list of places wealthy enough to bother with, and now these self-sufficient people protected by mountain ramparts showed they were adventurous as well as lucky and, like the Gauls, far from averse to the feel of other people's property. They had always worried their neighbours because they were tough and dangerous, looking with envy at the waving wheat fields, ample orchards and vineyards of their lowland neighbours. So soon drafts of young people who had grown to manhood in the years their monarch had been away arrived at the muster to bolster the army. Farmers, shepherds and drovers filled out the files of the phalanx and the sons of rich folk, with growing estates in the valleys of expanded Greater Epirus, beefed up the numbers of the cavalry.

Pyrrhus, finding nothing appealing in a life of ease, 'he had no greater delight in ruling than in warfare' and with a militarily refurbished tool to hand, knew there was a pressing need for funding, so naturally he cast around for a convenient war. The need to make conflict pay for itself was always the glittering prize for these Hellenistic warlords and Pyrrhus exhibited a towering confidence that it could be done. Whether this enterprise really started as just a great razzia to fill his coffers is a moot point; other records suggest he believed he had unfinished business in Italy, or why had he left troops with his son Helenus and an officer called Milon to hold Tarentum, and that his real aspiration was to conquer Macedonia and even West Asia to win the resources he would need to have another crack at the Romans. That this sounds far-fetched in the light of what happened is true, but of course thinking big was something that since Alexander had hardly been incredible, particularly for a man who very consciously followed the pattern of the all-conquering Macedonian.

Yet if his ambitions always soared to the heavens, even immediate policy was not exclusively about the need to pay his men; there had also been encouraging whispers from the wings. It seems Antigonus Gonatus had upset Ptolemy II of Egypt by flirting not just with Antiochus but also with the Egyptian ruler's greatest bugbear, Magus the rebel potentate in Cyrene, who looked to Alexandria almost like an existential threat when in 276 he began to march in arms on the Nile kingdom. So after receiving financial encouragement from African moneybags to harass the Macedonian ruler, Pyrrhus' eyes turned acquisitively south and east where any truly dominating presence had been removed since he had last stood on Balkan soil. Antigonus was in situ, but how strong was he? He intended to find out and had no trouble in unearthing an excuse. The king of Macedonia had been a natural to approach for assistance for his last Italian campaign, but now there was a very unsubtle threat: 'Unless he sent him some, he should be obliged to return to his kingdom, and to seek that enlargement of his dominions from him which he had wished to gain from the Romans.'[1] Antigonus had cold-shouldered him. Help was refused, despite many an advisor having muttered that it was in his interest to back the Epirot in more adventures over the Adriatic and keep him out of the Balkans. Pyrrhus was spoiling for a fight and hardly needed to trump up a pretext; it had been years since anything but might and opportunity made the difference in a world where revolution and disruption had made tenuous anything that might have been left to legitimacy or dynastic loyalty. Probably spending the winter at Ambracia with offspring raised to command and other officers eager to share in the glory, the Eagle king lingered until the weather allowed campaigning to begin.

It had been in 277 while Pyrrhus was shedding Carthaginian blood that Antigonus had recovered the throne of Macedon lost by his father just over a decade before and this was going to be his first and the most severe test of a reign that finally lasted almost forty years. Though he had benefited from a few trouble-free years in which to bed in his administration, still there existed no great reservoir of popularity to call on and he would have spent a twitchy winter waiting to receive the blow and gathering what fighting men he could to oppose an enemy led by undoubtedly the greatest general still left standing from the great Successor Wars. This precocious prince, a glamorous blend of Alexandrine chic and effective violence, had a reputation to be envied and even the great Hannibal would regard him as almost in the same league as Alexander himself in terms of martial talent. The threatened party's desperate need for troops would have meant that Antigonus called out some of the phalanx but not the full levy of the toughest warriors available; no one hoping to retain any popularity could afford to press troops willy-nilly among this key but depleted demographic. So much of his rank and file would have been his veteran mercenaries bolstered by thousands of those Gauls who had become so central to the military establishments of almost all Hellenistic rulers.

When Antigonus was sure the strategy Pyrrhus had mapped out was a direct assault on his kingdom, naked aggression from an expected quarter ensured columns of professional warriors mixed with farm boy soldiers and Macedonian and Thessalian gentry marched to meet the invader in battle. The direction of attack was from Ambracia, from where the route led north before following the Aous River through the pass it had cut in geological time, where intelligence agents had suggested any Antigonid garrisons or defence forces could be vulnerable. Turning to cross Tymphaea and through the Pindus Mountains towards Thessaly, Pyrrhus' spies proved prescient as arriving on the Macedonian borderlands the welcome was considerable, with several towns and 2,000 soldiers going over to the intruder, places and people who remembered that Pyrrhus had been their ruler in very recent times. Every day's journey into upper Macedonia persuaded the Epirot king that there was a real groundswell of support in the regions he was going through, emphasizing that much more than just a raid could be on offer here. Yet this was no undefended country, and emerging from the Aous pass, he ran into his enemy's army drawn up to defend a kingdom where the incumbent had been in possession for only a few years. It is clear from what occurred that Antigonus' confidence in the loyalty of his new subjects was not profound. He might have gained something of a standing with his victory over the Gauls, but he was still acutely aware that this might not count for that much, particularly when his father, as king of Macedon, faced Pyrrhus, it had ended very badly. Then the Macedonian levy had deserted and that exactly this might happen again was surely on his mind, particularly with several thousand of these soldiers already having gone over to the Epirot side.

After Pyrrhus drew up his ranks of Italian veterans, bolstered by the Gauls' Lagid money had help to recruit, they debouched from the narrow gorge to confront a shaky and reluctant Antigonus almost caught napping and now with little alternative but to face the risk of open battle. Quickly things went wrong as the invader ordered his men forward, an attack that threw the Macedonian army into disorder, causing the Antigonid command to order a withdrawal, leaving a rearguard of their own Gauls to buy the rest of the army some time to escape. So the attackers found themselves face to face with the dread warriors who had terrified the Balkans for more than half a decade behind a line of body shields, a barrier held solid by men with pot helmets or characteristic wild manes of hair lime-washed into spikes. Moustachioed faces glistening above bared chests were presented by men prepared to die for their salt. The veterans of the Epirot phalanx advanced over the no man's land between the two lines to the shrilling of high-pitched pipes with coloured flags raised to trigger the movements agreed in the command tent, while heralds attached to each almost 256-man unit (syntagma) transmitted the orders along, although if the clamour of battle made this impractical, the trumpeters and standard-bearer relayed instructions to lower pikes and advance. One of the manoeuvres drummed in by months of drill rocked the earth with the tremor of rhythmic steps of men who had bested Romans and Carthaginians in the past few years. A wall of bronze-skinned button shields and a hedge of 18ft pikes was chilling to behold, with colour provided by scarlet cloaks caught at the shoulders and the distinctive plumes on top of their helmets. Beside them, appearing out of the dust of battle, were Pyrrhus' own Gauls, brawny in body and brave to a fault; it was said that a belief in reincarnation, ditching concerns over eternity in the realm of Hades, made them laugh in the face of death. They certainly had no qualms at all about setting about their compatriots in the enemy ranks with great long slashing broadswords, showing no reluctance at all to tear into fellow countrymen holding the pass for a different employer.

The Antigonid rearguard, failing to hold its station against this smashing attack, was eliminated as a fighting force after a hard struggle, ensuring the defenders were now in real trouble. Never averse to a bold display of initiative, Pyrrhus ordered his men on towards the Macedonian elephants who they found caught in march formation. These put up no fight at all, with their Indian drivers surrounded, succumbing to threats from levelled javelins and hedged sarissas and happily adjusting their contracts of employment in the Epirots' favour. These men were as crucial as the beasts themselves; after all, it was not just anyone who could mount and control these temperamental animals. The relationship between the rider and mount was famously close, and on one later occasion would have fatal consequences for their new proprietor. Where Antigonus' corps of elephant had come from is never explained; that they were left over from the great herd that fought at Ipsus and escaped with Demetrius to be retained as part of his military over the years is possible but improbable. This is not because they might not have lived that long – elephants can survive for up to sixty or seventy years – but it is not likely that, running from the victorious enemy, he would have had the leisure to take many with him and, difficult and expensive in terms of upkeep, it would have made little sense to stable such animals for years in one of the Fetters of Greece. Nor do we hear of the animals being much used in Europe in the admittedly poorly-recorded decades after the battle of Ipsus took place. The more likely sequence is that these beasts were the remnants of the herd that came with Seleucus when he confronted Lysimachus and accompanied him across the Hellespont, only to be acquired by Ceraunus when the army proclaimed him king. That we know he had elephants when fighting the Gauls is suggestive, so if there was a small herd kept at the Macedonian court and some survived the vicissitudes of the Gallic nightmare, they would have been available to Antigonus once he inherited the Macedonian military establishment.

After this the attackers encountered the main Antigonid phalanx turning to fight, but these men despite showing a bristling hedge of pikes, had fear in their eyes, having just seen the huge animals who were the prestige arm of their military go over to the enemy and who might in no time turn against them. Already demoralized, there would be no fight to the bitter end here: when natural pauses in the fighting were caused by aching arms and stressed psyches, Pyrrhus hailed the men of Antigonus' army calling on them not to waste their lives in pointless resistance but instead accept an offer of wages and glory in his own forces. Soon their sarissas were raised, pointing to the sky, indicating pacific intent, while their officers approached their opposite numbers to formalize the agreement to change teams. In the rear of this confusion Antigonus could only look on in horror, despite him presumably being aware of these men's track record of turning coat. Facing not just defeat but obliteration, quick-witted attendants and loyal officers removed any insignia that might indicate his status to prevent his immediate capture and, covering him in common soldier's clothing to conceal who he was, cleared a path for their monarch to flee the scene of disaster. So soon after what must have seemed like the time he had finally come into his own, Antigonus, just like his father, 'divesting himself at once of all the marks of royalty', ran from Pyrrhus in disguise, and while looking back over his shoulder for the dust clouds of pursuit, was not even sure where he might be able to find adherents of proven loyalty who could help him salvage something from the wreckage of his fortunes. It had been a crushing defeat, showing once again the value of military reputation, the Epirot king having something of the Alexandrine glamour that really registered when it came to these Macedonian levy pikemen who had so happily switched allegiance to take orders from the coming man.

To exactly fathom the invader's intentions from the start is difficult; it may have been he was just looking to obtain the wherewithal to pay his men or he may have had high hopes of expanding Greater Epirus at the expense of a neighbour that had provided him with significant territory in past years. However, with the welcome he had received in a number of border communities and with the unconvincing attitude shown by so many of the men Antigonus had hoped would be motivated to defend their country, his ambitions grew. He had good memories of contesting with the Antigonids for control of Macedon, and if the expedition was originally planned to be limited in scope, such developments ensured the invader was bound to review his timetable. So with the first blow well struck, an overjoyed Pyrrhus, now definitely ratcheting up the level of his ambitions, pressed on deep into enemy territory, wide open now, his forces spreading over much of upper Macedonia and Thessaly before entering the antique capital of Aigai, after which successful incursions other cities soon followed suit in pledging their fidelity to the conquering warrior king.

The result of these decisive events was that he once again held most of the Macedonian kingdom from the upper cantons to the old heartland in the Axius valley, while Antigonus was left clinging on in certain coastal towns. Unfortunately he was not careful of his reputation when it came to this new constituency. He allowed some Gallic warriors to desecrate the tombs of Macedonian royalty situated near Aigai where recent finds at pristine internments show just what riches they would have found as they dug into the burial mounds, scattering hallowed bones while scrabbling for gold. That Pyrrhus probably could not have stopped them was not felt to be sufficient excuse, and reports were soon circulating that this was all calculation and he did not even try to curb these pet barbarians, seeing their activity as revenge for Lysimachus' desecration of Molossian royal burial grounds more than a decade earlier.

Pyrrhus' son Ptolemy had recently proved himself a chip off the old block. He had been only a teenager when his father left him in charge on leaving for Italy, but had already made a considerable splash by taking over Corcyra with an invasion force of only sixty and on another occasion, while in a naval engagement, leaped with a party of seven men into a fifty-oared galley, overcame the crew and captured it. This prince, with a considerable reputation from a young age, was rapidly becoming his proud father's strong right arm, so it was no surprise when he was left in command of the army of occupation in Macedonia while his father withdrew, probably returning to Ambracia to consider his next move. His enemy Antigonus had shown that he, like his father, knew how to run after defeat, though on this occasion he headed for Thessalonike. Here he proved just as resilient as his father, though he must have needed all his Stoic resolution to sustain not just the setback on the Aous but what turned out to be a double blow. Perhaps he had acquired a taste for regal trappings, sitting where Philip, Alexander, Cassander and his father had done before, that ensured he could not just sit it out in Thessalonica, but immediately on reaching safety had busied himself evaluating his assets. Outside maritime Macedonia he still had his Greek resources to fall back on, so stripping garrisons to the bare bones and ordering his treasurers to disgorge sufficient to hire a new band of Gauls, he soon had these mustering and eager to stake their lives on another martial gamble.

So despite the mauling he had just received, Antigonus resolved to carry on the fight. After receiving news that he would not have to face Pyrrhus in person, he convinced himself he might win against the son even if not against the father, so decided to strike immediately, leading out his mint new force for an autumn campaign, but all these endeavours foundered when history repeated itself and he discovered the young prince left holding the fort was himself too hot to handle. Antigonus had made a career out of circumspection, so he must have considered his prospects for victory at least reasonable, but he had miscalculated once again and this second army was so roughly treated, 'utterly defeated', that he had to flee the field again, this time with only seven companions. So the king of Macedon, almost disdainfully rebuffed, had now lost two battles against a people who were once their subjects and twice had to flee in terror, hiding his face from recognition. It suddenly looked like the victory at Lysimachia had been an aberration and that he too would be just one more on the long list of those occupying the Macedonian throne in the past years. There is even a report that he 'no longer indulged hopes of recovering his kingdom, but sought only hiding places for safety and solitary ways for flight', a reaction that hardly seems like the disciple of Zeno, the steady man whose most effective strategy in the past had been to stonewall and see what transpired.

Happy tidings of this latest victory fully repaid Pyrrhus' confidence in his son, meaning that it was a doubly joyous occasion when some of the spoils from the earlier victory were consecrated at Dodona.[2] The inscriptions on these dedications show the Epirot king had decided not to tread a well-travelled road. It might be expected he would have been thinking this was just like old times, and collecting enough of the Macedonian elite to arrange for some sort of election by the people assembled in arms; after all, the pro forma for this was well-known and he had done exactly that almost fifteen years earlier when Demetrius had fled his throne while he and Lysimachus divided the country. Probably his loyal Epirots expected this and some might have been looking forward to becoming important placemen in the larger and more considerable kingdom than their own land of savage herdsmen. Now Pyrrhus broke the mould, and the telling inscription 'Spoils of war, reft from much-vaunted Macedonia' showed it was as conqueror of the Macedonians that he wanted the world to see him. Nor can this be seen as aberrant as earlier when he took over Thessaly, this was not touted as any Macedonian return. He had dedicated the shields of the Gauls killed while fighting for Antigonus at the temple of Thessalian Athena situated between Pherae and Larissa, emphasizing again that he had destroyed an army led by the reigning king of Macedon. All this shouted that as king of Epirus, he revelled in crushing Macedonians, an idea he intended should seep south by word of mouth. This public relations onslaught was no mere caprice; his reasoning concerned the reception he hoped to receive among the Greek communities. Much depended on the stance he took. If he advertised himself as the new king of Macedon, he would be donning the garb of a generations-old bugbear and threat, but as the man who had humiliated them he would find it far easier to uncover friends in Boeotia, in Attica and the Peloponnese while also maintaining warm relations with the Aetolians. He needed these people as allies if he was going to dig Antigonus out of his Greek strongholds and completely neutralize him as a significant rival.

Pyrrhus might show withering condemnation, deriding Antigonus as a shameless man for still wearing the purple despite having no entitlement to the name or raiment of kingship, but even if he had beaten him convincingly in battle, he knew that this had not completely solved his problems. The Epirot, with hardly a navy at all, could not contest Antigonus' command of the sea, ensuring that not only could Antigonus hang on in the Fetters of Greece but also in those important Macedonian and Greek cities along the Thermaic Gulf that his garrisons still held. He wanted him out of Greece too, but how to achieve it? He certainly needed the locals on his side, and there were some signs that this was coming to pass. The Athenians for one, despite knowing that Antigonus would hardly approve their involvement in an Aetolian event, sent emissaries to Delphi to participate in the Amphictyonic council for the first time for years, while it is also probable that the Antigonids lost their control of the island of Euboea at this time, only regaining possession after campaigning around 270. The prospect of building on this movement was attractive enough to cause Pyrrhus to neglect finishing off the remnant of his enemies holding out in the tidewater communities.

Anyway, Pyrrhus was never a man to play things safe or be limited by the boundaries of his own backyard, so now he determined on making an impact in Greece, hoping that under threat of attack his enemy's friends and allies would disintegrate into discord. Yet it was a different man who influenced the details of strategy, the course of events being distorted by an individual whose baleful impact we have had cause to note before. The Epirot ruler was approached by that man of wrath Cleonymus of Sparta who, if far from one of the great power-players of the age, still had influence on events which was out of all proportion to his talents. Early in his life he had significantly impacted in the peninsula of Italy, causing a tourbillion that had been instrumental in sparking a Roman Samnite war, while in the late 90s it had been his arrival at Thebes that had brought down the vengeance of Demetrius on that unfortunate city. Now he arrived at the camp of the triumphant king of Epirus claiming considerable support back home for raising him to the Spartan throne and all that he needed was a powerful sponsor to see the project through. His reliability was bound to be very open to question; an exile's desperation could lead to wishful thinking of the most extravagant order, yet at Pyrrhus' headquarters there seemed little harm in recruiting him as an agent who might well be of use in the complexities of Peloponnesian power politics. After all, these Spartan grandees had always been backstabbers, prepared to tear each other apart since well before in the days of Demaratus, Leotychides and Cleomenes when they indulged in almost any skullduggery, even in the face of a massive and imminent Persian menace.

It had been more than thirty years since this Cleonymus had been blocked from following his father onto the Spartan throne, and on hearing news of what he was up to any survivors would have felt his squalid behaviour confirmed they had been right to deem him as something worse than just an unknown quantity. He had been considered too violent and irrational with little concern for the interest of his people back then and nothing since had given much reason for a reassessment. His record at Thebes had been poor and the current sequence of events that had led him into approaching a foreign king showed a malicious personality with few of the qualities hoped for in a national leader. As an older man he had married as his second wife a royal beauty called Chilonis from the Eurypontid line that conventionally provided one of Sparta's two monarchs. Tribulations of age differences were compounded because the young woman became attached to a young prince called Acrotatus. Bad enough in itself, the fact that the lover was the son of Areus I who had been given the throne in his stead made it intolerable, ensuring it was an opportunity not to be missed when an adventurer with a powerful army turned out very susceptible to his urgings. So the arrival back of Pyrrhus from his foreign travels and his success against Antigonus gave opportunity to this disgruntled character and he was not slow in taking it.

Cleonymus was on hand when the spring of 272 saw his new sponsor act. Pyrrhus' friends on the western marches of mainland Greece, particularly the Aetolians who had some maritime muscle in the Ionian Sea and the Gulf of Corinth, allowed him to choose his target in a way he simply could not on the Aegean side where the power of the Antigonid fleet was unassailable. Wherever he targeted he was coming in strength, emerging as a titan since his return from the west in a manner extraordinary for one who had so recently been turned out of first Sicily and then Italy. He now controlled country from Greater Epirus through most of Macedonia and Thessaly, and on top of this he decided to liquidate his Tarentine interests once and for all. His son Helenus, who had been sitting in the acropolis there for some time, was brought back with a garrison no longer required which allowed the accumulation of an army amounting to 25,000 infantry, 2,000 horse and 24 elephants. Nor was it just Helenus as his brother Ptolemy was also recruited, able to leave the country he had so recently defended successfully against Antigonus with reasonable confidence that that enemy's claws had been clipped for at least a season. So, acutely conscious that the alarm instilled by both his own name and the presence of Gallic mercenaries would significantly diminish any inclination to resist, he made his move.

Thus it was a family at war that slipped into the Corinthian gulf and crossed over to the southern strand, ships crunching onto the sand to disgorge an army of a size that had not been seen in the Peloponnese for many a long year. If Pyrrhus' enemy's position had crumbled in the north, any dissolution here had been less dramatic, so the region was a particular draw as the Epirot king could hope his arrival would inspire plenty of locals to get on board in helping to drive the Antigonids and their clients out of the peninsula. It was no surprise when the intruders found a number of emissaries waiting for them as they disembarked: envoys from

Achaea, Messenia and Athens crowded round the new arrivals, eager to get on the good side of a man whose military reputation had apparently only been enhanced by his wars against Rome and Carthage and who declared he had come to free those cities Antigonus dominated against their will, following the tradition started so long ago by the grandfather of his current enemy. With words of commitment from these new friends, they then took the road south to the centre of the peninsula to reach that key city of Megalopolis in a wide mountain-shaded valley, where the city fathers decided here was a bandwagon to join, despite previous close relations with Antigonus.

Settling down in the centre of Arcadia, more adherents arrived, travel-stained ambassadors from Elis committed themselves to the cause, even making a dedication to the Epirot ruler at Altis, the sacred grove of Zeus in Olympia.[3] Yet these were not the most significant visitors received at the royal headquarters; sober men from Sparta had turned up intent on knowing his purpose in what they still considered very much their bailiwick. The king was confronted by a difficult choice and his councillors were by no means unanimous in their opinions. Should he follow the advice of the exiled Spartan Cleonymus and turn against that perennially troublesome people or continue, where so many had failed before, to try to properly establish control in the rest of the Peloponnesus, extracting Antigonid partisans from Messene to the isthmus. After all, Sparta was no friend of Antigonus and on top of that they were close to the Ptolemies and if his old mentor the first Ptolemy was long dead, his successor had proved solid recently, helping to fund the army with which he had achieved so much. It was here in the heart of Arcadia that Pyrrhus first tried flattery on his latest guests, telling them that he greatly admired the ways of the great Spartan legislator Lycurgus and wanted to send his sons to be educated in the Agoge that for centuries had produced iron-hard Spartan warriors. There is a tradition that these honeyed words had their effect, and when later these same men discovered the king's army on their doorstep, recalling his words they accused him of duplicity, to which he replied with a smile: 'When you Spartans have decided on a war, it is your habit not to inform your enemy of it. Therefore do not complain of unfair treatment, if I have used a Spartan stratagem against the Spartans.'[4] Such a crack rings true from a commander who, despite a bellicose reputation, when it suited him would try to weaken any opponent's martial resolve by persuading them of the awful penalties of war, pushing arguments that showed their best interest lay in the path of peaceful subservience.

From the start, what Pyrrhus hoped for as return on his Peloponnesian investment was not obvious. There is no insight into his thinking to determine if he was planning to attack Sparta from the off, or had he arrived in the peninsula in a flexible mood, intending to judge what was the best strategy on the ground. We certainly know within his entourage that bad man Cleonymus' voice had remained loud as the invaders pushed through coastal Achaea and into the highlands of Arcadia, ensuring that by the time they reached Megalopolis the king had decided the time was right to play his hand by revealing his pretender to the Laconian throne. Hoping that, with this scion of a royal family at the head of his army, resistance in the Eurotas valley would be, if not absent, at least splintered and confused. So with this expectation in his heart he turned away from threatening the rump of Antigonid partisans in Arcadia to deal with the legendary city of extraordinary warriors and beautiful, independent women that had perhaps been his main target from the start.

These famous people whose peerless heroes had sacrificed themselves at Thermopylae had for centuries been the very home of contradictions, somehow contriving a sort of potpourri of respect for age combined with adoration of the military qualities of youth and an esteem for freedom and the imposition of the worst sort of helotage on much of their population. The latter double standard was common to some degree to most ancients, but the Spartan behaviour in enslaving a whole Greek people, the Messenians, to labour for them was seen even by contemporaries as odious. Their paradoxical attitudes showed particularly in respect of their women, some of which would show clearly in the days to come. In a society where the manly warrior virtues were the benchmark, still the female population was freighted with honour and respect not at all typical of the rest of Greece. Open sexuality was allowed as the handmaiden of procreation, while childbearing was the touchstone, where unlike in so many other places this was not just a burden to bear but a source of such prestige that potential mothers, from nubile youngster onwards, had a sort of emancipation that most of their Hellenic sisters could not dream of. They were expected, unlike most of their peers, particularly Athenians who would have been taunted as harlots if they appeared on the street, to show themselves as skilled athletes and dancers in the public eye and if the names of women were hardly mentioned in Athens, at Sparta the likes of the chariot-racing Euryleonis or Gorgo, courageous spouse of Leonidas, were lauded.

It was only a few days' march from Megalopolis for a force that found itself welcomed with provisions supplied from the depots of people who would have supported anybody on the way to have a thrash at their reviled neighbours. Pyrrhus pushed on over the Alpheus River first and then around the top of the Taygetus Mountains before descending the rugged hills and tramping onwards, pushing inexorably towards a city that while it had never been a place of great monuments to awe the senses, had still been so much in its time. Predatory Cleonymus, having finally arrived on the border of his homeland, was bullish at his sponsor's elbow as they passed down by the spur near Sellasia where, in a couple of generations' time, a Sparta of revolutionary kings would make its last stand in a world that had passed it by. There is an assertion[5] that while the king and the traitor pondered their strategy, out from the city precincts came the menacing sound of booted Spartan warriors emerging in their choreographed formations backed by regiments of Messenian and Argive allies to confront and be defeated by the invaders in open battle. To put it mildly, this is difficult to believe, with their main Spartan army in Crete and any likelihood of timely support from these usually deeply antagonistic neighbours being barely credible. More possible is that the invaders actually circumvented the town, coming up from the south where a place called Pyrrhus' camp is located[6] and it may well be that their approach to Sparta was from this direction.

From whichever point of the compass and whether bloodied or not, it was near evening when the outskirts were sighted and the returning exile was impatient and urged the king to attack at once, assuring him that, taken by surprise, his compatriots would fold at first contact, even telling everyone who would listen that he had ordered his servants to deck out his own town house for a party to celebrate their entering the city. However, if Pyrrhus had high hopes that a combination of flattery and his sponsoring of a home-town candidate would destabilize the defenders and might mean he would not have to fight his way in, he now knew differently and though a risk-taker, even for him an immediate assault smacked of imprudence. It was surely knowing the dangers of a night attack rather than the suggested concern that his men would get out of control and sack the place that counted. Any fight in darkness was fraught with danger, with men becoming hopelessly disordered, even ending up fighting each other and becoming easy prey for defenders who knew the streets and byways of the town far better than they.

As it turned out, it looks as if Cleonymus had done his homework and that an immediate assault might have been worth the risk as the Spartan king Areus was away campaigning on behalf of allies in Gortyn in Crete and the leadership left behind were a distracted and dithering pack of old men. The Gerousia (council of elders) gathered in an emergency night-time session were discussing evacuating the non-combatants to Crete for protection with the main army when it became clear that the Spartan women were having none of this. They were led by Archidamia, a queen who had been spouse to Eudamidas I until 305 and was mother of many more kings and queens. A hugely wealthy woman in her own right, in three decades' time, while in her 90s and finally at the cost of her life, she would support her grandson Agis IV in attempting to reclaim the city's Lycurgan past, being at the forefront in donating her wealth to subsidize a radical egalitarian reform programme intended to revitalize a Spartiate warrior class whose numbers had massively declined over the centuries. Possessed of a real sense of the dramatic, she stepped into the assembly, sword in hand, condemning those who were 'proposing that their wives and daughters should survive while Sparta itself perished'[7] and end up in the hands of the criminal lunatic Cleonymus.

The old gents of the Gerousia could not weather this verbal onslaught and, now convinced that there were plenty of people committed to defending the town, agreed to resist the coming attack with all their might and main. A plan had to be hatched because bone-deep xenophobia and contempt for the martial qualities of any who might threaten the city had ensured efforts at home defence had been deeply unfocused for many years. They determined to construct ad hoc protection that might stand in for the city walls the Spartans had always been so reluctant to construct, to dig a trench parallel with the enemy's camp 'and to strengthen at its ends by waggons buried up to their axles' to act as impediments to any assault by Pyrrhus' elephants. As soon as the work was begun, the women arrived dressed for labour, joining the older men in digging while the combatants were directed to get what rest they could to prepare them for battle the next day. This extemporized engineering corps with hardly any digging tools improvised almost 300ft of the whole 800ft long, 9ft wide and 6ft deep trench and leading the way was Chilonis, declaring she had already made arrangements to hang herself if it looked like the defences would be penetrated and she would fall into the hands of her husband, inspiring the rest to bring the young warriors food, drink and arms before urging them to conquer or die against an enemy who were beginning to stir and deploy for the assault.

With sun-up Pyrrhus was in no mood for prevarication after surveying the work that his decision not to attack straight away had allowed the enemy to construct in the night to thwart him. After taking an early breakfast and advancing through the earliest radiance of dawn towards this considerable entrenchment, the Epirot army found the Spartan defenders had taken up their place in the battle line, drawn up beside mess mates who had perhaps experienced some semblance of the exacting programme of the old Agoge, formed behind a shield wall in considerable depth on the lip of the recently-dug ditch. The attackers pushing forward found that even in the comparative cool of the morning, the exertions of advancing in heavy equipment combined with pre-battle tension meant their brows were soon beaded with sweat, while with their sarissas levelled they found purchase difficult: 'the freshly-turned earth gave his soldiers no firm footing'. While some stabbed across the breadth of the ditch with their long pikes, others stumbled down into the trench and once there even these veterans found it almost impossible to climb out again, to strike at the enemy line deployed above them who were hurling missiles down among vulnerable men, many of whom soon found themselves struck in unprotected thighs, arms and throats. With the first assault failing, Ptolemy, the king's son, tried a different approach: gathering together a couple of thousand Gauls and a picked force of Chaonians, he determined on an outflanking move by attacking the waggons that secured the end of the defensive line. We know the Gauls generally fought with short spear and sword and can assume the others, an Epirot people living north of the Molossians, would not have been phalanxites as such soldiers were not suitable for clambering over wagon barriers. They were probably peltasts who fought in loose formations and, encouraged by Ptolemy, they started digging out and dragging off the waggons towards the river to allow a passage for the rest of their comrades.

All this took time, and allowed a man with a point to prove to make a difference. It had been Acrotatus' behaviour that had lit the fuse that led to the presence of the invaders on Laconian soil. It was his affair with Cleonymus' young wife that had been the final straw, driving that poisonous prince to appeal to Pyrrhus to invade his homeland. This man, who would come to the throne in 265 but die in battle soon after, determined to make his mark. A lover and a fighter, he gathered 300 defenders to respond to the threat posed by the latest attack; moving in the cover given by the folds in the ground, this latest iteration of 300 heroes managed to get behind Ptolemy's men, taking them in the rear. It was a crunching assault and, despite the disparity in numbers, forced them to turn about and eventually drove the perplexed assailants in a disorderly crowd into the trench. The Spartans, from the edge, with the advantage of height now slaughtered their foes in numbers and eventually, despite being matched many times over, managed to drive them off. Bettering these valiant and numerous attackers had been an extraordinary achievement and as the young warriors, covered in the blood of their enemies, returned to the main Spartan line they received generous plaudits, while coarser spirits pressed Acrotatus to lose no time in begetting as many brave sons on Chilonis as he was able.

While this epic was unfolding fighting along the trench had also been fierce, with Pyrrhus desperate to lead his troops across this formidable obstacle. Easy to identify in his fine armour and sporting the distinctive wreath-girt helmet that can be seen represented on the wonderful head in the Naples Archaeological Museum, the king dismounted to try to force his way out of the fosse and into the ranks of the defenders lining the rim. Yet the hard-pressed men above would not concede an inch; one named Phyllius is particularly remarked dispatching a number of attackers who could not budge him from his position in the fighting line. Even if this hero fell at last, it was beside his companions and these loyal comrades fought like demons to stop the enemy despoiling his corpse, gallantry that so encouraged the rest that they were able to hold out until night covered the carnage and the attackers withdrew to lick their wounds. The Epirot king and his soldiers, dog-tired from their exertions, immediately took to their bedrolls to get some rest to be ready to continue the fight next day, but once stretched out on his camp bed the king had a vision, so that after awakening with a shock, he spread the word that the previous night he had dreamed of a Sparta levelled by thunderbolts from his own hands, enthusing his officers with reports of this omen before he strapped on his armour to lead the men drawn up in the dusty plain in a second day's assault on the stubborn city. This was another encounter so desperate that the Spartan women even joined the fighting line to bring food, drink and missile weapons to the men defending the ditch. Determined attempts were made to fill in the fosse: hurling in piles of wood chopped in the night and throwing earth over the corpses of the men who had fallen at the bottom, exertions they found countered by the defenders driving off those who were carrying the earth and stone needed to level out the pathways the Epirot attackers intended to follow. Eyeing up the situation, Pyrrhus himself led out some cavalry to defend these workers to discourage protagonists who were frustrating his efforts at every turn. For a moment the hero king, deciding there would be no crossing the trench, decided they must go round and, putting himself at the head of his household cavaliers, tried to press past the waggons until it seemed he might make a breakthrough and enter into the city itself, but it was not to be. Just as it looked like a path through the waggons had been won, a Cretan archer loosed a missile that drove into the belly of the king's warhorse and with morale badly affected by seeing their leader thrown into the ditch, a shower of missiles from the Spartans turned the attackers back.

There was a pause all along the trench with the defenders covered in the gore of both themselves and the men they were fighting. They had kept the enemy out, but the cost had been high with almost every man holding the line suffering from wounds inflicted by the spears, swords and missiles of their adversaries. Pyrrhus for one considered the sagging line of defenders could not possibly hold out much longer and, sure that they would soon be forced to send out emissaries with offers of surrender, he called off further onslaughts, but this turned out to be a decisive miscalculation; far from tightening the screw on a depleted foe, the defenders had won themselves crucial time. Exertions by Sparta's friends now made the difference as Ameinias the Phocian, the pirate famous for his capture of Cassandreia, who was now one of Antigonus' officers at Corinth, rode to the rescue. This active man had drawn a significant force of mercenaries from the garrison of the Acrocorinth and force-marched them down through the Argolid, past Mantinea and

Tegea, reaching Sparta just after the second day's assault. Slipping into the town, these timely arrivals gave an extraordinary fillip to a garrison on its last legs, though this turned out not the best of it for the flagging veterans, youths and women who had held out so far. Hot on the heels of the first relief column came King Areus himself at the head of 2,000 soldiers from the army with which he had been campaigning in Crete. For Ameinias to arrive in so opportune a fashion is believable, answering the call after receiving news of the attack on Sparta, but for these men to get back from Crete surely must have meant the urgent petitions for recall were sent by prescient heads much earlier, when the threat from Pyrrhus was imminent rather than immediate. Honeyed words at Megalopolis had clearly failed to completely convince, as it must have been as early as this that word was sent to recall Areus, but it had been enough and he had acted directly; knowing his home would soon be a target, he aborted his Cretan project and gathered his warriors and ships for the voyage home. This journey must have taken some days to prepare transports, load up his men and cover the 150-odd sea miles from the island to disembark at the port of Gythium before double-timing up the Eurotas valley.

However they had heard that they were needed, these reinforcements were extraordinarily welcome to a people who surely could not have stood alone for another day. Now the wounded and the older men were relieved and a defensive perimeter organized of fresh and eager men, many the very best of Areus' Spartans. So now Pyrrhus found himself confronted not by a battered and broken remnant of resistance as he had expected but by steady veterans lining the defensive trench supported by many of those who had already given his men such a hard time. Yet this tenacious fighter did not blanch but threw his formations back into the attack, trying again to fill the trench so his phalanx could roll across and take the town, but it was to no avail; casualties multiplied and still no real progress was made until the attackers decided that it no longer made tactical sense to just keep on upping the ante. There is something strange here that a makeshift defence in front of an unwalled city could keep at bay the kind of army that had come against it, and a couple of incidents should warn us that we are not getting the full picture. There is clearly an inclination to laud the Spartans' ability to protect their city from a terrible danger even with so many of the army away and what is certain is that it was not just old men and youths who held the line; we know that there were Cretan archers present, professional soldiers, one of whom brought down the Epirot king's horse. More than this, there is a suggestion[8] that it was just bravado that no one had ever bothered to construct defences for their valley home; that in fact there was already some protection in place that had been constructed in the face of Demetrius' invasion a few years earlier and it is more than probable that there were some in the city with engineering experience able to improve these ramparts with those earthworks that proved so effective against the assaulting troops.

It must have been a frustrated group that gathered in Pyrrhus' command tent after he had called his senior officers together now that another attack had failed to break the defenders' will. While their leader had never been a man for a cautious approach, just as pertinently he had never been known for constancy and staying power either. He had ducked out before in his life when things became too difficult, but perhaps more mature now, he showed he had learned and, having the resources to keep at his task, decided that if he could not batter his way in he would put the town under siege. To prepare the ground, his predation included the ripe lands of the Eurotas valley, gathering in whatever was growing to supply an army that was intent on seeing the business through. However, as it turned out, events in other parts of the Peloponnesian peninsula ensured that the acclaimed city of Sparta was to be spared any further destruction.

It was Argos, almost 70 miles by road to the north from Sparta, that drew him away; a community that claims itself as the oldest in Europe and certainly existed since Neolithic times, showing a potent triplet with Tiryns and Mycenae in the age of Diomedes, the local hero and 'winter torrent' who scattered the hosts of Troy, grazed the pretty skin of Aphrodite and skewered the war god Ares with his ashen spear.[9] Bitter rivals of Sparta, they had supported the Messenians in attempting to throw off the yoke of helotry at a time when the infantry phalanx was coming into fashion in the seventh century and contested the battle of 300 champions against them over the plain of Thyrea in 546. Now it turned out that a people whose feelings of detestation for the Laconians had been bleeding through the years should be instrumental in lifting the pressure on their hated enemy. This city was currently being torn in two between a couple of local strongmen called Aristeas and Aristippus, the unanticipated annoyance being that the latter supported by Antigonus was looking set to win out. This place was one of the great cities of the peninsula, important enough to ensure that Pyrrhus, when messengers arrived pleading for aid, was persuaded to intervene.

To decide was one thing; getting to Argos was another as the king of Sparta was determined to make the exit of the enemy who was trashing his country as problematic as possible. The retreating regiments set out on the road to cross the 30-odd miles of rough terrain to reach the flat country around Tegea with a rearguard made up of trustworthy Molossians and Gauls. However, the trailing column of soldiers, horses and elephants soon found themselves assailed along the road by Spartan troops who, knowing the country, had found paths to beset them at difficult sites along the route. Coming at them from above, they even cut off some of those rearguard units posted to protect the departing army's vulnerable marching ranks. Indeed, the threat was sufficient for Pyrrhus to dispatch his son Ptolemy with some squadrons of the royal horse guard to relieve the pressure, while he himself led the main body, urging them out of the hilly defiles and into the plain of Tripoli, level country where they would be far less menaced by their opponents' harassing tactics.

This dispatch of his eldest son, a warrior prince only in his mid-20s and named for his honoured friend and sponsor Ptolemy of Egypt, had been ordered, despite the portentous warnings of diviners that sacrifices had foretold the death of one of the king's kindred. Now he, like so many others of his impulsive ilk, reaped the consequences of flouting such warnings. As the prince rode to the rescue at the head of his father's gorgeously-accoutred retainers, driving forward to break through to the men cut off in the rear, he came face to face with an elite force led by a captain called Eualcus. A 'fierce battle developed' and among the Spartans were a number of Cretan warriors, one of whom was called Oryssus from the town of Aptera in the west of the island who was well-known for both his bodily strength and his fleetness of foot. It was this man who was able to get around Ptolemy, high on his mettlesome horse, and while approaching from the flank assail his unshielded side. He hurled a javelin that downed the prince with a fatal strike, horrifying his followers who saw him collapse from his mount. Morale was badly dented, with many losing heart and falling back with Spartans pressing on after them. The whole mixed bundle of combatants – the rearguard, the dead Ptolemy's guardsmen and their Spartan foes – descended almost together out of the hills where they had been fighting and found themselves on a level plain where the main Epirot army could be seen through the dust drawn up in serried ranks. So before they had time to reorganize themselves, the Spartans were themselves threatened with being cut off by a much larger force. The man in charge of the army facing them was in 'an agony of grief' and desperate for revenge, having just heard from the returning men that his eldest son had fallen.

Never loath to lead from the front and infuriated now, Pyrrhus took his place at the head of his Molossian cavalry in preparation to ride down those men who had killed Ptolemy. 'His daring and fury surpassed everything' as the bereaved father bore down on the Spartan commander and Eualcus only managed to avoid the king hurtling his way by cutting his horse's reins with his sword as he passed him by. However, this adept swordplay failed to save him as the assailant pierced his body with a lance, although if his burnished armour did not provide protection, the impact unseated his attacker who found himself on foot in wild combat with the men defending the Spartan leader's corpse. Yet desperate rage gave the king's arm superhuman strength with his followers making short work of the defending crowd and causing the enemy, after having suffered considerable losses, to recede back into the hills. This had been a bloody and frantic affray and the intruders were desperately glad to be out of the rugged hills of the Parnonas where they had been at such a disadvantage and at last rid of their gadfly enemies, able to reorganize for the remainder of the march to Argos.

The rationale for this move to the Argolid had not been just the apparent ascendency of Aristippus; it was an understanding of the real danger of Antigonus Gonatus being on the move. This great rival was not just sending his generals to make life difficult; he had come himself with his main army and had occupied the heights above the town not far from the sanctuaries of Apollo and Athena and menacingly commanding the plain. The capacity of Antigonus to raise another significant army after two defeats is the most convincing evidence that the realm based around the Fetters of Greece that he had nurtured for decades was economically robust, allowing him to continue to fund expensive wars that since his exclusion from most of Macedonia had to be fought almost exclusively by his own mercenaries. Even if it is accepted that there was some truth in the contention that he had reconquered parts of Macedonia,[10] it is improbable that he could have been sufficiently in control to call out any of the levy for a foreign war. That he was prepared to again risk his limited military resources against a man who so recently crushed him in battle shows how important he considered it was to defend his place in the Peloponnese. Aristippus was far from his only powerful protégé in the region and he knew to retain their loyalty he must be on hand to defend their interests. Getting there was easy, commanding as he did the Aegean seaways and the isthmus crossing, and becoming aware of his rival's travails in Sparta, he had been able to chose the most convenient time and place to intervene.

Pyrrhus, having completed his forced march to the Argolid, was frustrated on realizing he had been beaten to the best ground and had little option but to march onwards to set up camp on well-defended terrain above Nauplia 3 miles to the east, past the historic mound that covered the Mycenaean fortress palace of Tiryns. That place, great between the years 1400 to 1200, stood where humans had lived for more than 5,000 years with incredible Cyclopean walls and rock tunnels that also claimed with a few others the honour of being the birthplace of the demigod Heracles. It was alternately menace then action as his men settled down in camp and, exasperated in his desire to reach his foe, he sent a herald to challenge Antigonus to come out and fight, only to receive the reply: 'When he was conducting a campaign, he chose his own moment to fight, and that if Pyrrhus was weary of life, he could find many ways to die.'[11] If Antigonus was not biting, exchanges in Argos itself soon ensured that the stalemate would not go on forever. The faction troubles that had brought both dynasts to the area took centre stage again. If the Argive hard men had first welcomed the appearance of their sponsors in force, now they were not so sure, becoming concerned at the presence of two large armies devastating the countryside where they and their supporters had their estates. This was not what they had bargained for; a more discreet involvement to give a local edge had been what each had hoped, but with it looking like their country would become a battlefield, they joined forces, mobilizing their adherents to make representations to the kings that if they removed themselves, the citizens would remain neutral in the struggle and be on good terms with both sides. This approach was received with some sympathy by the contenders, with Antigonus even handing over a son as hostage; after all, he had everything to gain by this proposal as with Pyrrhus' army gone, he would endure to dominate the region from his base at Acrocorinth. Yet if he had good reason to be sincere, his rival had double-dealing in mind: rather than preparing to leave, he had persuaded his man Aristeas to open the gates and allow him to bring his men in to take control of the city.

If residents had informed Pyrrhus about another local demigod who, incensed by Zeus' lustful intentions towards his daughter Io,[12] had hurled curses at the father of the gods and ended so tormented by him he drowned himself in the river that drained the western Argive plain, then perhaps he should have had pause, as it seems the loss of his own offspring was encouraging his own rashness. His enemy Antigonus described him as a dice-player who threw many good throws but did not know how 'to exploit them when they are made'[13] and now he prepared his last toss. The coup was hatched in nocturnal obscurity with the Epirot army descending from the hills above Nauplia, making as little noise and showing as few lights as possible as they crossed the Argive plain in the face of awful omens registered by the augers at the commencement.[14] In contravention of this haruspication, they covered the dark miles to the walls with the Gauls in the lead, reaching 'the gate known as Diemperes' in the city's southern walls before any guards on the battlements noticed. The order was given to enter, and in fact these nimble warriors had penetrated down the night-black streets to the market place before the town watch glimpsed spectral figures entering and raised the alarm. Pyrrhus was elated; success seemed imminent, so that when the inevitable 'friction of war' intervened to wipe the smile off his face it was even more galling. The Gauls were already inside and other troops too, but when the elephants approached the entrance it was discovered that the howdahs on their backs made them too tall to get through. The animals were also fractious after travelling so far in darkness, so the process of removing their burdens was even more time-consuming than usual, particularly as they needed to be put back in place after they had passed through the gates.

Once the alarm was raised, the local response was emphatic with obdurate Argives arming themselves and rushing to key strongpoints, particularly the hill of Aspida, 250ft high and once functioning as joint acropolis with Larissa, site of the old king's palace and named by the citizenry from being shaped like an Aspis shield, while word was rushed to Antigonus' camp begging for aid so the city would not fall to the intruders. This king's response was not only unequivocal, with his son and other officers leading the men immediately available to help, but king Areus, still eager for payback, had also arrived leading a strike force of 1,000 lightly-armed Spartans and Cretans. These doughty fighters, displaying murderous steel, entered from the other side of the town and encountered Pyrrhus' Gauls in the unlit streets who, not expecting such severe resistance, were thrown into confusion. Milling around in the agora, some had even turned to looting, stripping the houses for trophies as the newcomers struck them hard. While his men suffered, the Epirot king was trying to reach the scene of fighting, leading his horsemen from the gymnasium outside the walls where they had concentrated, then through the gate, all shouting their war cries to alert their friends of their coming. The response from the Gauls was not encouraging, but disregarding this, these cavaliers pushed on as hard as they could, although the presence of drainage channels crisscrossing the town slowed them down. It soon became clear that horsemen were far from the ideal troops for a night-time urban conflict and the effect of those who reached the fighting was to confuse even more an utterly chaotic combat.

Soon that was not the limit of Pyrrhus' anxieties. There was no sense and no order, 'men about and lost their direction in the narrow alley-ways, and amid the darkness, the confused noise and confined spaces',[15] and generalship was entirely negated in the chaos. So both sides at full stretch now paused to wait for the break of dawn when the Epirot king was shocked to see so many enemy troops drawn up in the market place around a bronze statue of a bull and wolf attacking each other. A proper sight of his foe, on top of a memory of a prophecy that foretold his death when he saw just such a combat of animals, apparently for the first time gave him pause. We need not believe this usual bizarre oracular foreboding that attends the death of so many great men; much more likely with his night-time coup having failed, he realized any decision to remain to fight in the unfamiliar streets of Argos was ripe with peril and likely to rebound against him. Recalculating, the Epirot leadership decided to back out as best they could. Orders were sent to prince Helenus waiting outside with the bulk of the army to break down the walls and defend the breach so those men in the city could withdraw safely. However, in a moment ominous and inauspicious the message was garbled and instead the young general tried to enter the city with his best men and the rest of the elephants to buttress the combatants already inside.

Some of these newcomers managed to reach the main square where the conflict had become increasingly hot, but once there, their presence only managed to increase the pandemonium. Pyrrhus had been holding his own in the cut and thrust of the fight, but as the new arrivals approached the Gauls and others still with him began to fail and were withdrawing from the open space back into the narrow streets already choked with men. The king rode into their ranks yelling orders to keep this retreat orderly, but with little success; his men were barely able to hear the orders and, in jostling each other and attempting to retire towards the gates and extract themselves, they were halted by new units pressing in the opposite direction along the same road they were taking out of town. Then to compound matters an elephant called Nicon, careening through the city streets in an effort to find his wounded mahout, began crashing into the escaping men and, as many of these fell crushed under his massive feet, another lumbering monster, the largest of them all, in trying either to enter or exit the gate fell over, blocking the road to everyone else. It was a nightmare with Pyrrhus' men borne along, hardly able to turn to fight an enemy who was infiltrating their ranks and attacking them from the rear. Indeed, the confusion with friend and foe packed in a solid mass of grappling humanity was such that many died from friendly fire, with comrades pressed against each other's unsheathed swords or spears. It was during this bedlam that the animal called Nicon intervened again:

> Having found the body of his master, he took it up with his proboscis, laid it across his two tusks, and turned back as if crazed, overthrowing and killing those who came in his way. Thus crushed and matted together not a man of them could act at all for himself, but the whole multitude, bolted together, as it were, into one body, kept rolling and swaying this way and that.[16]

Extraordinary accounts were subsequently told of this milling affray. The king, we learn, in an effort to bring order out of anarchy and with no inkling that he was riding to his doom, 'seeing the stormy sea that surged about him' removed the gold crown that wreathed his helmet and handed it to an aide before charging into the pursuing enemy in a last attempt to get his men to turn and fight. Depending on his horse to keep him safe from the enemy around him, initially he was only grazed by a spear thrust through his breastplate and was also able to deal a blow with his own weapon against his assailant. This Argive hero was a desperate guardian of hearth and home whose bravery was fostered by the presence of his mother observing the action from the roof of a nearby house. Yet this vigorous matron was not satisfied with just encouraging from afar and when she saw the terrible enemy on his magnificent warhorse threatening her offspring, she tore off a tile from the roof and with both hands threw it down at the king. It seems she may not have been the lone Amazon there and that many of the local women threw whatever they could find at the intruders, but hers was certainly a lucky shot. Striking below his helmet, the heavy slate crushed one of the vertebrae in Pyrrhus' neck 'so that his sight was blurred and his hands dropped the reins. Then he sank down from his horse and fell near the tomb of Licymnius',[17] a place that is mentioned by Pausanias as being on the straight road to the gymnasium commemorating the offspring of a legendary king of Tiryns who was killed by Heracles' son Tlepolemus.[18]

A number of Antigonus' soldiers, seeing the enemy officer fall, dragged him dazed and defenceless into a nearby doorway. Their intention had initially been to capture this potentially valuable prisoner, but when he began to come round and struggle against his captors, one named Zopyrus decided that in the middle of battle the safer plan would be to kill him. He sliced at the head with an Illyrian short sword, but it seems just the stare of the belligerent king terrified his assassin and an ill-aimed blow failed to strike off the head, only wounded him so severely around 'the mouth and chin' that he suffered a long-drawn-out and painful death before the head was finally separated from his torso. The news of his demise could not but travel swiftly from mouth to mouth until Antigonus' illegitimate son Halcyoneus, the fruit of his dalliance with a courtesan during a lengthy youthful residence at Athens,[19] who was commanding men in the street-fighting heard and arrived to collect the bloody trophy Zopyrus and his comrades were still safeguarding. This young man, looking to his reputation, left the fight to find his father sitting with his staff behind the battle line and triumphantly flung the remains of the Antigonids' terrible enemy on the ground at his feet. The prince did not, however, get the reception he expected: his father hit him with a staff and kicked him out without ceremony, with charges of barbarism and impiety ringing in his ears. It had been too much for the king, who burst into tears from the memories that were brought back of his own family's misfortunes, with his grandfather Antigonus dying in battle and Demetrius rotting in captivity. He wanted no taint of failing to respect his fallen foe, although we can perhaps question the sincerity of his feeling that the remains of this man who had given him so much anxiety really deserved a better fate, so collecting the head and body he had the proper rites observed, dressing him in royal accoutrements for burial and dispatching him back to Epirus.

Now the earlier mockery of the humbled Antigonid was flung back in the teeth of its originator with the Epirot king just a dust-strewn corpse while Gonatus was well on the way to regaining his throne. It was a complete turnaround from the earlier outcome on the Aous River with Pyrrhus' followers rudderless without their charismatic leader, surrendering themselves and their camp to Antigonus. The victor was magnanimous, 'he dealt mildly with the friends of Pyrrhus' and indeed was unable to stay angry with his son when he found Halcyoneus had discovered prince Helenus 'in an abject state and wearing a paltry cloak', and treated him well before bringing him to Antigonus' tent. The rehabilitation of the young man was shown to be incomplete when the king declared that his conduct, although better, was still a disgrace as he had not provided his royal captive with a proper wardrobe.

A far-off campaign had ended as tragedy for the whole Epirot royal family with the father and one son dead in bloody battle, but the tremors felt from these events would be wide-reaching for the whole Balkan world order. Helenus was returned to his homeland after an agreement was reached to relinquish Epirot control of all Thessaly and any of Macedonia still in their hands. Antigonus must have hoped that in returning the prince, it might put his family under obligation, a solid win as opposed to some other candidate who might prove troublesome in a world that remained confused and dangerous. If so, his calculation did not immediately prove correct as another son of Pyrrhus, by Agathocles' daughter Lanassa, called Alexander who had been left in charge when his father marched south, in less than a decade became involved in fighting against Antigonus until the latter's own son Demetrius defeated him and drove him into exile. Beyond this brief time of troubles, in the long run the sweet, short years of distinction for Greater Epirus were comprehensively in the past, built as they had been on the back of an extraordinary monarch who had been wiped out by a lump of plain undecorated terracotta. So the Stoic monarch of Macedonia could finally contemplate a future that held little threat from over the Pindus Mountains. Antigonus had been perhaps 18 or 19 when his grandfather lost a world kingdom, then a couple of years past 30 when his father had been turned out of Pella, and now at almost 50 the times had turned full circle. A man who had learned to shrug his shoulders at the ups and downs of fortune during the era of Demetrius and during his own career could finally believe that he had come into his own in a world safe at last for a blighted people and an understated ruler.

Epilogue

The first few decades of the third century in Macedonian Europe seemed peopled by folk of extremes. It was a time when the depths of wickedness were plumbed. Ptolemy Ceraunus, no one was in any doubt, was an iniquitous man whose behaviour over more than a decade not only showed consistently egregious but ushered in an appalling crisis for not only his own homeland but for the countries all around. Yet even his depravity, wallowing in assassination, familial murder and deepest treachery, was trumped by the likes of Apollonius who, when tyrant of Cassandreia, is accused of orchestrating cannibal feasts. They were up to their necks in a kind of behaviour redolent of exotic eastern courts that had occupied palaces at Sardis, Babylon, Ecbatana or Susa with even a suggestion that they might represent a falling of standards that some would claim as a hallmark of what is called the Hellenistic age. Cassander and Lysimachus, if reported as more solid citizens, still emerge as pretty unlovable, if not worse, though it must be understood that their reputations are largely transmitted via a prism that was attached to the entourage of their bitterest enemies. There were other extraordinary characters around like Cassander's brother Alexarchus who invented a solar religion and is mentioned as the founder of a utopian community called Ouranoupoli in Chalcidice, and amazing women like Arsinoe who, first as Lysimachus' queen, was deeply implicit in his dreadful downfall before returning to Egypt to marry her brother Ptolemy II and act as a crucial player at that prince's remarkable court for several years before her death sometime in the 260s.

Apart from descent into iniquity or eccentricity, it was the extremes of ambition and risk-taking and the ups and downs of fortune that characterized the two individuals for whom we have the most detail in these years. They had been a pair, these two kings, even if they did play in slightly different leagues. To continue the analogy, Demetrius is easy to see as the Real Madrid of the Galactico era, always competing for world domination and occasionally reaching the heights for a time but still so essentially unbalanced; all glitz and glamour with little heart for the mundane routine fare, so any position at the very pinnacle of the domestic game was seldom long sustained. Pyrrhus, like Ajax of Amsterdam during the twenty-first century who, despite being supremely talented and always ambitious, just did not have the resources, apart from very occasionally and for very short periods, to ever be able to compete at the highest level. Both had sat on the Macedonian throne, both imagining a great Balkan state and more, but failing in the end to achieve it. There was also ignominy at the end of both these lives. Demetrius had terminated by drinking himself to death in a morass of ennui, and hardly ten years later Pyrrhus had been vanquished, not honourably by a foeman's spear or sword but by a roof tile; not only that, but one flung by of all things an old lady or, if Cassius Dio is to be believed, the even greater indignity of the old lady slipping off the roof and falling on top of him. The Eagle king being dead obviously did not have to worry personally, but it is easy to imagine the embarrassment his shade felt as he contemplated his earthly reputation from any afterlife.

The lives of Demetrius and Pyrrhus had been a picaresque of power, and with the death of the latter it seemed the end of an era when larger-than-life characters stalked the Hellenistic stage, the butt end of an epic, yet an epic nonetheless. They had been unscrupulous, dangerous and unpredictable, but had painted in broad brush strokes that impacted so many in the world both near and far. It also marked the demise of the only truly formidable enemy of the man who sat on the Macedonian throne when the sands settled. He was a new sort of ruler who had never seemed to fit naturally into a world of grand schemes and castles in the air; so different from both his father and his greatest enemy, he existed on a much more human scale. This ruler who condescended to encourage his soldiers to play ball games[1] fitted better into the cultural milieu exemplified by the New Comedy where family troubles and love affairs took over from the great themes of the mythical past. The character who emerges is less physically imposing than his father and from several anecdotes showed considerable humour and self-awareness, quipping that the man who emptied his chamber pot had not noticed he was a god, regarding the royal diadem as just a rag and the life of kingship as one of glorious servitude, glorious certainly but servitude nonetheless, nothing like the extravagant pageant envisaged by his father.

He would not initiate any monumental extravaganza to commemorate the survival of a barbarian Armageddon such as the Athenians eventually constructed on their burned Acropolis to celebrate the endurance of their home twice razed by the Persians. Despite Thermopylae being central to both campaigns and however hard the likes of Pausanias tried to draw parallels, the contest with the Gauls never garnished the glory of the earlier epic and its aftermath was never wreathed in the same garlands of triumph. After Xerxes' defeat the victors proceeded to centuries of impressive political, cultural and military achievement, but the world that survived the Gallic wreckage never hit such highlights. Antigonus also left it to the rulers of Pergamon to put up great altars to commemorate victory over the Gauls and, despite a penchant for collecting philosophers, he saw no need to establish a great cultural centre like Alexandria, Antioch or Pergamon; any cities that he planted were modest affairs, Antigoneas whose stories hardly rang down the centuries.

Whether psychology or happy coincidence, Antigonus appears as the polar opposite of his father, so unlike the anti-role model that was Demetrius; only in his filial affection did he show those traits that had been legend in the family. It was even there in their looks: taking few of his father's genes when it came to appearance, Demetrius was almost beautiful while his son was snub-nosed and not much to look at, but it was in personality and policy that the chasm was most marked. There was no thirst for deification and he did not crave the visibility of his handsome father or the overweening power of his grandfather, while his interested, versatile mind was reflected in the coterie of thinkers with whom he was to be found during all his long life. He could certainly practice realpolitik, showing cunning and cynicism, particularly when late in his reign he proposed an arrangement with the Aetolians to invade and partition the Achaean League. Yet this was inevitable for a man in his position and anyway, never covered in any envelope of reserve, he would often unbend to show a far from unusual Macedonian tendency to indulge in heavy drinking, and the lavish birthday party he gave for the prince Halcyoneus was infamous. However, despite imbibing unwatered wine in all-night parties, like his father he did not let such inclinations much affect his actions. It was an off-duty interest and one that Demetrius only took to extremes when fortune ensured that he had no more duties to perform.

Antigonus himself would probably have wanted to be remembered as a sort of philosopher prince if anything; after all, he had trained with Zeno in his turbulent early years and if, when the balmy times came at Pella, he could never persuade the old man to visit himself, his spirit certainly travelled, personified by the presence of Persaeus of Citium who had come at Zeno's request to substitute for his teacher. This stand-in seems to have been very much a man of the world who loved heavy drinking with Antigonus and, after tutoring the king's son, ended in control of Corinth where he was killed when Aratus took over there. An idealistic appeal to other thinkers made for something of a Cynic and Stoic admixture at the court of this cerebral monarch, and sending out invitations to great names in philosophy was intended to give his headquarters real kudos, perhaps in an effort to compensate for a realized decline from earlier days. It ended by garnering the likes of Bion of Borysthenes, a Pontic Greek and real globe-trotter who sampled every variety of Philosophic school in Athens before staying a while at the court of the royal intellectual, Timon of Phlius, a one-eyed octogenarian who began as a dancer and ended as a renowned thinker of sceptical leanings. There was a coterie of philosopher-poets too, like the eel-loving Antagoras of Rhodes, Alexander Aetolus who had supped at the Alexandrian muse for years before arriving at Pella, and Aratus of Soli, famed for cosmological verse and praise-singing about the great victory over the Gauls at Lysimachia.

This was the man who would steer Macedonia into largely peaceful waters in an extravagantly long reign of almost forty years, ending in 240 or 239 when he was 80 years of age, although there is something of a conundrum about what occurred in Macedonia at the start of Antigonus' latest and final stint as ruler of the country. How much ground had he recovered after his two defeats while Pyrrhus was away in the Peloponnese? Was he largely re-established before heading off to confront his adversary at Argos? We cannot be sure, but certainly after his rival's death the veil lifts to reveal Antigonus fully in control, ready to consolidate the opportunities that had become available after Pyrrhus' ignominious dispatch. Not that much detail can be discerned by peering into opaque and trifling sources for the last decades of his reign. We can recognize that he retained a tenuous hegemony in much of Greece, with the Fetters, the forts in Attica, Megara, perhaps Troezen, Epidaurus and Hydra to control the entrance of the Saronic Gulf and make life difficult if the Lagids fancied stirring the pot by flexing their naval muscle, while the old trick of Antipater and Cassander of sponsoring friendly tyrants was not infrequently played, particularly in the Peloponnese. Antigonus was also fortunate that of the four most significant Greek powers – Aetolia, Athens, Boeotia and Sparta – only two ever joined against him at any one time, although when Sparta and Athens did conjoin, it resulted in one of the major conflicts in his last thirty years of power.

One slight island of information stands out a little in the murky ocean that is the period after Pyrrhus' death and appropriately it centred around that city where Antigonus had received much of his education and spent many years of his young life, a place he understood perhaps much better than most of his forebears on the Macedonian throne. This man who loved to spend so much of his time among philosophers, many of whom had strong links with, if they did not actually come from Athens, would end remembered and vilified for this war against the city and indeed his general intrusion into the Greek world. Athenian war aims remained what they had been for years: to regain Piraeus and the other forts that had been retained in Antigonid hands after the revolution of 287. They had hoped Pyrrhus might have helped with removing these muzzles to their independence when their envoys approached him in the Peloponnese in 272, but he had other things on his mind at that time and now a few years later he was no longer a factor. However, the conflict hotted up within that other perennial context within which so many Macedonian rulers had to try to exist: hostility from the incumbent at Alexandria. This Chremonidean war was sparked sometime in the mid-260s, named for an Athenian diplomat who had spent much of his career as a condottieri in the employ of the Ptolemies. If the conflict was partly a proxy business fuelled by Ptolemy II, when it came to fighting the Lagids did little more than send an admiral called Patrocles who camped on a small island opposite Cape Sunium and largely remained quiet after discovering that Antigonus saw no benefit in fighting a sea battle. Yet at least on land Lagid agents with bottomless pockets had sponsored a considerable coalition with those beyond the Attic capital who answered the call including Sparta, the Achaeans, Elis, the Tegeans, Mantineans, Arcadians and a few Cretans, all of whom signed up after seeing the glint of Lagid gold.

The Spartan king who had given so much trouble to Pyrrhus took the lead, initially making an abortive attempt to pass the isthmus defensive line based on the Acrocorinth to aid an Attic ally who was bound soon to be threatened by Antigonid armies once they had dealt with the distraction of an Epirot raid led by Pyrrhus' son Alexander. The next year Areus was killed after again committing to battle against Antigonus outside Corinth, an occasion when his son Halcyoneus[2] may also have lost his life. A defeat that saw not just the decisive termination of the Peloponnesian League efforts, particularly after the next king of Sparta, Acrotatus, the hero of Pyrrhus' siege, was himself killed in a defeat against the forces of Megalopolis, but also the withdrawal of the Lagid fleet. So with two more Spartan kings perishing in battle, siege lines, already in place since 263, had been drawn tight around Athens, such that late in the summer of 262 the defenders surrendered with a Macedonian garrison re-established on the hill of the Muses and a state of dependency made apparent with the induction of the grandson of Demetrius of Phalerum to partly reprise the role of his forebear who had managed Athens in the interests of Cassander; a punctuation mark in the city's story emphasized by the death around this time of Zeno, the last of the great initiators of philosophic institutions in ancient Athens. Antigonus' hegemony over Greece had never been complete, particularly tight or oppressive; far more a thing of manipulation, of personal connections rather than Ptolemaic-style direct administration, but the Chremonidean War had made it clear that none of the other Hellenistic kings could effectively compete with him for influence in this particular arena. They might like to make friends among the great historic cities but the only man who really counted ruled at Pella, who if he eschewed direct rule in most places and accepted his prerogatives were considerably constrained by the Achaeans and Aetolians flexing their muscles, still remained the context and could not be crossed with impunity.

Not that the years after the submission of the Athenians were ever likely to be problem-free, and if the evidence is gossamer-thin, we know that the late 250s saw rebellions by Craterus' son Alexander ensuring that for quite some time Antigonus lost control of Acrocorinth, Chalcis and Eretria. This Alexander, so unlike his faithful father, declared himself king in his own right after suborning the commanders of the Euboean fortresses, allied himself with the Achaean League and made trouble for

Antigonus' friends in Athens and Argos before being bought off. Yet this turned out to be only a blip, if a five-year one, and on Alexander's death Antigonus, his cunning little blunted by age, duped his widow Nicaea with an offer of his son's hand in marriage. During the festivities and despite his almost seventy summers, he walked up the steep path to the Acrocorinth with some steady men to be let in by the celebrating garrison before taking over the crucial citadel. This key stronghold always seemed to be at the centre of things in Antigonus' later years and 243 saw the ageing king suffer a considerable blow with the emergence of Aratus of Sicyon heading up a resuscitated Achaean League that permanently dented the Macedonian Peloponnesian presence.

This man had been a friend of Antigonus in the past, but this did not stop him, flush with Lagid money, from taking the Acrocorinth by a coup de main. He climbed at night ninja-like into the fortress with the help of some bought members of the garrison, taking over and killing the officers Antigonus had left to hold the place. Nor was this the end as he wooed the likes of Troezen, Epidaurus and even Megara into his expanding league. Whether these places had been garrisoned by the Antigonids is not known, but what is clear is that the king's relations with other Peloponnesian big hitters like Elis, Megalopolis and Argos were far less steady after this time, though that they were never stern enemies is made probable by their distaste for a Sparta which always regarded Antigonus as a dangerous foe. What was not in question was that Macedonian power and influence in the key region of the Argolid, Isthmus and Megarid which had been so solid and so important for so long was now at least shared with a rising Archean polity.

Not that the long years of entrenchment involved just looking south. Antigonus in many ways had a personality more suited to the normal role of commanding a marcher state than many of his recent predecessors and if his concerns were greater than just defending the civilized littoral from savage men to the north, still he knew that he needed to keep an eye on the ambitions of not just Gauls but other older bugbears populating the borderlands. Antigonus would have appreciated as much as an Achaean historian

> how highly should we honour the Macedonians, who for the greater part of their lives never cease from fighting with the barbarians

for the sake of the security of Greece? For who is not aware that Greece would have constantly stood in the greatest danger, had we not been fenced by the Macedonians and the honourable ambition of their kings? The best proof is this. The moment that the Gauls after defeating Ptolemy Ceraunus conceived a contempt for the Macedonians, Brennus making light of all other opponents, marched into the middle of Greece with his army, a thing that would often have happened if our frontiers were not protected by the Macedonians.[3]

Yet despite making every effort to hold the line against anybody trying to follow in the steps of Bolgius and Brennus, he was never able to completely reconstruct the barrier that had been broken with the demise of Lysimachus. Dardanians, Illyrians and Thracians and Celts would occasionally crack the brittle northern carapace of his kingdom, though no further existential menace emerged in the lifetime of this man who as often stood guard by the unhealthy freshwater lake of Pella, watching his polities' northern fringes, as he did attending to the southern world of Hellenes from his other capital of Demetrias.

It was from that city at the head of the Pagasaean Gulf that the armadas were dispatched to do battle against the Ptolemies at Cos and Andros during the 250s and 240s before Lagid attention was drawn again to interminable conflicts with the Seleucids over Coele-Syria. This was a contest that matched the other two long-lived monarchs whose lives and reigns closely mirrored that of Antigonus Gonatas. Ptolemy II Philadelphus was made joint king with his father around 283 and lasted until 246. Apart from bothering Antigonus, Africa took much of his attention, with his half-brother Magus of Cyrene a source of trouble, while he also found time to invade Nubia, devoting considerable resources to opening up the Red Sea, founding trading posts to cash in on the Arabian and Indian ocean spice trade as well as getting African bush elephants to beef up his military. Antiochus I Soter, like the other two, had also served an apprenticeship under the progenitor of his dynasty. He had been Seleucus' co-ruler responsible for the Eastern Seleucid territories since around 292 before starting a solo reign in 281 that lasted through to 261. Apart from his duel with Ptolemy, problems with rampaging Galatians, independent Anatolian dynasts and Eastern provinces that were never secure ensured he had plenty to occupy a reign which, after the brief confrontation of the early 270s, was pretty quiet on the Macedonian front. Equally, if ideas of going east to secure an effective border or to gain control of the key trade routes and cities may have attracted his descendant Antiochus III, such grand strategic thinking that always fell foul of those old enemies' time and distance, was not a possibility in the middle of the third century.

After decades of war, treachery and trauma, the empire that the great Alexander had secured had finally settled into three discrete entities, each conveniently established on the different continents of Europe, Asia and Africa. The dynasties that ruled them had each sprung from one of those great marshals who had found themselves heir to a considerable portion of the whole when the first dismemberment occurred at Babylon in 323. Ptolemy had received the satrapy of Egypt, and apart from expanding into the lands of the Levant and the waters of the East Mediterranean and Aegean, there he largely remained. Seleucus had initially continued as second-in-command to Perdiccas before being designated as governor of Babylonia at Triparadisus in 321. From then came exile and return before winning for himself an Eastern realm sufficiently puissant that with his partners Lysimachus and Cassander he could wreck the high ambitions of Antigonus the One-Eyed at Ipsus, a victory that first won for him most of west Asia outside Anatolia before the final campaign of the old adventurer took his frontiers to the shores of the Hellespont. The last of the three was the grandson of the same man defeated at Ipsus, but the road that took him to Pella was so topsy-turvy, convoluted and chaotic that it is suggestive of the whole story of the particular section of the Macedonian Empire of which he ended being in charge.

What of this state nurtured by such a conscientious and long-lived monarch? The legacy of the Imperial years and the contests of colossi that came after, all ensured that despite the wealth that had seeped back after the conquests of the Persian Empire, his kingdom was considerably weaker than when Philip had passed it to his son as a tool to shape a new world. There were no more gold strikes in the Pangaion Mountains above Amphipolis or gold coins minted, with only amounts of silver, iron and lead still being processed in the last king Perseus' time; a condition of economic weakness that is emphasized by the claim that his yearly revenue amounted to only an unbelievably derisory 200 talents.[4] This was despite there having been some territorial recovery with the retrieval of the rump of the upper cantons, including the strategically crucial Aous pass, after the defeat of the Epirots by Antigonus' son Demetrius and with Paeonia and other posts on the northern frontier reclaimed. And what had always been very apparent was that if Antigonus Gonatus had survived terrible trials in his first decade in power, it was not so much due to the resources of the northern kingdom but largely because of the vigour of his holdings in Greece and the effectiveness of his old strategy of waiting out others who might be more talented and powerful.

That just the phrase 'grassy knoll' conjures up a whole world of conspiracy is not only because of the glamour of J.F. Kennedy, the strangeness of the lone gunman Lee Harvey Oswald and the years of investigation into what really happened; it is partly because the assassination of a world leader is not a very frequent event. The death of Philip II was also wrapped in mystery, with stories of the perpetrator having had a personal gripe because Philip had scornfully dismissed his claims of being raped by a great man of the court or that Olympias or even Alexander had been involved in urging the assassination. What is common to both is that they were not inevitable: Kennedy might easily, if events had fallen out differently, have lived to serve two terms and Philip could have enjoyed a couple more decades or longer to see out his already launched Persian project. If the former circumstance had not occurred, it would probably not have made a massive difference to how the 1960s panned out in America and the world after. Johnson would likely have carried out his civil rights legislation as vice president and all the evidence suggests that Kennedy would not have resisted being sucked into the morass of Vietnam. No president would have been prepared to preside over another Communist success in the Far East on the model of China until years of awful bloodshed had made inevitable what the evidence had always indicated.

With Philip, the situation was different. If he had not been killed, the Macedonian Persian war might have taken a significantly dissimilar direction; he was, after all, a very different man from his son, far less astonishing in his inclinations. The invasion of Darius III's empire would have been headed up by Philip, no doubt with Parmenion as a steady second and Alexander in the same kind of subordinate role he had occupied at the Battle of Chaeronea. In these circumstances it is easy to imagine significantly different outcomes for the great enterprise. It is probable that Philip would have achieved much the same as his extraordinary son in the first few years, defeating the satraps and mercenaries who would have faced him over the Hellespont and gone on to overrun most of Anatolia; after all, 100 years earlier a king of Sparta had showed this level of ambition.[5] Equally, that the allure of the Levant and perhaps Egypt would have drawn him is quite credible, taking over territory that it would take years to suppress, organize and digest, but would he have gone further? This is impossible to know, but what is surely certain is that he would have called a halt well before Macedonian arms had reached the Zagros highlands, never mind the Hindu Kush or the Indus valley. Most of his followers could not have conceived that the high walls of Babylon or the palaces of Persepolis would not mark an end to what by any standards had been unparalleled and almost unbelievable achievements. With Philip we cannot envisage him dreaming of reaching the ocean at the end of the world and dragging his dazed and crazed Macedonians on a journey through Mesopotamia, Iran, Bactria, Sogdiana and the Punjab, actions that even contemporaries certainly saw as those of a man either not quite sane or touched by deity.

Like Parmenion, Philip might well have been happy to agree to a peace with the great king that would have established a Macedonian frontier west of the Euphrates and would have avoided the final showdown that eventually occurred at Gaugamela. This would have left a rump Persian Empire ranging from Mesopotamia to Bactria and Sogdiana but still would have ensured that the sunburst banner of Macedonia would have flown over country stretching from European Macedonia, through the massively wealthy provinces of Anatolia to the Levant. This much less stretched realm, each part easily and swiftly able to communicate via the sea lanes, would surely have been less frangible than the one that was eventually bequeathed by Philip's son. Alexander, growing older as a crucial military subordinate but not allowed to have his latent megalomania run free, might with the passing years have become something closer to what was expected of a Macedonian monarch, perhaps fathering an heir who could, by the time Philip had died and certainly when his son had, would have been sufficiently mature to accrue all the benefits of legitimacy, sufficient to keep the new Macedonian Empire from splintering apart.

This established Macedonian dynasty could conceivably have retained control, maintaining the loyalty of its conquering marshals, and been puissant enough to sufficiently suppress centrifugal tendencies, either independence movements by conquered peoples or attempts by ambitious commanders and officials to set up as independent rulers. Even if Mesopotamia had been conquered with the treasure houses of Susa, Babylon and Ecbatana emptied, it is still possible to imagine a unitary state surviving. Antigonus almost achieved this himself with no golden glow of legitimacy to smooth his way and in a world where the poison of faction fighting was already well established. Yet even he was unable to keep hold of the upper satrapies or Babylonia for long and the same would surely have been the case, even if an heir of the legitimate line had come into his own. To illustrate this possibility, a version of this kingdom did emerge just before the final shattering. Lysimachus, having taken over the throne of Macedon from Pyrrhus in 284 and incorporating Paeonia and Thessaly into his realm, possessed just such a state stretching from Epirus to the Taurus and almost from the Danube down through much of the north Aegean. If the old king had not indulged in such poisonous familial machinations but instead handed over this extensive rich and powerful realm to his mature and talented son Agathocles, it is conceivable that a strong legitimate line could have retained control of this extensive, powerful but tight imperial entity.

A reasonable orthodoxy suggests that much of Rome's success in taking over the Hellenistic East forty years after the demise of Antigonus Gonatus had been, just as it had been in winning the Hannibalic War, dependent on her ability to draw on the resources of the numerous and warlike peoples of Italy that she had brought under her sway over the previous couple of centuries. It was a matter of arithmetic; she had the numbers: she could afford the awful bloodlettings of the Punic War years when so many of her armies were eliminated by an opponent whose soldiers might not have individually been better than the legions, but in combination and led by the likes of Hannibal were devastatingly effective. This was due to an ability to recruit from both an expanding pool of citizens and subject allies from central and south Italy: fighters from the plains of Apulia, the hills and glens of Lucania, Bruttium, Samnium and north through Latium, Samnite country up to Cisalpine Gaul, north of Etruria and Umbria, who provided at least half the infantry and much more of the horse that saved the city from Hannibal and fed the conflicts that took Roman power across the Adriatic and as far as the Taurus Mountains of Anatolia in less than a generation. This was a polity that could send 40,000 men across the Adriatic, then send another when the attrition of several years' campaigning in mainland Greece against Philip V of Macedonia had worn it out, so that when a final great battle was fought at Cynoscephalae she could, with a small number of local allies, field an army slightly larger than her enemy in their own back yard. Then, within a very few years, dispatch even larger forces to take on Antiochus III, the Seleucid monarch of Asia who had just returned from a great conquering promenade around the upper satrapies of Iran, Bactria and Sogdiana that had earned him the sobriquet 'the Great'.

However, something else is demanded other than just maths; numbers might have been absolutely crucial in allowing Rome to expand so swiftly and decisively east into the Greek and Hellenistic heartland, but it had been about division too. In dealing with these two Hellenistic powers, Rome had been able to take them on one at a time, indeed with encouragement from the non-belligerent who welcomed the idea of a regional rival being taken down a peg or two without anticipating that such encouragement would end with the fox taking up residence in the hen coop. What must exercise the imagination is what would have occurred if the Hellenic power that Rome faced comprised the kind of compact but extensive East Mediterranean power that might have developed without a world-conquering Alexander as the driving force. A Macedonia controlling Macedonian Europe, Anatolia and perhaps even the Levant and Egypt with all the resources monetary, military and naval these would have provided might have been able to face with greater success the Roman storm from the west. Certainly such an entity would have been able to raise another army after a defeat even as total as Cynoscephalae, just as Rome had after the Trebbia, Lake Trasimene and Cannae, while control of the Hellespont and, perhaps being the major naval power in the Aegean, in the way Philip V or Antiochus III never were, might have suggested a different outcome. Such a polity that was more dominant in Greece and Anatolia also might have meant the Romans would have had less opportunity to exploit the potential of places like Aetolia, Achaea, Pergamon and Rhodes as significant auxiliaries in the wars against the Hellenistic kings. That all this might have made a difference is predicated on the existence of a form of Macedon very much beefed up from the entity that stood exposed as resource-weak and fairly friendless against a Rome able to call on the hundreds of thousands of warrior peoples of central and south Italy, honed and hardened after more than fifteen years of warfare against the terrible Hannibal. Such a single Hellenistic kingdom could mobilize her deep barrel of military manpower from not just the Macedonian heartland, with the sarissa-wielding soldiers of the phalanx and the urban foundations of soldier settlers around some of the most fertile and strategically significant sites in the Eastern Mediterranean, but from the Greeks of Anatolia and Europe whose ethos always saw the citizen as solid warrior when the time required. On top these would have been seconded by hordes of tough warriors from the tribes of Thrace and hard-fighting Galatians; a military potential seconded by a first-rate marine founded on a combination of Greek Aegean and Phoenician and Levantine talents and assets, all defending a state that might perhaps have the wherewithal to buy sufficient time to learn the techniques and find a weakness in the juggernaut of hatchet-wielding killers coming their way.

Counter-factual yet interesting, it is possible to make reasonable calculations about the sort of military response that such a Macedonian could mobilize in the face of the direst threat, but was there perhaps something else that made the difference? Can a case be made that it was the particular military system of the Romans that ensured success? This matter had been under discussion since the days of Polybius, who saw Rome as deploying a political system that produced both the leadership and the military machine particularly suited for world conquest, while Livy could happily speculate on the likelihood of a Roman victory had Alexander turned from his eastern conquests to invade the Italian peninsula. These mechanistic explanations saw the Roman military way as the key; that those states that fell to Rome practised an art of war that just could not take what the legions could throw at them, particularly that the Roman soldier organised in centuries and maniples had the edge over the phalanx in a way that was always bound to be decisive. History clearly indicates that on occasions military systems can be decisive; that ways of fighting in particular settings and particular contexts can frequently be pivotal. Thus, while the Roman legion proved impressive against so many of the enemies it encountered in Europe, Africa and Asia, the systemic use of horses, archers and cataphracts practised in armies from steppe nomads through to the Parthians and Sasanian Persians generally proved very effective against this same enemy when deployed on their home ground.

So it is possible that even if a Macedon with the manpower resources of a much greater European and Asian state could have faced up to Roman numbers, this other factor would have ensured their defeat anyway. Polybius stressed that the peculiarities of the legion, its flexibility and that it could fight in uneven terrain in large or small bodies were the explanation of what most considered its extraordinary achievement in defeating the Macedonian-style phalanx. He contended the secret was that within its three lines, each legion had reserves that would not engage with the phalanx when contact occurred and that when the phalanx moved, either in difficult ground or in forcing its foe back or retreating, it would become disordered and move away from the auxiliary troops supporting it, so the spare Roman warriors could occupy the ground in the phalanx's flank and rear to attack the pikemen where they were vulnerable. It was the phalanx's inability to act and fight in separate smaller squads that meant they were unable to counter this threat.

Yet that the phalanx was so easily disarranged and only truly effective on flat, level ground does not seem to fit with the evidence from the whole career of the Macedonian phalanx from Phillip II through to the great second-century battles. Here there are multiple examples of it staying solid and functioning effectively in all sorts of country, from Philip's phalanx marching backwards uphill to entice the Athenians to follow them at Chaeronea, to Alexander's phalanx fighting against Illyrians and Thracians in hilly wooded terrain. Then in his Persian Wars, his phalanx attacked successfully across both the Granicus and Issus rivers and many years later the phalanx of Antigonus III Doson advanced uphill to get at the Spartans at Sellasia with little loss of effectiveness. There does seem to be enough evidence to squash the well-held contention that the only place where the phalanx was effective was on level ground. This is not to say that the formation might not suffer on difficult terrain or when trying to push forward rapidly; in these circumstances their ranks would certainly have become disordered and gaps appear in the bristling hedge of pikes. However, the key factor in most of these contests was that the troops opposing the phalanx were unable to effectively exploit this tendency.

Yet in the heavily-armoured swordsmen of Rome, the phalanx found a kind of nemesis almost designed to exploit its weakness and enabling the legion to hand out an almost unbroken line of defeats. The process was simple but devastating for a soldier who knew how to fight as an individual duellist. The legionary, after gaining sufficient experience to realize the ploy was possible, could, after pulling his shield to cover his front, push down between the rows of pikes facing him and, once reaching the phalanxite, stab him with his heavy short sword. Having downed the man in his front and perhaps more, this would have then made the gap between the pike heads larger, allowing more of his comrades to penetrate. This intruder would be well-placed even if his opponent dropped his pike and defended himself with his own short sword, a circumstance in which the legionary's skill as a swordsman would give him an edge while his body shield provided much better protection than the other's smaller round pelte. Not only would it be probable that he would beat his man, but the very fact that the other had dropped his pike would be bound to cause disruption among his comrades on each side, ensuring even more gaps for enemies to pour in. It is easy to see that it would not take many swordsmen wrecking havoc among almost unprotected phalanxites to cause fatal disorder in the heart of the formation.

This would not generally have been the case for the other opponents faced by the phalanx. A Persian bow and spear man, a Greek hoplite, a Thracian peltast, a Gallic warrior or the later ubiquitous thureophoroi, peltasts with larger Gallic-style shields, faced with a gap in the lines of pikes facing them were none of them especially well equipped to exploit it. Persian infantry were not generally close-quarter combatants, while the hoplite used to fighting as a unit would not naturally push between rows of spear points, even if his large round shield didn't make it physically difficult. Then, just like a peltast with his javelin, the hoplite with his spear would, if he could penetrate the hedge of pikes, find it more difficult to strike his opponent when he defended himself with his own short sword. The same problem would face the thureophoros, and as for the Gallic warrior, he would have little room to swing his long slashing sword among a forest of sarissas. So while the phalanx worked well against these various warrior types, even on terrain that did not ideally suit it, when it came to facing the legionary it was different, although this had not been the case straight away. When they faced Pyrrhus' veteran Epirot phalanx in three battles, the Roman swordsmen either were defeated or failed to achieve complete success. They needed experience to learn how to deal with the formidable hedgehog as it approached them; indeed, even at Pydna their commander Aemilius Paullus would declare his own terror just at the sight of the glistening hedge of spear points.[6] Fortunately for him, his men proved less intimidated and with more than a century of phalanx-fighting experience to draw on, they saw off a very high-quality Macedonian phalanx on a battlefield, much of which was flat and clear.

It seems that Rome's legionaries exposed a fatal flaw in the phalanx system for which they were never able to find an answer, but nothing is a given; chance can take a hand and a larger, more resource-rich Macedonian kingdom might have benefited from an ability to learn from defeat. What is noticeable is that in each of the great Roman campaigns against Hellenistic enemies at Cynoscephalae, Magnesia and Pydna they were decided by one great battle, after which Rome's enemy was never able to come back for a second and third round in the way the Romans themselves had done against first Pyrrhus and then most famously against Hannibal in the Second Punic War. The legions failed in battle at both Heraclea in Magna Graecia and Asculum in Apulia, while Benevento in Samnium was perhaps something like a draw, but that they could return to battle meant they were able to work out methods of dealing with the novel test posed by great phalanxes, elephants and well-armoured cavalry that they found themselves facing. The Hellenistic kingdoms never had this luxury, but had there been a state founded on the resources of a great Balkan and East Aegean empire to face the threat from over the Adriatic, things might have been different. It is interesting that a capacity to learn might be distinguished in the war between Rome and Antiochus fought only a few years after the Second Macedonian War. Realizing the danger from the terrible butchers with their short Spanish swords noticed by their own observers or officers transferring from Philip's defeated military, it is interesting that the Antigonids' first response in 191 was to face the new enemy at the pass of Thermopylae where they could establish a static defence with their flanks protected. In this place, standing strictly on the defensive with legionaries throwing themselves onto its spears, the phalanx worked well:

Battle being joined, the light-armed troops assailed Manius first, rushing in from all sides. He received their onset bravely, first yielding and then advancing and driving them back. The phalanx opened and let the light-armed men pass through. It then closed and pushed forward, the long pikes set densely together in order of battle, with which the Macedonians from the time of Alexander and Philip have struck terror into enemies who have not dared to encounter the thick array of long pikes presented to them.[7]

The problem with this bulwark was, as with Xerxes and the Gauls in earlier instalments, a way was found around when Cato the Elder with a strong detachment turned their flank and, once exposed, Antiochus' men blocking the pass had no choice but to withdraw. Anyway, Thermopylae was not a normal battlefield and it was hardly possible to fight the Romans only in mountain passes and in very specific circumstances where flanks were absolutely covered and the Romans prepared to attack them frontally. Equally a purely defensive strategy was bound to hand the initiative to the enemy, exposing the homeland to being ravaged and its cities to being besieged without any response. Apart from these obvious disadvantages for the civilian population, for the army it would bound to have a damaging effect, not just on the esprit de corps of the men but on the reputation of the commander, with the imminent danger of allies deserting to an enemy who seemed far more active, more likely to win and more capable of defending their friends. So for a Hellenistic high command to stay perpetually on the tactical defensive was bound to be hugely problematic. The project also depended on the Romans attacking an essentially static phalanx head-on and, apart from against an opponent without any sort of military brain, this was unlikely to occur. Most Roman commanders were well aware of how dangerous this was likely to be, so the best that might be expected was a stalemate until the defenders were manoeuvred out of their position, as however well-protected a defender's flanks might be, finally almost any position could be turned.

Failure at Thermopylae did not subtract from concerns already felt about the propriety of deploying a phalanx in the open against legionnaires, particularly as the fact that Seleucid soldiers had only been present in small quantities was part of the reason for fighting there. Not that paucity of numbers would be in the least the case in the next great test at

Magnesia on the plains of Lydia, yet here again it is clear that Antiochus and his generals were sufficiently concerned to deploy their phalanx in an innovative manner. They split up the pikemen into a number of blocks with elephants deployed between the sections in a manner described as being like towers in a defensive wall. The great advantage of this deployment with individual phalanxes having a shorter front would mean it would be less likely that order would disintegrate as they moved into the attack. That they chose elephants must have seemed high-risk to any who knew the propensity of such beasts to run amok, but presumably it was expected that with their accompanying light infantry they would be sufficiently intimidating to stop enemy troops slipping between the bodies of phalanxites and threatening their vulnerable flanks, a tactic not too dissimilar to that employed by Pyrrhus at Asculum when he deployed his allied Italian infantry between blocks of Epirot pikemen. Even if at Magnesia the phalanx performed reasonably well for most of the battle, with the final defeat assured by events in other parts of the field, whether a learning process would have been effective is doubtful, particularly as a glimpse into the few generations after may suggest a general failure to find a formula to combat the legion. Seleucid and indeed Mithridatic militaries would come up with no satisfactory answers, and the only truly significant development was the tendency to just try to replicate, to produce sorts of ersatz legions, many of which in the Mithridatic Wars were trained by Roman officers but none of which seemed to have had a significant impact in the conflicts in which they were employed. Not that the victors held the defeated in contempt: Alexander's phalanx kept its aura of world-conquering glamour down the ages, with attempts at resuscitation of the antique formation being tried by several Roman emperors from Nero onwards.

Yet in following up some of these ideas, the obvious must not be forgotten: that Rome never did have to contend with that larger, wealthier, more populous state that has been posited. The Macedon of Antigonus Gonatus, Philip V and Perseus was no such grand polity; the extraordinary character of the founder of the Macedonian Empire had ensured this. It had been Alexander's particular curse upon his homeland; functioning as he did like very few men in history, it was always likely that his impact would be commensurate with his character; but for him, things might have been different. Extravagant ambition is not unusual or military talent, but for the most extreme of these to be combined in one man whose crazed narcissism conditioned a whole world is uncommon. The nature of the individual who had generated the Hellenistic world ensured that no unified Macedonian Empire could exist to be tested by a future that included a rampant Italian power. The upshot of his extraordinary life was that despite allowing the development of a Greek *koine* (shared language) from southern France to the Indus, he also ensured an enfeebled homeland that, if it enjoyed the immediate baubles of conquest, never benefited from the usual long-term dividends of empire. A great conqueror he had been, but not a great consolidator, partly because he had no great interest in such prosaic stuff, partly because he died too young to establish a stable succession, but also because the colossal entity he had conquered was just so big there was almost no chance that anybody following him would be able to hold the most significant parts of it together. So his own people hardly experienced that flowering that the progenitors of empire usually do, at least for a few generations, and despite the extraordinary expansion of the Macedonian world, the actual state based on the conqueror's homeland had ended reduced and feebler than in the reign of his father. It was a state in which the economic base was considerably reduced, and the Philippine ascendency in Thrace reinforced and expanded by Lysimachus was long gone. Even the Odrysians were broken, with only the smoking wrecks of Seuthopolis showing what once had been, and just indigenous local entities left with the Gallic kingdom of Tylis plumped down in the middle. The story of decline had been about much more than the Gallic intrusion that had broken the mould; it had been the decades of brutal and destructive conflict that consumed so much of Greece and the Balkans that had undermined the edifice. This outcome of ages of chaos synchronized with a considerable outbreak of kakistocracy, that surfacing of the corrupt, incompetent and shameless rulers with which we are not unfamiliar in our own time.

Notes

Introduction
1. The gestation of the Macedonian phalanx is comprehensively discussed in C. Matthew, *An Invincible Beast.*
2. Most recently proposed by J.D. Grainger in *Alexander: The Great Failure.*
3. Arrian, *Anabasis*, 7 2.

Chapter One
1. Herodotus, 5 34-40.
2. Arrian, *Indica*, 18.
3. Pseudo-Lucian in *Macrobii.*
4. Plutarch, *Alexander*, 40.
5. Diodorus, 19 57.
6. Pausanias, 1 13.
7. Polyperchon had allied against Cassander with both Olympias and her cousin Aeacides, king of the Molossians, to restore her to power in Macedon as guardian of Alexander's son, but after she was killed at Pydna and the war lost, both found refuge in Aetolia.
8. Plutarch, *Demetrius* 17.
9. Diodorus, 19 64.
10. Diodorus, 19 67.
11. Ibid.
12. Diogenes, *Laertius*, 5 79.
13. Strabo says that the harbour of Aulis could only hold fifty ships, and that therefore the Greek fleet must have assembled in the other ports in the neighbourhood.
14. Flavius Josephus, *Against Apion*, 1 21.
15. A.B. Bosworth in *The Legacy of Alexander* demonstrates this description of them is not strictly accurate.

Chapter Two
1. Polybius, 18 11.
2. Diodorus, 20 45.
3. Plutarch, *Demetrius*, 9.
4. Diodorus, 20 45.
5. Diogenes, *Laertius*, 5 79.

6. These two heroes had slain Hipparchus, the brother of the tyrant Hippias in 514, who was himself overthrown four years later preparing the way for the introduction of democracy.
7. Plutarch, *Demetrius*, 11.
8. Plutarch, *Demetrius*, 13.
9. Diodorus, 20 102.
10. Diodorus, 20 103.
11. Plutarch, *Demetrius*, 25.
12. Diodorus, 20 110.
13. Frontinus, 1 5 11 describes a camp constructed by Lysimachus: 'Fearing that the enemy would attack from above, he dug a triple line of trenches and encircled these with a rampart. Then, running a single trench around all the tents, he thus fortified the entire camp.'
14. Arrian, *Anabasis*, 1 3.
15. Strabo, 9 5.

Chapter Three
1. Plutarch, *Pyrrhus*, 8.
2. Diodorus, 19 105.
3. Diodorus, 20 28.
4. Pausanias, 9 7.
5. Cartledge, *Thebes*, p.247.
6. Athenaeus, 1 34.
7. Justin, 12.
8. Pausanias, 1 15.
9. Pausanias, 1 9.
10. Appian, *Syrian Wars*, 10 64.
11. Diodorus, 19 73.
12. Diodorus, 19 106.

Chapter Four
1. Plutarch, *Demetrius*, 24.
2. Plutarch, *Demetrius*, 31.
3. Polyaenus, 4 12.
4. Plutarch, *Demetrius*, 32.
5. Plutarch, *Demetrius*, 20.
6. Plutarch, *Demetrius*, 33.
7. Plutarch, *Pyrrhus*, 3.
8. Herodotus, Book 2, 55-57.
9. Homer, *Iliad*, Book 16.
10. Justin, 16.
11. Plutarch, *Demetrius*, 38.
12. Plutarch, *Demetrius*, 53.
13. Diodorus, 19, 53.
14. Plutarch, *Pyrrhus*, 10.

Chapter Five
1. Justin, 9.
2. Plutarch, *Demetrius*, 43.
3. Plutarch, *Demetrius*, 41.
4. Plutarch, *Aratus* 31 and 32.
5. Plutarch, *Pyrrhus*, 11.
6. Pausanias, 1 26.
7. Plutarch, *Demetrius*, 46.
8. Pausanias, 1 11.
9. Plutarch, *Pyrrhus*, 12.
10. Appian, *Illyrian Wars*, 2 7.
11. Justin, 16 2.
12. Pausanias, 1 10.
13. Pausanias, 1 9.

Chapter Six
1. Diodorus, 20 19; Justin 15.
2. Polynaeus, 4 12 3.
3. Diodorus, 21 13.
4. Memnon, 5.
5. Ibid.
6. Memnon, 13.
7. Appian, *Syrian War*, 63.
8. Memnon, 4.
9. Ibid.
10. Memnon, 8.
11. Justin, 24.
12. Ibid.
13. Ibid.
14. Austin, *The Hellenistic World from Alexander to the Roman Conquest*, 270.
15. Justin, 24.
16. Strabo, 7 5.
17. Justin, 24.
18. Ibid.

Chapter Seven
1. Arrian, *Anabasis*, 7 15.
2. Xenophon, *Hellenica*, 7 20.
3. Polyaenus, 7 42.
4. Barry Cunliffe, *The Ancient Celts*.
5. Livy, 38 16 3.
6. Memnon, 11.
7. Justin, 24.
8. Polyaenus, 7 35.

9. Pausanias, 10 19.
10. Pausanias, 1 4.
11. The epitaph left a Thermopylae to commemorate the 300 Spartans and the king who died there in 480.
12. Habicht, *Athens from Alexander to Antony*, p.132.
13. Pausanias, 10 21.
14. Ibid.
15. Ibid.
16. Ibid.
17. Ibid.
18. Pausanias, 10 22.
19. Homer, *Odyssey*, Book 19.
20. Justin, 24.
21. Ibid.
22. Ibid.
23. Ibid.
24. Propertius, *The Elegies*, 3 13.
25. Pausanias, 10 23.
26. Pausanias, 1 25.
27. Justin, 24.
28. Stabo 4 1; Dio Cassius, Frag, 90.

Chapter Eight
1. Plutarch, *Demetrius*, 53.
2. Ibid.
3. Plutarch, *Demetrius*, 49.
4. Justin, 24.
5. Memnon, 4.
6. M. Austin, *The Hellenistic World from Alexander to the Roman Conquest: A Selection of Ancient Sources in Translation*, 259.
7. Memnon, 10.
8. Justin, 25.
9. Ibid.
10. Ibid.
11. Ibid.
12. Syll. 207 = Michel 1482.
13. Justin, 24.
14. Diogenes, *Laertius*, 2 142.
15. Polyaenus, 4 17.
16. Justin, 25.
17. Diodorus, 22 5.
18. Ibid.
19. Polyaenus, 4 18.
20. Pausanias, 2 30.

21. Frontinus, 3 6-7; Polyaenus, 2 29.
22. Aegium took over the territory of nearby Helike, which was both destroyed by an earthquake and buried by a tsunami in 373 BC, and is suggested as a possible origin for Plato's *Atlantis*.
23. Polybius, 2 41, 13-15.
24. Polyaenus, 4 6.

Chapter Nine

1. Justin, 25.
2. Plutarch, *Pyrrhus* 26; Pausanias, 1 13.
3. Pausanias, 14 9.
4. Polyaenus, 6 6.
5. Pausanias, 1 13.
6. Polybius, 5 19.
7. Plutarch, *Pyrrhus*, 27.
8. Pausanias, 1 13.
9. Homer, *Iliad*, Book 5.
10. Pausanias, 1 13.
11. Plutarch, *Pyrrhus*, 31.
12. There are many tales about King Inachus for whom the river is named and his daughter Io, from Aeschylus to Ovid.
13. Plutarch, *Pyrrhus*, 26.
14. Plutarch, *Pyrrhus*, 31.
15. Plutarch, *Pyrrhus*, 32.
16. Plutarch, *Pyrrhus*, 33.
17. Plutarch, *Pyrrhus*, 34.
18. Pausanias, 2 22 8.
19. Athenaeus, 13 578.

Epilogue

1. D. Karunanithy, *Macedonian War Machine*, p.27.
2. Plutarch, *Moralia*, 119c.
3. Polybius, 9 35.
4. Plutarch, *Aemilius Paulus*, 28.
5. Agesilaus II of Sparta campaigned with some success in Achaemenid Asia Minor from 396 to 395.
6. Plutarch, *Aemilius Paulus*, 19.
7. Appian, *Syrian Wars*, 4.

Bibliography

Ancient Sources:
Appian, *Roman History*
Arrian, *Anabasis and Indica*
Athenaeus, *The Deipnosophists*
Cassius Dio, *Roman History*
Diodorus Siculus, *Universal History*
Frontinus, *Stratagems*
Herodotus, *The Histories*
Homer, The *Iliad* and *Odyssey*
Flavius Josephus, *Against Apion*
Justin, *Epitome of Philippic History of Pompeius Trogus*
Livy, *The History of Rome*
Memnon of Heraclea
Pausanias, *Guide to Greece*
Plutarch, *Parallel Lives and Moralia*
Polyaenus, *Stratagems*
Polybius, *The Histories*
Strabo, *The Geography*
Xenophon, *Hellenica*

Modern Sources:
Adcock, *The Greek and Macedonian Art of War* (Berkeley, 1967)
Anson, E.M., *The Siege of Nora: A Source Conflict* (Historia 37, 1988)
Austin, M., *The Hellenistic World from Alexander to the Roman Conquest* (Cambridge, 2006)
Austin, M., *Hellenistic Kings: War and Economy*, in CQ 36 (1986)
Bennet and Roberts, *The Wars of Alexander's Successors*, Vol. I and II (Pen & Sword, 2008)
Billows, *Antigonus the One-Eyed and the Creation of the Hellenistic State* (Berkeley, 1990)
Bosworth, A.B., *The Legacy of Alexander* (Oxford University Press, 2002)
Browne, E.L., *Antigonus Surnamed Gonatus* (Arktouros Hellenic Studies, 1979)
Burstein, Stanley M., *The Hellenistic Age from the Battle of Ipsos to the Death of Kleopatra VII*, Translated Documents of Greece and Rome, Series Number 3, paperback, 26 September 1985
(Cambridge Ancient History, Volume 7, Part 1, The Hellenistic World, 1972)

Campbell, Duncan B., *Greek and Roman Artillery* (Osprey, 2003)

Campbell, Duncan B., *Siege Warfare in the Ancient World* (Osprey, 2006)

Carey, B.T., *Warfare in the Ancient World* (Pen & Sword, 2005)

Carney, E.D., *Arsinoe Before she was Philadelphus* (Ancient History Bulletin 8, 1994)

Carney, E.D., *The Curious Death of the Antipatrid Dynasty AM*, VI (Thessaloniki, 1999)

Cartledge, Paul and Spawforth, A., *Hellenistic and Roman Sparta* (Routledge, 1989)

Cartledge, Paul, *Thebes* (Picador, 2020)

Champion, Jeff, *The Tyrants of Syracuse*, Vol. II (Pen & Sword, 2012)

Champion, Jeff, *Pyrrhus of Epirus* (Pen & Sword, 2009)

Chaniotis, A., *War in the Hellenistic World* (Oxford, 2005)

Connolly, *Greece and Rome at War* (Frontline Books, second edition, 2016)

Cunliffe, B., *The Ancient Celts*, Second edition paperback (OUP, Oxford, 26 April 2018)

Ellis, J.R., *The Assassination of Philip II* (Studies in honour of Charles Edson, London, 1981)

Errington, R.M., *Diodorus Siculus and the Chronology of the Early Diadochi 320–11 BC* (Hermes 105, 1977)

Ferguson, W.S., *Hellenistic Athens* (London, 1911)

Fox, Robin Lane, *Alexander the Great* (Penguin, 1973)

Gabbert, J.J., *Antigonus II Gonatus* (Routledge, 1997)

Gabbert, J.J., *The Career of Olympiodorus of Athens* (The Ancient World 13, 1986)

Gardiner, R. (ed.), *The Age of the Galley* (Conway Maritime Press, 1995)

Garoufalias, Petros, *Pyrrhus* (Stacy International, 1979)

Grainger, John D., *Alexander the Great: Failure* (Hambleton Continuum, 2007)

Grainger, John D., *The Galatians* (Pen & Sword, 2019)

Grainger, John D., *Antipater's Dynasty* (Pen & Sword, 2019)

Grainger, John D., *Seleukos Nikator* (London and New York, 1990)

Grant, Michael, *The Hellenistic Greeks* (Weidenfeld & Nicolson, 1982)

Green, P., *Alexander to Actium* (London, 1991)

Griffiths, G.T., *The Mercenaries of the Hellenistic World* (Cambridge, 1935)

Habicht, C., *Athens from Alexander to Antony* (Harvard University Press, 1997)

Hammond, N.G.L., *The Macedonian State* (Clarendon Paperbacks, 1992)

Hammond, N.G.L., *Alexander the Great* (London, 1981)

Hammond, N.G.L. and Walbank, F.W., *History of Macedonia*, Vol. III (1988)

Hanson, *The Western Way of War: Infantry Battles in Classical Greece* (Oxford, 1989)

Hanson, *Hoplites* (Routledge, 1993)

Head, Duncan, *Armies of the Macedonian and Punic Wars 359–146 BC* (Wargames Research Group, 1982)

Heckel, W., *The Marshals of Alexander's Empire* (London and New York, 1992)

Heckel, W., *The Last Days and Testament of Alexander the Great* (Historia Einzelschriften 56, 1988)

Hornblower, Jane, *Hieronymus of Cardia* (Oxford University Press, 1 January 1982)

Karunanithy, D., *The Macedonian War Machine* (Pen & Sword, 2013)

Leon, C.F., *Antigonus Gonatus Rediscovered* (Ancient World 20, 1989)

Lund, H.S., *Lysimachus* (Routledge, 1992)

Manolis, Andronicus, *The Royal Tombs and Other Antiquities* (Athens, 1984)

Matthew, C., *An Invincible Beast* (Pen & Sword, 2015)

McCurdy, G., *Hellenistic Queens* (Baltimore, 1932)

Rankin, H.D., *The Celts and the Classical World* (London and Portland, OR, 1987)

Rosen, K., *Political Documents in Hieronymus of Cardia* (Acta Classica 10, 1967)

Rostovtzeff, M., *Social and Economic History of the Hellenistic World*, Vol. 3 (Oxford, 1953)

Scullard, H.H., *The Elephant in the Greek and Roman World* (London, 1974)

Shipley, G., *The Greek World after Alexander* (London and New York, 2000)

Simpson, R.H., *The Historical Circumstances of the Peace of 311* (JHS 74, 1954)

Simpson, R.H., *Antigonus the One-Eyed and the Greeks* (Historia 8, 1959)

Tarn, W., *Hellenistic Military and Naval Developments* (Cambridge, 1930)

Tarn, W., *Antigonus Gonatus* (Argonaut, 1912)

Tarn, W., *Heracles, Son of Barsine* (JHS 41, 1921)

Usher, S., *The Historians of Greece and Rome* (Hamish Hamilton, 1969)

Walbank, F.W., *The Hellenistic World* (Fontana History of the Ancient World, paperback, 24 September 1992)

Waterford, R., *Dividing the Spoils* (Oxford, 2011)

Wilkes, J., *The Illyrians* (Blackwell, 1992)

Woodhead, A.G., *Athens and Demetrius Poliorcetes at the end of the Fourth Century BC* (Studies in honour of Charles Edson, London, 1981)

Worthington, *Ptolemy I* (Oxford, 2017)

Index